Birthing
a Nation

Birthing a Nation

Gender, Creativity, and the West in American Literature

Susan J. Rosowski

University of Nebraska Press Lincoln & London

Portions of this work have been published previously, in slightly different form: chapter 2 as "Margaret Fuller, an Engendered West, and *Summer on the Lakes,*" *Western American Literature* 25 (summer 1990): 125–44; chapter 8 as "Molly's Truth Telling, or Jean Stafford Rewrites the Western," *Reading the West: New Essays on the Literature of the American West,* ed. Michael Kowalewski (Cambridge: Cambridge UP, 1996), 157–76; and chapter 9 as "The Western Hero as Logos, or, Unmaking Meaning" *Western American Literature* 32.2 (November 1997): 269–92. Reprinted with the permission of *Western American Literature* and Cambridge University Press.

The figure on page 35 is reprinted from *The World of Willa Cather* by Mildred R. Bennett, by permission of the University of Nebraska Press. Copyright © 1961 by the University of Nebraska Press. Copyright © renewed 1989 by the University of Nebraska Press.

Library of Congress Cataloging-in-Publication Data
Rosowski, Susan J.
    Birthing a nation : gender, creativity, and the West in American literature / Susan J. Rosowski.
        p.   cm.
    Includes bibliographical references and index.
    ISBN 0-8032-3935-1 (cl.: alk. paper)
    1. American literature—West (U.S.)—History and criticism. 2. American literature—Women authors—History and criticism. 3. National characteristics, American, in literature. 4.Cather, Willa, 1873–1947—Knowledge—West (U.S.) 5. Stafford, Jean, 1915– Knowledge—West (U.S.) 6. Women and literature—West (U.S.)—History. 7. Frontier and pioneer life in literature. 8. Western stories—History and criticism. 9. Gender identity in literature. 10. Nationalism in literature. 11. West (U.S.)—In literature.   I. Title.
PS271.R67   1999
810.9'3278'082—dc21   99-14233
                                                              CIP

For Jim

Contents

Preface

This is a book about national identity and the American West, a broad claim for work that began with an apparently simple and decidedly personal question. While serving as president of the Western Literature Association and preparing to address my colleagues, I wondered why I felt so at home in a field that was prototypically male. I knew full well that Frederick Jackson Turner's indefatigable frontier thesis provided the subtext for scholarship in the field. Its premises are familiar to every schoolboy—or girl. With the prospect of free land, Europeans coming to America moved to the edge of civilization where they confronted an alien wilderness and native peoples. Settling there they were transformed into a new identity as Americans. Meanwhile, the frontier moved westward and the process repeated itself. Not surprisingly, our interpretation of literature has echoed Turner's interpretation of history as the conflict between wilderness and civilization, the rugged individualistic hero, and the return to origins from which the uniquely American, American Adam was reborn. From it all have grown conventions in our literature that celebrate male experience—variations upon the idea of boys lighting out for the territory to escape the civilizing threat of women.

These generalizations do not explain my reading of western American literature in which female experience seems central. Hester Prynne, Ántonia Shimerda Cuzak, Molly Fawcett, and Sylvie Fisher inhabit the landscape of my literary West so profoundly that their traces remain, deeply residing far beyond their immediate presence in *The Scarlet Letter, My Ánto-*

nia, The Mountain Lion, and *Housekeeping.* No figure is even remotely equal to displacing them—certainly not the hero of the Western, who in his various permutations has attempted to take possession of the field and to whom so many critics have looked when defining the literary West.

To understand the discrepancy between the literary West as it has been told to me and that which I experienced, I began reexamining the premises by which I was reading. I set aside Turner and the historians for the moment and returned to early American literature. There the charge to writers was clear, and it had nothing to do with mapping a territory or breaking sod. Instead, writers were challenged to give birth to a nation, and they were to do so by looking to the West. By positing a female model of creativity at the genesis of American literature, the metaphor suggested its own question: what are the consequences of this literary challenge to give birth within a culture (American generally and the West specifically) so decidedly hostile to women?

In pursuing this question, I turned to those writers who most directly and deeply took up the challenge of giving birth to a nation—the women who believed in literature as a serious and noble form of art and wrote to influence how the United States perceived itself. For designedly public literature to be written by culturally marginalized authors is a paradox that has the potential to become an oxymoron since gender assigns authors to genre, and we are unaccustomed to recognizing epic seriousness in women. To further complicate matters, facing west meant engaging with a cultural and literary discourse that rendered women Other and fulfilled itself to the extent that it rendered women a silent and distant "other."[1] In *The Virgin Land* Henry Nash Smith traced ways in which the female is the metaphorical Other through which an unsettled West is represented, and in *The Resisting Reader* Judith Fetterley interpreted a politics of male empowerment in which the female reader entered the "masculine wilderness" of canonical American literature. In *The Lay of the Land* Annette Kolodny (Smith's student) pursued gendered implications of male writers' metaphorical experience of the land-as-woman, and in *The Land before Her* she interpreted women's own representations of the West—the diaries and journals that offer the historical experience of settling the West.

My own approach differs from theirs in that I have looked to those writers who belied their cultural alterity and spoke for themselves in responding to the challenge to give birth to a nation. My premise is that its literatures offer a culture's most passionate involvement in issues central to it and that it is by engaging with those literatures that we might best learn of the deep cultural forms and structures of feeling with which we construct our personal and national identities. With this premise in mind, I have focused upon four writers. The number at first startled me, for I began the project expecting that an extended list of possibilities lay before me only to see the field narrow in my preliminary reading. I now wonder why I was surprised. "Until recently, only a tiny proportion of literary women aspired to artistry and literary excellence in the terms defined by their own culture," writes Nina Baym (5); the percentage is even smaller when that aspiration includes the epic ambition of articulating national identity. Once engaged with these four writers, however, my field expanded again as I came to realize that for Margaret Fuller, Willa Cather, and Jean Stafford, writing of national identity and destiny was the purpose of a lifetime, and Marilynne Robinson gives every indication of similar commitment. No survey would have accommodated their seriousness, and I adapted my plan accordingly by including multiple chapters on Cather and Stafford complemented by single chapters on Fuller and Robinson. To establish a context my introduction lays out literary responses to the charge of giving birth to a nation. To suggest some consequences of this charge a later chapter interprets how the popular Western subverts female creativity by denying the generativity of language, and an afterword offers conclusions and speculations.

Any study of gender, creativity, and the West builds upon the ongoing process of reclaiming women's voices, and mine is no exception. I am thinking particularly of important scholarship on the noncanonical texts of female communities, private writing, and domestic rituals that provides a basis for my reevaluation of women who sought to influence and join the literary canon. Elizabeth Hampsten's *Read This Only to Yourself* prepared me to read women's private writing and led me back to the Cather family letters. By testing stereotypes and myths against women's private writing, Glenda Riley's *Frontierswomen* prepared me to recognize ways in which women writers resisted stereotypes in their fiction. I have turned gratefully to other scholars for surveys of birth myths. Marta Weigle's *Creation and Procreation* provides a starting place for recognizing the central place that conception, gestation, and childbirth played as symbolic acts in cosmogonic myths, and Paula Gunn Allen's *Grandmothers of the Light* demonstrates the ongoing power of Native American goddess stories. Similarly, other writers are revisioning our national discourses by writing against a western masterplot. In *Why I Can't Read Wallace Stegner and Other Essays,* Elizabeth Cook Lynn objects to claims that western history ended in 1890 and that the Plains Indians were a vanishing people, and in *Beloved* Toni Morrison writes the black reenactment of the birth of a nation in a southern landscape. Though these and other texts lie outside the parameters of my subject, they invite extensions of and alternatives to it in significant and productive ways.

My gratitude to others is more personal, for it has to do with chapters read, questions answered, advice offered, and friendship enjoyed. Tom Quirk and Joe Urgo generously gave of their time and expertise in reading the manuscript, and I am deeply grateful for their suggestions and corrections. Kristin Harpster demonstrated that good copyediting is intelligent as well as careful. Others who figured into the long background of this project are, I now realize, reminders of ways in which categories collapse and free possibilities. Past and present, woman and author, fiction and fact, personal and professional—a conclusion of my afterword is embodied in the people who figured most importantly in reaching it. Sensitive to how a historical past informs the present, Ann Billesbach and Kari Ronning bring Willa Cather's Nebraska background alive; by their living knowledge of Willow Shade, Susan and David Parry have a similar effect with Cather's Virginia. Helen Cather Southwick brings the actual Willa Cather very near, a welcome antidote to the scholarly tendency to flatten her into "Cather." In her scholarship as in her personal life, Ann Romines illuminates ways in which women's creativity figures in domestic plots and family lives, Melody Graulich and Merrill Skaggs model possibilities of pro/creativity while John and Sally Murphy, Bruce and Karen Baker, Charles and Mary Mignon, and John and Cheryl Swift demonstrate how family and scholarship may merge. Bob Thacker confirms the richness of friendship lived through generations, from when we were students to now, when we look to other students as they enter the field.

Some of those emerging scholars provided research assistance that was particularly important to this project. I thank Joy Currie, Audra Dibert-Himes, Deb Forssman, Susan Jagoda, Margie Rine, and Jerry Whelan. Others, having graduated, figured in the project in critical ways: Lynn Beideck-Porn by providing invitation into and expertise about the University of Nebraska Archives and Special Collections, and Steve Hayes, whose fine editorial eye and computer wizardry are my notion of a modern-day deus ex machina. Over the years students in seminars on Willa Cather and on gender, creativity, and the American West confirmed the power of literature to challenge and inspire and also the power of conversation to change the way we read a text and see the world.

Through it all, there are those who sustain communities: at the University of Nebraska, Robert and Virginia Knoll, Fred and Peggy Link, and Steve Hilliard; in Cather studies, Jim and Roberta Woodress. At the core, Bill and Alice Campbell and David and Scott Rosowski. And—always—Jim.

Introduction

The Birth of a
Nation as
a Literary Charge

From the beginning of discussions about American literature, writers identified its "Americanness" with the West. In defending a plain style, Thomas Hooker, in 1648, reminded his reader that "a homely dresse and coarse habit . . . *comes out of the wildernesse,* where curiosity is not studied" (preface); in 1782 J. Hector St. John de Crèvecoeur adopted the pose of a simple western farmer, a writer who composed as he followed his plough; and in 1786 David Humphreys saw "the brutal rudeness" (23) of the wilderness as a promising subject for the writer, advising that among the "untrodden scenes" (24) of "these western climes" (23) the writer might find a worthy subject:

> For here vast wilds which human foot ne'er trod,
> Are mark'd with footsteps of a present God; (24)

By 1800 Charles Brockden Brown (the editor of the *American Review and Literary Journal*) was specifying the western materials that would best engage an American reader's sympathy: "The incidents of Indian hostility, and the perils of the western wilderness, are far more suitable" subjects for American writers than inherited Old World manners and Gothic castles (3). And by 1815 a shift in perspective had occurred—from looking backward, toward the East and beyond, to Europe, to looking westward. "Only after the War of 1812, with relations with Europe more or less settled, could America turn its attention westward" (McKinsey, *Western Experiment* 2).

With this turn came heightened interest in what the writer was to *do* with the West, which was not to map a new country, break sod, or return to an original state but to create a new national identity. Correspondingly, the birth metaphor—there from the beginning—shifted westward also. Whereas Hooker had focused upon New England and stressed its similarity to other creations ("Only as in other births, so here . . . depend meerly upon Gods good pleasure; who opens and shuts the womb of truth fro bearing, as he sees fit, according to the counsell of his own will" [preface]), Humphreys extended the birth metaphor westward by invoking "the Genius of the western world" for an original conception by the writer:

> Rise, daring muse, with bolder flight explore,
> The heav'nly wonders for these climes in store;
> Sing nature lab'ring with her latest birth,
> And a new empire rising on the earth! (24–25)

In 1818 John Knapp, noting the speed with which lands were being "cleared of their heaven-planted forests," called to American poets to take in the "stupendous frame of nature . . . feel its life-breathing motions . . . and listen to its supernal promptings," then let it out again in an original national poetry (176). In 1839 the *Democratic Review* referred to "the beginning of a new history . . . which separates us from the past and connects us with the future only" as "our national birth" (426), and in 1846 Margaret Fuller wrote of America's soul "yearning" for "that riper time [when] national ideas shall take birth, ideas craving to be clothed, in a thousand fresh and original forms" and regretted the "abortions" theretofore seen ("American Literature" 124).

Such descriptions, so familiar that we unthinkingly accept them, posed a radical charge, for they redefined creativity in American terms by placing writers in a metaphorically female position. Writers were to take America (i.e., the West) into themselves, as if by insemination; to carry it about within themselves, as if in gestation; and to create something original, as if giving birth to new life. This charge by the early writers was taken up and expanded upon by later writers, who created a literature in which they treated the West by adapting, assisting in, celebrating, and subverting the female experience of giving birth.

The transcendentalists laid the philosophical foundation and demonstrated the gendered implications of this charge. In "The Poet" Emerson linked the birth of a poet and the birth of a nation as he elevated the writer's calling to sacred and prophetic heights. "All that we call sacred history attests that the birth of a poet is the principal event in chronology," Emerson wrote (3:7). Once born, poets will go to the origin of things, to "an original relation to the universe and from that act as "liberating gods," creating life by putting "eyes, and a tongue, into every dumb and inanimate object" (3:12). Transcendental ideals of independence, self-reliance, and nature readily translated into the myth of the West, and in the same year that he wrote "The Poet" (1844) Emerson wrote in "The Young American": "Luckily for us, now that stream has narrowed the Atlantic to a strait, the nervous, rocky West is intruding a new and continental element into the national mind, and we shall yet have an American genius. . . . Our logrolling, our stumps and their politics, . . . the western clearing, Oregon, and Texas, are yet unsung. Yet America is a poem in our eyes; its ample geography dazzles the imagination, and it will not wait long for metres" (1:21–22).[1] As importantly as by his words, by his actions Emerson turned the nation's attention westward when, "[b]eginning about 1850, coincident with the development of railroad travel in the West, he made almost yearly lecture tours which, in the course of the next twenty-one years, took him to every one of the states—then twelve in number—west of the Alleghanies, north of the Ohio, and east of the Rockies, and to most of them many times" (Marchand 149).

Emerson issued the charge. It was left to others to carry it out—most famously Margaret Fuller and Henry David Thoreau.[2] Both considered moving to the West, both proposing to support themselves there by teaching school. As early as 1833 Fuller asked her friend James Freeman Clarke, who was pioneering a western branch of transcendentalism in the Ohio Valley, to help her find a position (he refused, saying she would find the West too raw); five years later Thoreau made similar inquiries, proposing to his brother John that they "start in company for the West" to teach school there, saying that whatever John decided, "Go I must, at all events!" (17 March 1838; *Familiar Letters* 22). What is interesting in their requests is not their personal inclinations (neither was particularly suited to frontier living) but the seriousness with which they accepted that the West was the American Muse.

In 1843 Fuller traveled to the frontier, going first to Niagara Falls, then to Buffalo, Chicago, Milwaukee, and the Wisconsin Territory (Wisconsin was not admitted as a state until 1847); upon her return, she wrote an account of her travel, published the following year (1844) as *Summer on the Lakes. Summer,* routinely referred to as an early historical account of frontier conditions, is also Fuller's *Künstlerroman*, for Fuller traveled west as an American writer invoking the Muse, trusting "perhaps to foresee the law by which a new order, a new poetry, is to be evoked from this chaos" (*Summer* 22). Rather self-consciously situating herself in the transcendental manner, ready for the loss of self that would precede rebirth as an artist-poet, Fuller remained for eight days at Niagara Falls, calling it "a magnificent prologue to the as yet unknown drama" (6). She may have not known specifics of that drama, but she knew what she expected of its effects upon her. Traveling to the West, she was going to the source of America's identity, and she expected nothing less than "a new existence" (7).

What Fuller found on that trip was not a new existence but heightened awareness about the bonds of convention, particularly upon women—both those she met living on the frontier and also herself. She returned to the East realizing that the West as Muse had remained closed to her and issuing a call to younger, freer women to carry on the adventure she had begun:

> I shall not enter into that truly wild and free region; shall not have the canoe voyage, whose daily adventure, with the camping out at night beneath the stars, would have given an interlude of such value to my existence. I shall not see the Pictured Rocks, their chapels and urns. It did not depend on me; it never has, whether such things shall be done or not.
>
> My friends! May they see and do and be more; especially those who have before them a greater number of birthdays, and a more healthy and unfettered existence! (96)

At approximately the same time that Fuller was calling to women to form a new order, Thoreau was forming his own poetic aspirations in terms of the West. His essay "Walking" is the most sustained, fevered call to the West in our literature. The walking of the title, as Thoreau establishes at the outset of the essay, is toward sacred sources. Adopting the pose of a saunterer, Thoreau describes walking as going to the Holy Land ("à la Sainte Terre"), explaining that for him the Holy Land lies in the West (205). Inevitably, the needle of his instinct points him "between West and South-southwest," for those are the directions of freedom, the future, and progress: "I must walk toward Oregon, and not toward Europe. And that way the nation is moving, and I may say that mankind progress from east to west." (218). Blazoned against the horizon, every sunset beckons the walker "to go to a West as distant and as fair as that into which the sun goes down," only to reappear each morning to "migrate westward daily, and tempt us to follow him. He is the Great Western Pioneer whom the nations follow" (219).

What will he find in such a West? For his answer Thoreau falls back upon sweeping affirmations of what awaits his saunterer. The West will inspire the spirit and provide "the means for man to grow to greater perfection intellectually," he writes, so that his thoughts will be as vast as the country itself (222). Inspired by that country's vastness, Thoreau's prose expands to reflect it: "I trust that we shall be more imaginative, that our thoughts will be clearer, and more ethereal, as our sky,—our understanding more comprehensive and broader, like our plains,—our intellect generally on a grander scale, like our thunder and lightning, our rivers and mountains and forests,—and our hearts shall even correspond in breadth and depth and grandeur to our inland seas" (222–23). A tall order, yet one that Thoreau expands further as he includes the ideas of Genesis and Manifest Destiny:

> To Americans I hardly need to say,—
> "Westward the star of empire takes its way."
>
> As a true patriot, I should be ashamed to think that Adam in paradise was more favorably situated on the whole than the backwoodsman in this country. (223)

Edwin Fussell has written that "Walking" "contains what is probably the longest sustained meditation on the West in American literature." He then goes on to note that "Actually, 'Walking' is one long tissue of clichés" (181). I would agree, adding only that it is as cliché that the essay confirms my point: it is a commonplace that the West figures in our cultural discourse as the sacred source to which the writer pays homage. "The West of which I speak is but another name for the Wild; and what I have been preparing to say is, that in Wildness is the preservation of the World" (Thoreau, "Walking" 224).

In its invocation to the West as Muse, "Walking" complements *Walden*, America's most famous account of self-reliance in nature. Long interpreted as a pioneer how-to book, a naturalist's guide, and a seeker's spiritual quest, *Walden* has entered our national mythology as paradise found (Joseph Wood Krutch) and Thoreau as an American Adam (R. W. B. Lewis). Seen within the context of gender and national creativity, *Walden* is also Thoreau's exploration of the peculiar demands placed on the American writer, in which the writer casts off a conventional male stance of explorer or discoverer and assumes a female one of gestation and birth.

Thoreau shaped his sojourn in nature into the female version of creation demanded by the American challenge to give birth to a nation. He
compressed the actual time he lived at Walden—two years, two months,
and two days—into one year, and he shaped that year into two parts. The
first is a brief, prefatory period of three months during which Thoreau accomplishes conventionally male pioneer tasks: he clears the land, hews
timber, and constructs a cabin. The second consists of his nine months'
residency, and it culminates in multiple births—of spring, of himself as a
writer, and of a new nation. It is this nine-month second period that is the
heart of *Walden*. Appropriately, Thoreau begins it on Independence Day, 4
July, for following that day Thoreau is indeed independent from men's
ways. One of the last revisions to his proofs was to record the date that
Walden "was completely open," his criterion for seeing "spring come in"
(244).[3] While living by Walden Pond, Thoreau shapes his days by domestic
ritual: he plants a garden, keeps house, goes on walks, and entertains visitors. Descriptions of this period celebrate the conventionally female life
he has adopted: Thoreau reflects that "housework was a pleasant pastime,"
then proceeds to describe how he scrubs his floor. Days are passed "hoeing
or perhaps reading and writing in the forenoon," then bathing, smoothing
out the wrinkles of his labor, and in the afternoon, strolling "to the village
to hear some of the gossip which is incessantly going on there" (146).

   More than in such details, however, *Walden* is a creation myth that
Thoreau writes as if in confinement (his term; see, e.g., 87). He shapes his
experience to correspond to that of a pregnancy by choosing a nine-month
residency and also by the way in which he describes his perceptions being
altered during that period: it is as if time is suspended and he is at the center of the world, experiencing life with heightened senses. "This is a de-
licious evening, when the whole body is one sense, and imbibes delight
through every pore" (118); "I have, as it were, . . . a little world all to myself"
(119); "Sometimes, in a summer morning, having taken my accustomed
bath, I sat in my sunny doorway from sunrise till noon, rapt in a revery"
(105); and "I grew in those seasons like corn in the night" (105). These are
feelings of some women during pregnancy, when their measure of time,
view of the world, and keen awareness of sensation reflect the life growing
within.

   It is natural that *Walden* ends with a labor and birth. As the earth has
been pregnant with the idea and leaf of new life, so Thoreau has been pregnant with the idea and language of this new world, America, and in the

end Thoreau describes his own labor to give birth. As words are pressing forward to be born, Thoreau's language is brilliantly one with its content in its extended linguistic punning:

> No wonder that the earth expresses itself outwardly in leaves, it so labors with the idea inwardly. The atoms have already learned this law, and are pregnant by it. The overhanging leaf sees here its prototype. *Internally*, whether in the globe or animal body, it is a moist thick *lobe*, a word especially applicable to the liver and lungs and the *leaves* of fat, ($\lambda\varepsilon\iota\beta\omega$, *labor, lapsus*, to flow or slip downward, a lapsing; $\lambda o\beta\acute{o}\varsigma$, *globus*, lobe, globe; also, lap, flap, and many other words,) *externally* a dry thin *leaf*, even as the *f* and *v* are a pressed and dried *b*. The radicals of lobe are *lb*, the soft mass of the *b* (single lobed, or B, double lobed,) with a liquid *l* behind it pressing it forward. In globe, *glb*, the guttural *g* adds to the meaning the capacity of the throat. (247)

Thus Thoreau describes his version of the birth of a nation. In succeeding paragraphs Thoreau reflects upon its significance, comparing his experience to "the creation of Cosmos out of Chaos and the realization of the Golden Age . . . [when] 'Man was born'" (252–53). This new life (the New World) is but young, "groping for expression, blindly and ineffectually perhaps, like a new-born instinct" (252), yet in such a way "the Golden Age was first created" (254). The seasons continue, and, Thoreau writes, "thus was my first year's life in the woods completed" (256).

Thoreau reinforces the linking of the West and a female version of creativity in his conclusion, which is framed by two ideas. In the first, Thoreau defines the West, that source of an American identity, not as a geographical place but as our internal potential: "What . . . does the West stand for? Is not our own interior white on the chart? . . . be a Columbus to whole new continents and worlds within you, opening new channels, not of trade, but of thought. . . . Start now on that farthest western way" (259). Thoreau concludes with a story of life within us, "an egg deposited . . . many years earlier . . . [and] buried for ages," finally warming, quickening, taking form, and unexpectedly coming forth "to enjoy its perfect summer life at last!" (266).

Fuller and Thoreau demonstrate gendered implications of the charge that American writers give birth to a nation. From this time on American literature was marked by birth strategies characteristically identified with the West. In *The Scarlet Letter* (1850) Hawthorne created a woman who embodies the peculiarly American form of creativity. He placed his community "on the edge of the Western wilderness" (57) and then created Hester Prynne, "a fully developed woman of sexual age" (Baym 13), as the woman who enters the wilderness of the forest, opening herself to it and to her own passion. The power of the novel lies in Hester Prynne's independence, even autonomy. Because she assumes responsibility for and authority over her pregnancy and birth, the conventional question of paternity (who is the father of this woman's child) becomes secondary, so that the community seems a grotesque version of a patriarchy—outmoded, ineffectual, and in sharp contrast to Hester's strength and integrity. While on the scaffold, for example, Hester hears words from above, "Hearken unto me, Hester Prynne" (64), as if they are from God rather than Governor Bellingham. Similarly, Chillingworth and Dimmesdale offer two versions of the Old World idea of man: Chillingworth, the scholar, and Dimmesdale, the "young clergyman, who had come from one of the great English universities, bringing all the learning of the age into our wild forest-land" (66). Their scholarship and religion are impotent because Hester places herself outside and beyond their authority (I never quite believe that Dimmesdale is the father of Hester's child; at some level I believe that she actually took the wilderness itself as her mate). As Hester refuses to speak and give her child a father, so Pearl refuses to say that her Heavenly Father made her. Out of herself Hester has given birth to Pearl, and Pearl signifies the New World: "skipping, dancing, and frisking fantastically among the hillocks of the dead people, like a creature that had nothing in common with a bygone and buried generation, nor owned herself akin to it. It was as if she had been made afresh, out of new elements, and must perforce be permitted to live her own life, and be a law unto herself, without her eccentricities being reckoned to her for a crime" (134–35). With the A on her breast that announces not only adultery but the beginning of an alphabet, Hester announces a line of American women who live in the margins, unpossessed and independent—Willa Cather's Ántonia, Jean Stafford's Molly, and Marilynne Robinson's Sylvie.

Whitman took another route. Convention has it that in *Leaves of Grass* he created himself, but he did so as a midwife assisting in America's birth of a nation. Whitman opens *Leaves of Grass* with multiple applications of a birth metaphor that he repeats as he describes his origins ("Starting from fish-shaped Paumanok where I was born"). He then turns to his poetic Muse—"Solitary, singing in the West, I strike up for a New World." America, the West, and the birth of a nation—again they are linked, for Whitman too describes an American creativity by metaphors of labor. After an introductory catalog, for example, he writes the birth of a nation:

> This then is life,
> Here is what has come to the surface after so many throes and
> convulsions. (sec. 2, "Starting from Paumanok")

But instead of claiming that labor for himself, as Thoreau had done, Whitman describes it in America. Then Whitman addresses America as her midwife, giving back to her poetry as her own "progeny" that he has assisted into life:

> Take my leaves America, take them South and take them North,
> Make welcome for them everywhere, for they are your own offspring.
> Surround them East and West, for they would surround you,
> And you precedents, connect lovingly with them, for they
> connect lovingly with you. (sec. 4, "Starting from Paumanok")

As her midwife, Whitman takes America into himself by loving her, then lets her out again in his "song":

> Democracy! near at hand to you a throat is now inflating itself and joyfully
>   singing.
> My femme! for the brood beyond us and of us,
> For those who belong here and those to come,
> I exultant to be ready for them will not shake our carols stronger and
> haughtier than have ever yet been heard upon earth.

> I will make the songs of passion to give them their way,
> And your songs outlaw'd offenders, for I scan you with kindred eyes, and carry
> you with me the same as any. (sec. 12, "Starting from Paumanok")

Whitman's poetic stance as midwife was a shrewd response to the charge of giving birth to a nation. By placing the creative impulse in America and assisting her in giving birth, Whitman freed himself from anxieties over possession or paternity: "These are really the thoughts of all men in all ages and lands, they are not original with me," he specifies in "Song of Myself" (sec. 17).

Twain wrote yet another version of the charge to go to the wilderness and give birth. In *Huckleberry Finn* (1884) he set in opposition two impulses or desires (to use Peter Brooks's terminology), toward birth and toward death represented as abortion. As various critics have pointed out, from the time that Huck stages his own death on Jackson Island, *Huckleberry Finn* is a story of would-be rebirths and reincarnations. Harold Beaver, who has counted them, reports that Huck takes on nine different identities: as Sarah Williams, Mary Williams, Sarah Mary Williams, and George Peters (at Mrs. Judith Loftus's); as Charles William Albright, alias Aleck James Hopkins (in the Raftsmen's Passage); as Mary Ann's brother (confronting the two slave-hunters on the river); as George Jackson (on parleying with the Grangerfords); as Adolphus (English valet to the king and duke); and finally as Tom Sawyer (*Huckleberry Finn*).

By their sheer number, these identities (one scarcely knows what to call them) undermine the idea of rebirth, however, for the pattern that emerges is of lives that have only the briefest and most precarious reality before they are cut short and discarded. Huck's final and most disturbing rebirth, as Tom Sawyer, confirms that pattern. It "was like being born again, I was so glad to find out who I was" (282), Huck says upon learning that Aunt Sally Phelps believes he is Tom; by welcoming rebirth as Tom Sawyer, Huck repudiates all he had learned on the river and confirms the basic pattern of the novel: *that of abortion*. The novel thus contradicts the reader's desire for rebirth, and by doing so it asks that we reconsider the setting and plot we had looked to with such hope. The narrative's Mississippi River, for example, has been compared to a maternal force, a natural mother, and even a birth canal; yet the setting's promise of conception and birth is disproved by the plot's unremitting return to death. Again, Beaver has counted the bodies. By the end of Huck's travels on the Mississippi, Pap and Miss Watson are dead, the king and duke are missing or dead, Buck Grangerford and Mary Jane are dead. Moreover, "Young Huck had survived at least nine attempts on his life. Within less than six months it had been threatened: by Pap with his claspknife; by the *Walter Scott* gang; by the steamship pilot who slices through the raft; by the Grangerfords when they first discover him; by the gun-happy Shepherdsons; by the blustering Boggs; by the mob at Peter Wilks's grave; by the king, who reckoned he'd drown him; and by the posse at the Phelps farm that shoots Tom" (119). Huck's "rebirths" are in response to aborted earlier selves, his own and others'. By the novel's end the Mississippi itself "is awash with corpses. On his journey downstream Huck had encountered some thirteen" (Beaver 119).

Against all this, there is, so far as I can determine, not one birth in *Huckleberry Finn*. Not a single literal birth counters the staggering number of literal deaths, and not a single symbolic rebirth is vital or solid enough to last. I would suggest that the power of *Huckleberry Finn* lies first in Twain's sending Huck into the wilderness to form (that is, to conceive of) an original relation to nature and then in Twain's following through to reveal the difficulty—even impossibility—of Huck's carrying this conception to term and giving it birth.

Two events in 1902 signaled the twentieth-century's gendered responses to giving birth to a nation. Owen Wister published *The Virginian*, a runaway bestseller invariably cited as the text that inspired the genre of the Western novel and announced the Western's obsessive concern over "the problem of what it means to be a man" (L. Mitchell, *Westerns* 3). That same year, Willa Cather published her first story, "Peter," and with it announced her own commitment to freeing women from the alterity of the Western's script. For the next decade and a half, Cather's western fiction formed a countervoice to the fledgling Western. In 1912 Zane Grey published what would be his most popular novel, *Riders of the Purple Sage*, the book that "firmly established the modern Western by offering a convincing sequel to Wister" (L. Mitchell, *Westerns* 122). Also in 1912 Cather published "The Bohemian Girl," in which she introduced her central character as a lone rider who, emerging upon a crest of high land and silhouetted against the western sky, "seemed . . . an inevitable detail of the landscape" (*Collected Short Fiction* 6–7). The image is so consistently identified with the Western that it is sufficient to announce the genre and its conventions of gender, against which Cather explores the difference that it makes when that lone rider is a woman. *O Pioneers!* followed in 1913, and in 1918 *My Ántonia*, American literature's most fully realized response to the challenge to give birth to a nation.

Three points about *My Ántonia* are especially relevant. First, Cather was writing with an Emersonian seriousness conventionally reserved for men, positioning herself in the epic tradition by repeating Virgil, "for I shall be the first, if I live, to bring the Muse into my country" (256). Second, she fulfilled the gendered charge to American writers by identifying the West with a female principle of creativity for the birth of a nation. Like Whitman, she placed fecundity in America itself, and like Hawthorne, she privileged a woman's independent creativity. And third, Cather freed her narrative from conventions that would limit a woman's creativity. A descendent of Hester Prynne, Ántonia gives birth independently; her creativity, fecundity, and sexuality are in all but the most literal, biological ways independent from men. Similarly, Cather's narrative establishes its independence from the Western. Coming to the West on the railroad, Cather's narrator Jim Burden is reading a Jesse James novel, and when he alights from the train, he reads the West as fictionalized in a genre that is, as Lee Mitchell indicates in the subtitle of his book, obsessively concerned with "making the man." Cather's narrative disabuses Jim of that fiction, then displaces his authority by returning language to a woman's principles of storytelling as cooperative and communal.

Though Cather may have freed *her* birth myth from the Western, the genre remains frontally and pervasively hostile to female creativity both in its obviously pulp spin-offs and in its "higher" mythic reincarnations. It is significant, for example, that Walter Van Tilburg Clark's short initial version in 1935 of *The Track of the Cat* was without any female characters and that the finished version, published in 1949, articulates responses to threatening female sexuality. A western *Long Day's Journey into Night*, Clark's novel tells of in(ti)mates who, while snowbound, play out their drama of hatred and love in compressed and heightened forms. The repressed mother reads the Bible, the ineffectual father escapes through alcohol, the spinster sister is neurotic, and the three sons are engaged in a struggle for dominance that takes the form of a hunt. Into the family Gwen Williams enters as the disruptive force, for by embodying qualities conventionally expected of men, she defies boundaries of gender. She is self-possessed, independent, competent, and quiet; most important, she is both sexual and responsible for her own sexuality.

The narrative's surface plot about the brothers' hunt of a black cat provides a vehicle through which sexual tensions are played out. Sitting in the kitchen where they hear Gwen and Grace laughing together in the bedroom, the men perceive both a cloistered purity and an illicit seduction in the women's laughter, so that for them sister/fiancée/wife/whore become powerfully and dangerously merged. As the cat is simply itself, called evil "only with the conscious and inventing mind" of men (Clark, "On The Track" 183), so Clark depicts women as the threat of that which cannot be possessed. What is particularly significant is the role of language in the narrative's hostility to female sexuality. Through naming, distinctions are erased and meanings are conflated: father, mother, and son (Curt) call Gwen a whore; the father calls the mother a whore; one son (Hal) thinks his mother is a whore; the father calls all women whores.[4] A hallmark of the Western, I argue in chapter 9, is its hostility toward language generally and toward the generativity of metaphor specifically.

Jean Stafford confronted the Western's violence toward women—or rather toward girls, for that violence denied the growth of Stafford's girls into womanhood. Her western stories tell of would-be writers growing up gifted and female, claiming language, and by doing so, challenging western narratives from the position of "other"—which is to say, in the Western, of prey. Finally, Marilynne Robinson challenges the divisive premises of national discourse represented in the Western—subject versus object, hunter versus prey—with their plots of opposition and confrontation. By casting herself as an anthropologist of language, Robinson excavates the birth metaphor and retrieves in its deep narrative structure an alternate epistemology of genesis. By putting connection rather than isolation, kinship rather than autonomy at the center of her story, Robinson challenges notions of the United States as having a unique destiny, questions its claim to happiness as a worthy ideal, and reclaims the metaphor of birth from its fragmented and divisive appropriation as "the birth of a nation" by American jingoists.

As we slouch toward the millennium, media stories of western survivalist encampments are merely the latest chapter in a national myth defined by variations of a frontier thesis. As Richard Slotkin has so persuasively argued, America is characterized by its "regeneration through violence," with the frontier West as the site of our "face-to-face meeting with the Enemy. . . . the fulfillment of a destiny or fate, pregnant with meaning" (*Fatal Environment* 12). Yet even so—with masculinist westering myth so firmly identified with America that it carries the face of a Marlboro man—the challenge to give birth to this nation remains viable as a metaphoric presence. Slotkin titles one book *Regeneration through Violence* and writes in another of the "pregnant" meaning of confrontation as our national destiny, his language recalling the challenge to give birth to a nation.

A myth of violence is unarguably one response to the challenge to give birth to this nation, but as I hope to demonstrate in the following pages, a birth myth of a profoundly different character remains viable. It waits for readers to provide the attention necessary for it to survive and, under favorable conditions, to develop a mythic life of its own.

1

Fuller
and the West
as Muse

Like a literary version of an American pop hero, Margaret Fuller is readily granted superlatives, then as readily dismissed. At the time of her death Fuller was acclaimed the most famous woman in America; a century later she was hailed as "the most distinguished advocate of the Feminist cause in America" (Wade 135) and later still described as "one of the greatest humanists of her century, one of the greatest America has ever produced" (M. Allen 178). Yet *Woman in the Nineteenth Century,* "the only one of her works which is generally remembered," is "little read today" (Wade 135); the single other book she wrote, *Summer on the Lakes,* has until recently been ignored or, at best, treated as an aside. Reinforcing the notion that Fuller is interesting primarily as a personality, early critics stressed biography, seeking to distinguish the woman from the myth. More recent critics, seeking to explain her place in intellectual movements of her day, have stressed her ties to the East and the Old World: transcendentalism, Emersonianism, Goethean self-culture, and behind that, Europe. Curiously, even while acknowledging that Fuller was above all dedicated to self-culture, critics have overlooked her most developed autobiographical account of personal change, *Summer on the Lakes.*[1] Even while describing Fuller as the quintessential American, critics have given short shrift to her ties to the West, the region (and idea, for the two are intertwined) most distinctly American.[2]

It seems inevitable that the West figured in Fuller's plans for self-culture, for it was a natural extension of two major influences upon her—the

Jeffersonian thought she learned from her father and transcendentalism. There was the West's broad promise of individualism, free from restrictions imposed by society, and there were personal ties. With Unitarian settlements in Cincinnati, Louisville, and St. Louis came a need for clergy. Three of Fuller's friends—James Freeman Clarke, Christopher Pearse Cranch, and William Henry Channing—went to the Ohio Valley to serve. A rite of passage rather than a lifelong commitment, "this western branch of Transcendentalism did not long survive. Cranch returned east in 1839, Clarke followed in 1840, and Channing, despite his declaration that he should never go west at all unless it were for life, likewise retreated in 1841" (McKinsey, *Western Experiment* 7).[3] Yet the fact of their going reaffirmed the West for Fuller as the wellspring of original American thought, as is evident in her correspondence with Clarke during his sojourn in St. Louis and Louisville (1833–40). Beginning with a letter written on the Ohio River, 31 July 1833, Clarke revealed to Fuller his aspirations and disappointments, a chronicle of one man putting self-reliance to the test. "I came here with the hope of being more free," Clarke wrote from Louisville 12 August, then went on to lament his inability to act. By December he was writing, "I like the West, but the West does not like me. I could be very happy, were it possible to be happy without the feeling of effectual action," for "my culture has been of a too universal kind to be a good preparation for action in any department" (70). Finally Clarke issued his own call:

> You know why I came West. I thought that here was real freedom of thought and opinion, and that it was . . . a more favourable scene for the development of a mind which wished to have the power to express individual convictions. I have so found it. We are free to speak here whatever we think—there is no doubt of it. Public opinion is not an intolerant despotism, for there is no such thing as Public Opinion. The most opposite and contradictory principles, notions, opinions are proclaimed every day. Every variety of human thought here finds its representatives. All is incongruous, shifting, amorphous. No spirit of order broods over this Chaos. The old Virginian chivalric sentiments are dying out, and a motley group of modern notions is rushing in. The conviction is gaining ground that as the knights are dust, and their good swords rust, that their ways and fashions may be buried with them. Here is the place for a bold and self-possessed mind to step in, and lay the foundations of a new and strong edifice of thought on the basis of sentiment and feeling. But for one who like myself has no mental self-possession there is a difficulty. (15 Dec. 1834; 86–87)

Fuller's apparent stance was the classically feminine one of confidante, from Massachusetts eagerly learning from Clarke as her surrogate on the frontier: "Is the promised freedom joyous or joyless? Which do you learn most from the book of Nature, Goethe or St. Paul—and are you going to stay in the West always?" Fuller wrote to Clarke on 1 February 1835. Yet throughout the correspondence runs the tension of Fuller's straining to leave the sidelines and participate. As if in counterpoint to Clarke's feeling unable to act, Fuller proposes involvement and is determinedly optimistic, declaring that her "desire to go to the West is revived by the doings at Lane Seminary," which "sounds from afar so like the conflict of keen life" (Fuller, *Letters* 2:221). Clarke never encouraged her impulse toward action, however: when she asked him to help her find a teaching position at Lane Seminary, he discouraged her by writing, "This western country is a wild country and I would advise no female friend of mine to come to it in any capacity which would bring her into collision with the natives as you would be as a teacher" (Clarke 73). When Clarke began editing the *Western Messenger,* Fuller contributed to it. Yet she continued to write of her own westering impulse, sometimes directly and sometimes in the playful tone of drawing-room conversation—as when she reminded Clarke she "always had some desire to be meddling with the West" (9 Dec. 1838; Fuller, *Letters* 1:354).[4]

Inclination became reality when, a decade after suggesting the trip to Clarke, Fuller went west with him and his sister Sarah. Traveling from late May into mid-September, they went first to Niagara Falls and to Buffalo. There they took a steamboat to Chicago, where they were met by another Clarke brother, William, who accompanied Margaret and Sarah through northern Illinois. The women went on their own to Milwaukee and Wisconsin Territory, and Fuller traveled alone to Mackinaw Island, where Ottawa and Chippewa tribes were assembled to receive the government's annual payment. After nine days at Mackinaw, Fuller returned to Chicago, where she rejoined Sarah for the journey home.

What did she expect to find? Though acknowledging the chaos that Clarke had described, Fuller set for herself more far-reaching goals than his. She proposed "by reverent faith to woo the mighty meaning" of the West and "perhaps to foresee the law by which a new order, a new poetry, is to be evoked from this chaos" (*Summer* 22). Such is the tone of the opening passages of *Summer on the Lakes,* which rings with the high seriousness of the transcendentalist calling to the Muse. Niagara was nothing if not sublime, as Elizabeth McKinsey writes, and "for Fuller as for other Romantic artists, the effect of the sublime in nature or in great genius was always artistic inspiration" (*Niagara Falls* 226). The conventions are there, certainly: in Fuller's description of "the weight of a perpetual creation," her anticipation of "a new existence," and her rather self-conscious looking into a whirlpool as into a vortex of constant creation (*Summer* 7). Above all, there is her high seriousness. Like a novice taking religious vows, Fuller approaches the falls with "a solemn awe," knowing it was "the aspiration of my life's hopes" and feeling hesitation, perhaps from "a feeling of my unworthiness to enter this temple which nature has erected to its God" (11).

Fuller makes the conventions hers, however, in giving them not only an American but a gendered slant. The essential element for American rebirth is authentic (i.e., original) experience, and Fuller carefully distinguished between that which she got secondhand and that which was her own. She described her disappointment that paintings and descriptions had prepared her for the British waterfall, especially as seen from the Terrapin Bridge. She was reassured though that wilderness remained for her to discover for herself: "But from the foot of Biddle's Stairs and the middle of the river and from below the Table Rock, it was still 'barren, barren all'" (12). The pioneering impulse was as basic to the American writer as it was to the settler, and Fuller was laying claim to new experience. "The fountain beyond the Moss Islands *I discovered for myself*," she wrote (8; emphasis mine). Then she developed further the pioneering metaphor: "Happy were the first discoverers of Niagara, those who could come unawares upon this view and upon that, whose feelings were entirely their own" (12).

Seeking to embrace the new and to leave the past behind, Fuller used complementary scenes to contrast orders of things and ways of seeing: the transcendentalist's law of love and self-forgetfulness versus the age's "love of *utility*" (8) and "habits of calculation" (15). While at the falls, for example, Fuller described the experience she liked best. Carefully selecting her site, sitting "on Table Rock, close to the great fall," she gave herself up to nature until "all power of observing details, all separate consciousness, was quite lost" (8). She immediately followed the description with a contrasting one. While she was sitting there, "a man came to take his first look. He walked close up to the fall, and after looking at it a moment, with an air as if thinking how he would best appropriate it to his own use, he spat into it" (8). And she overhears immigrants on the boat with her, "talking not of what they should do, but of what they should get in the new scene" (16). Fuller suggests, though does not specify, gender distinctions in the contrast—her sympathy at odds with his utilitarianism.

As she approached Niagara Falls, so she approached the West. She was venturing into a country stripped of "the old landmarks" and awaiting new ones in the chaos between the past and the present. Early episodes are variations upon the idea of original creation, with Fuller casting herself as a creator. In a game of mythological identities, Fuller chooses to be a gnome who works in secret "to feed the veins of mother Earth with permanent splendors. . . . passing a life, not merely in heaping together, but *making* gold. Of all dreams, that of the alchemist is the most poetical" (13–14). And when she describes the land and water meeting, she writes of their mingling so that "a new creation takes place" (15). Initial passages culminate in Fuller's dedication of herself to the West:

> I come to the West prepared for the distaste I must experience at its mushroom growth. . . . The march of peaceful is scarce less wanton than that of warlike invasion. The old landmarks are broken down, and the land for a season bears none, except of the rudeness of conquest and the needs of the day, whose bivouac-fires blacken the sweetest forest glades. I have come prepared to see all this, to dislike it, but not with stupid narrowness to distrust or defame. On the contrary, while I will not be so obliging as to confound ugliness with beauty, discord with harmony, and laud and be contented with all I meet, when it conflicts with my best desires and tastes, I trust by reverent faith to woo the mighty meaning of the scene, perhaps to foresee the law by which a new order, a new poetry, is to be evoked from this chaos, and with a curiosity as ardent but not so selfish as that of Macbeth, to call up the apparitions of future kings from the strange ingredients of the witch's caldron. Thus I will not grieve that all the noble trees are gone already from this island to feed this caldron, but believe it will have Medea's virtue and reproduce them in the form of new intellectual growths, since centuries cannot again adorn the land with such as have been removed. (22–23)

Here ideas from her correspondence with Clarke reappear, especially those of chaos and violence; yet Fuller changes the metaphor. Although he had used images of battle (knights' swords are rusting) and building (a bold mind could "lay the foundations of a new and strong edifice of thought"), she writes of courtship and reproduction (an ardent wooing that will yield new life) and thus redefines the West in female terms. By trusting that the

West "will have Medea's virtue" of reproduction, Fuller describes it as a powerful woman using the magic she alone possesses to destroy the usurping king and to create something new.[5]

Contrasts continue between utilitarianism and a law of love. As if in opposition to white settlers who were approaching nature in a warlike invasion, Fuller describes how she learned to love the prairies. While settlers leave wanton destruction behind them, she leaves poems. Gender distinctions are implicit in this contrast between barbarism, which is (closely associated with men), and love (closely associated with women). As Fuller advances into the West she focuses increasingly upon women's roles: "The great drawback upon the lives of these settlers at present is the unfitness of the women for their new lot," Fuller writes, for women frequently have followed their husbands' choices rather than moved independently, and on the frontier "their part is the hardest and they are least fitted for it" (44). They can rarely find help with domestic work, they have few resources for pleasure, and they have been educated as ornaments of society not suited for "wildwood paths" (45). Fuller would look to the little girls "and hope they would grow up with the strength of body, dexterity, simple tastes, and resources that would fit them to enjoy and refine the Western farmer's life" (45). Applying ideals of self-reliance to women, Fuller advocates casting off European standards of "fashionable delicacy" (45) and learning skills for the West—developing the "bodily strength to enjoy plenty of exercise," learning to play the guitar rather than the piano, and learning vocal rather than instrumental music. The result would be a new elegance for girls (46).

The gendering of the narrative is the most interesting and significant characteristic of *Summer.* It lies behind Fuller's increasingly explicit identification of women as the hope of the West and also her attitude toward her own role in this rebirth. Instead of experiencing the transcendental oneness with the West that she had envisioned, Fuller found herself an outsider. As she did so, her rhetorical stance became one of a reticent, even apologetic visitor, and her tone became ironic. After hearing an amusing account of a farmer's adventures among the Indians, Fuller demurred, "But I want talent to write it down, and I have not heard the slang of these people intimately enough"; "There were many sportsman stories told, too," but "I do not retain any of these well enough . . . to write them down" (99). The word "pleasant" recurs through the final scenes as an ironic reminder that Fuller's experience did not result in the ecstatic loss of self she had anticipated: "How pleasant it was to sit and hear rough men tell pieces out of their own common lives," she remarks (99). In the letters she wrote during her tour, Fuller openly described the loneliness she was feeling, for the erasure of personality she experienced meant uselessness and invisibility, not rebirth. She wrote to Channing from Chicago:

> Always it has been that I should hear from them [the people she has met] accounts of the state of the country, in politics or agriculture, or their domestic affairs, or hunting stories. Of me, none asked a question. Like Mr Es lonely poet
>
> What she has, nobody wants
>
> I have not been led to express one thought of my mind with warmth and freedom since I have been here, and all I have ever learnt or been is useless as regards others in the relations in which I meet them as a traveler or visitor. (16 August 1843; *Letters* 3:141–42)

Thus Fuller the creator gives way to Fuller the recorder as her belief in possibility gives way to awareness of limitations. The climax of *Summer* is Fuller's statement of *impossibility*. Establishing her situation as solitary and her mood as thoughtful, Fuller makes the reflection dramatic by a play of emotion—first acknowledging that the course along a new river is pleasant, then regretting that the experience of it is closed to her. She had hoped to glimpse the rapids by daylight, yet when they passed "the beautiful sunset was quite gone, and only a young moon trembling over the scene when we came within hearing of them" (96). In place of the original experience she had sought, she now hopes merely to hear the sound of the rapids; in place of a new birth, she remembers the birthday of a friend. The passage builds to her painfully direct acknowledgment that the West is forever closed to her:

> I shall not enter into that truly wild and free region; shall not have the canoe voyage, whose daily adventure, with the camping out at night beneath the stars, would have given an interlude of such value to my existence. I shall not see the Pictured Rocks, their chapels and urns. It did not depend on me; it never has, whether such things shall be done or not.
>
> My friends! May they see and do and be more; especially those who have before them a greater number of birthdays, and a more healthy and unfettered existence! (96)

By turning toward the future with hope for other, younger women, Fuller anticipates the serious argument of *Woman in the Nineteenth Cen-*

tury. In concluding *Summer,* however, Fuller transposed her disappointment into one of her most developed comic vignettes, using ironic humor as an escape from the captivity myth in which she found herself (see Kolodny, *The Land before Her,* for a discussion of that myth). After acknowledging that she will never have the canoe trip she had imagined, she describes the one that she does have. Sarah and she "had a mind for a canoe excursion," Fuller wrote, and so "asked one of the traders to engage us two good Indians, that would not only take us out but be sure and bring us back, as we could not hold converse with them" (100). Gendering the classic western humor of easterner versus westerner, Fuller wrote of the incongruity of women's manners in a man's world. For it was as a lady that Fuller "shot the rapids," a contradiction in terms that she recognized was rich with comic potential. By her action, diction, and imagery, she told her story as the pretend adventure of a lady who entrusts herself to Indian guides she cannot talk to, who approves of them because they are wearing pink calico shirts, and who seeks "terror and delight" while sitting comfortably and safely on a mat in the canoe:

> When they came to me, they spread a mat in the middle of the canoe; I sat down, and in less than four minutes we had descended the rapids, a distance of more than three quarters of a mile. I was somewhat disappointed in this being no more of an exploit than I found it. Having heard such expressions used as of "darting" or "shooting down" these rapids, I had fancied there was a wall of rock somewhere, where descent would somehow be accomplished and that there would come some one gasp of terror and delight, some sensation entirely new to me; but I found myself in smooth water before I had time to feel anything but the buoyant pleasure of being carried so lightly through this surf amid the breakers. . . . these men are evidently so used to doing it and so adroit that the silliest person could not feel afraid. I should like to have come down twenty times that I might have had leisure to realize the pleasure. (97–98)

With its play on gender, Fuller's account of shooting the rapids is characteristic of the sort of humor found throughout *Summer,* including in her story of "a young lady" who wouldn't accommodate herself to makeshift beds arranged for the women at an inn where rooms were booked. Sitting up all night in a neat lace cap "so that she would have looked perfectly the lady, if anyone had come in" (31) may have protected her reputation, but by doing so she made herself unfit for travel the next day. Eventually, Fuller cast herself in a similarly comic role of a lady, carrying a sunshade among

Indians at Mackinaw Island and demurely shooting the rapids. Comic resonances deepen when Fuller's experiences contrast with her expectations. Approaching the West Fuller had been haunted by images of "naked savages stealing behind [her] with uplifted tomahawks" (7); on the frontier she found Indians who were accomplished guides in her mock adventure.

Humor in a mood of understated irony dominates the return to Buffalo, for the deflation Fuller felt after her canoe adventure resembles what she feels while traveling home. "In the boat many signs admonished that we were floating eastward," Fuller observes, then quietly surveys the human comedy about her: a shabby phrenologist laying hands on every head that would bend, knots of people discussing theology, and a bereaved lover turning to Butler's *Analogy* for religious consolation but distracted by a pretty face. "It seemed a pity they were not going to rather than from the rich and free country where it would be so much easier than with us to try the great experiment of voluntary association," Fuller reflects with fine irony (103).

Summer's overall structure of departure and return reinforces this sense of irony. Though she did indeed progress from company to solitude, Fuller found neither independence nor firsthand, original experience. The second part of *Summer* is her testimony to the discrepancy between what she envisioned as a human being and what she experienced as a woman. It was, in other words, as traveler, creator, and adventurer that Fuller departed, and it was as a woman that she returned. As she deepened her awareness of the role gender was playing in her journey to the West, she increasingly spoke directly as a woman to other women. In her final poem, titled "The Book to the Reader," Fuller addresses her reader as "madam" and instructs her to place the book in a domestic setting, to

> try a little with the evening-bread;
> Bring a good needle for the spool of thread (104)

From the perspective provided by its ending, we recognize that throughout *Summer* runs a female text of a woman addressing other women. When she approached the West, Fuller's dominant mood may have been one of transcendental high seriousness, but beneath that she described conventionally female fears of a wilderness—her apprehension over dirt and poor food, her anticipation of dangerous isolation, and her fear of being stalked by natives. Such fears stem from remembrance of captivity myths that Fuller brought with her to the West and to which she responded by describing the familiar (see *The Land before Her* for an alternate reading). For even as the West disproved Fuller's personal aspirations for creating great art, it offered the reassurance of ordinary women living familiar lives. Within a barren log cabin, "female taste had veiled every rudeness" (42); despite the hardship of her husband's illness, a settler's wife was keeping her family neat and clean; and though they spoke different languages, Fuller "held much communication by signs" (75) with Indian women. Such ordinariness was not congenial to the artist in Fuller, but by writing of it she made the West accessible to the imaginations of other women.

The method as well as the content of *Summer* offers reassurances, albeit sometimes conventional ones, for behind its descriptions lies a law of love that encourages sympathetic identification. Fuller wrote that she came to love the prairie as she came to know it (26–27), and she used metaphors of intimacy to describe that growing closeness. She tells of coming to appreciate the lake scenery, for example, "only after a daily and careless familiarity," "for Nature always refuses to be seen by being stared at," making herself expressionless to the gaze "of impertinent curiosity" (21). "But he who has gone to sleep in childish ease on her lap," she writes, "or leaned an aching brow upon her breast, seeking there comfort with full trust as from a mother, will see all a mother's beauty in the look she bends upon him" (21). By such metaphors Fuller domesticates the frontier: "the tall trees bent and whispered all around, as if to hail with sheltering love the men who had come to dwell among them" (29), and a little log cabin with a flower garden in front of it disturbed the natural scene "no more than a stray lock on the fair cheek" (56).

Most important, and most characteristic of Fuller, *Summer* offers an invitation to women by its form—that of the conversation. Since childhood known as a brilliant talker, Fuller had by 1839 formally identified the conversation as the genre in which she would assemble women "desirous to answer the great questions. What were we born to do? How shall we do it? which so few ever propose to themselves 'till their best years are gone by'" (27 Aug. 1839; *Letters* 2:87). Together, women would "pass in review the departments of thought and knowledge and endeavor to place them in due relation to one another in our minds. To systematize thought and give a precision in which our sex are so deficient, chiefly, I think because they have so few inducements to test and classify what they receive. To ascertain what pursuits are best suited to us in our time and state of society, and how we may best make use of our means for building up the life of thought upon the life of action" (*Letters* 2:87).

The structure behind Fuller's Conversations encouraged participation by all its members. Fuller would open a subject with a general statement—at first doing a great deal herself, she would gradually lead "others to give their thoughts upon it" (*Letters* 2:88), drawing them into an increasingly active role, first within the conversation itself but eventually in the world. Fuller's objective was "a life of action" in which women work "to reproduce all that they learn" (*Memoirs* 1:324, 329; see Chevigny, "Growing" 83). Ironically, the qualities for which Fuller is often faulted are ones that enabled her success in conversation. Instead of demonstrating mastery over her material or her audience, she demonstrated sympathy with both; she excelled not in an individual performance but rather in the cooperative spirit of communal discourse. As a participant in the Conversations recalled, Fuller "never could remember what she had said, never could repeat a brilliant saying, and, if obliged to read any illustration, read it, as all her friends admitted, very badly." But she was at her best when she was "conversing with one sympathetic person," or with others in her Conversations, or especially, when her Conversations were with "her young women" (Dall 8). This selection of a forum resonates with implications of power and gender: unlike the lecture, in which power remains in the speaker, the conversation involves an exchange of thoughts and feelings made possible by mutual sympathy and respect. Presciently, Fuller identified the conversation as a genre especially well suited to values held by women; it would be basic to women's consciousness-raising groups 130 years later. Interestingly, "her conversations were highly successful save for the one time when she included men in the group" (*Letters* 2:89).

Fuller's journey to the West and writing of *Summer* occurred within the period of the Conversations (1839–44), and not surprisingly, she wrote *Summer* in their manner. Her voice—impossible to define but nonetheless recognizable in its individuality—unifies *Summer*. It was a contemporary who, having heard Fuller speak, recognized her conversational voice when he met it in print. Quoting a representative passage of *Summer*, Edgar Allan Poe remarked, "Now all this is precisely as Miss Fuller would speak it. She is perpetually saying just such things in just such words. To get the conversational woman in the mind's eye, all that is needed is to imagine her reciting the paragraph just quoted" (qtd. in Margaret Vanderhaar Allen 68–69).[6]

Fuller encourages her reader "To get the conversational woman in the mind's eye" by various means. She establishes a stance of friendship at the outset by addressing the reader directly as one who is "to share with me such footnotes as may be made on the pages of my life during this summer's wanderings" (6); she then proceeds in the casual, spontaneous, and flexible manner of conversation. As in her Boston talks, so in *Summer* Fuller introduces a subject, then draws her reader out, often addressing her directly and inviting her to take an active role: "You have only to turn up the sod to find arrowheads and Indian pottery" (38); "the town . . . seems to grow before you. . . . a few steps will take you into the thickets" (55); "do not blame me that I have written so much suggested by [my reading], while you were looking for news of the West" (69). Driving her point home, Fuller ends *Summer* with an imagined conversation between herself and her reader that is incorporated into a poem, addressed to the reader, in which Fuller specifies that she wants her book to be read as an exchange of ideas.

The conversation between Fuller and her reader provides the thread unifying *Summer*. Upon it are strung like beads stories from literature and anecdotes from life, moral reflections, poetry, and occasionally, descriptions of the land and its people. As Elizabeth McKinsey notes, "Fuller's most characteristic metaphor for nature's expressiveness [is] . . . aural," described by her brother as "the spirit of each scene . . . ever speaking" (*Niagara Falls* 218). Transitions extend this quality and suggest the spontaneity of spoken rather than written discourse: "Let me here give another brief tale of the power exerted by the white man over the savage" (88); "I shall say more upon the subject by and by" (34); "I have wished to say these few words" (53); and "I have mentioned that" (101). In her content, too, Fuller privileges conversation, making travel its occasion. On board the steamboat that will take her from Buffalo and into the West, Fuller describes not the scene but a conversation between herself and her traveling companions; upon reaching Mackinaw Island, Fuller postpones describing its beauty and instead quotes an extended conversation told to her by a fellow passenger. Taking refuge in a farmhouse in the Wisconsin Territory, Fuller notes only "here was a pleasant scene" (63), then moves immediately to a dialogue she imagined between herself and three persons, personified as Free Hope (Fuller), Old Church, Good Sense, and Self-Poise. When Fuller at last describes Mackinaw on her return trip, she does so largely by a series of conversations. She tells of often "having a good guess at the meaning of [the] discourse" of Indian women by their talk and variety of gesture, and

she reflects upon the role of women by quoting one woman quoting another woman: "Mrs. Grant speaks thus of the position of woman amid the
Mohawk Indians: Lady Mary Montagu says . . . " (76). She also argues for
human rights by imagining a conversation between an old, fat priest and
an Indian. The effect is of Fuller weaving together a community of voices as
she "converses" with her reader, her traveling companions, their fellow
passengers, persons she met and about whom she heard, authors she read,
and voices she imagined.

Following her journey to the West, Fuller continued to live the ironies
that resulted from a woman's pursuit of the American dream of self-reliance and independence. Needing reference materials as she prepared her
travel journal for publication, she became the first woman reader Harvard
College Library admitted to its holdings. As the trip had given her access to
a frontier dominated by men, so writing *Summer* gave her access to knowledge considered the preserves of men, with the result that Fuller was again
a pioneer—for women. Published in June, *Summer* attracted the attention
of one of the West's more enthusiastic boosters, Horace Greeley, who
asked her to join the *Tribune*'s staff as chief reviewer-critic. And so the pioneering theme continues, for "women had been associated with journalism in one or another capacity before her, but no woman had ever invaded
the world of the fourth estate as a member of the working press" (A.
Brown 73).

Fuller's journey west was important to her work in other ways, for it
served as a crucible for her most influential writing, drafted and published
as "The Great Lawsuit: Man vs. Men, Woman vs. Women" immediately
before her trip, then revised and published as *Woman in the Nineteenth
Century* immediately after it.[7] *Woman* is Fuller's Declaration of Independence for women. If readers can penetrate the dense style and mind-
numbing detail in *Woman,* they will find that Fuller rewrote national
myths, making them accessible to women. She gendered history by first
tracing human development as masculine and feminine, then arguing
that old civilizations developed by men are outmoded, and finally by
charging women to create a new civilization in America. "Man in the order
of time was developed first; as energy comes before harmony; power before
beauty," she wrote (212). But it is now time for woman to come forward, to
take her natural place and, by doing so, to move human beings toward the
ideal (213). Addressing "women of my country," Fuller charges "let not slip
the occasion, but do something to lift off the curse incurred by Eve" (210).

As Fuller gendered history with her interpretation of America's past, she gendered transcendentalism with her charge for America's future, urging "upon the [female] sex self-subsistence in its two forms of self-reliance and self-impulse, because I believe them to be the needed means of the present juncture" (216). In the process, she gendered too the central American principle of independence by charging women to be independent from men: "I believe that at present women are the best helpers of one another," she stated (213). While she affirms as an ideal "the harmony of common growth" (178), Fuller recognizes that reality is another matter altogether, for women have been long dependent upon men, and men long in the habit of instructing women. Because "souls, whether of Man or Woman, must be able to do without them in the spirit," Fuller "would have Woman lay aside all thought . . . of being taught and led by men" (179). Self-reliance, according to Fuller, means that "women must leave off asking [men] and being influenced by them, but retire within themselves, and explore the groundwork of life till they find their peculiar secret" (180). As elsewhere, Fuller links America's promise to the West, here by undergirding her argument with frontier metaphors such as "Let her put from her the press of other minds, and meditate in virgin loneliness" (180).[8]

While the content of Fuller's argument is revolutionary, its rhetoric is conciliatory. Fuller affirms ties of women to their fathers, husbands, sons, and friends, and by placing those ties in the long perspective of history, she argues that men and women are equal—two sides of human nature. By changing her title from "The Great Lawsuit: Man *versus* Men: Woman *versus* Women" to *Woman in the Nineteenth Century,* she further avoided confrontation. But under the conciliatory rhetoric lies an argument for women's ascendancy. It is not nature but society that has crippled women's (and therefore human) development, for society has cast the man as creator and the woman as Muse. Looking beyond society's precedents and arguing from principles of nature, Fuller casts the woman as creator and the man as Muse: "The Woman might have sung the deeds, given voice to the life of the Man, and beauty would have been the result. . . . The sounding lyre requires not muscular strength, but energy of soul to animate the hand which would control it. Nature seems to delight in varying the arrangements, as if to show that she will be fettered by no rule; and we must admit the same varieties that she admits" (153). Thus Fuller wrote her own version of America as the New World: the Old World was worn out in terms of gender roles, and a New World would be an Eden in which Eve would have her chance.[9]

Following the publication of *Woman,* Fuller responded to the objection of its "exhibiting ills without specifying any practical means for their remedy" ("The Wrongs of American Women" 226) by once again linking American women to the West. In an 1845 book review, "The Wrongs of American Women. The Duty of American Women," Fuller recognized that women face great difficulty earning their subsistence, and the solution she endorsed was that society prepare women to teach children, "especially in the West" (217). She then discussed a plan for this mass movement of women westward, perhaps acknowledging by its specificity that she had had no such mechanism when she had proposed moving to the West herself:

> The plan is to have Cincinnati as a central point, where teachers shall be for a short time received, examined, and prepared for their duties. By mutual agreement and cooperation of the various sects, funds are to be raised, and teachers provided, according to the wants and tendencies of the various locations now destitute. What is to be done for them centrally, is for suitable persons to examine into the various kinds of fitness, communicate some general views whose value has been tested, and counsel adapted to the difficulties and advantages of their new positions. The central committee are to have the charge of raising funds, and finding teachers, and places where teachers are wanted.
>
> The passage of thoughts, teachers and funds, will be from East to West—the course of sunlight upon this earth. (224)

In 1846 Fuller also returned to the idea of a national literature with which she had approached the West in *Summer,* where she sought "the law by which a new order, a new poetry, is to be evoked." "American Literature: Its Position in the Present Time, and Prospects for the Future" is her most sustained statement of prospects for American literature; for it, Fuller uses a birth myth.

The charge to American writers to give birth to the nation was a familiar one; by using it Fuller was acknowledging another convention she had inherited. What I find interesting is that just as Fuller had gendered such conventions—geographically, by writing a woman's version of the American West; philosophically, by teaching transcendentalism through the woman's forum of her Conversations; and politically, by charging women to be independent from men—she develops the idea of giving birth to a nation as distinctly female. She distinguishes two stages of development: first, the presumably male physical exploration and settlement basic to the moral and intellectual freedom she considered necessary to an American literature, and second, the creativity by which national ideas shall "take birth." Far from being gender neutral, Fuller's metaphor of giving birth suggests a woman's experience of the stages of pregnancy—"the symptoms of such a birth may be seen in a longing felt here and there for the sustenance of . . . [national] ideas." The birth "shows itself" at present in attempts at social reform, she writes, but before America can have poets, there must be a quickening by which it "needs to penetrate beneath the springs of action, to stir and remake the soil by the action of fire" ("American Literature" 124).

While the birth metaphor forms the rhetorical heart of her essay, it is "national ideas" that are key to Fuller's argument, which asserts that "without such ideas all attempts to construct a national literature must end in abortions" (124). No one yet has met the test, Fuller concludes after surveying the literature that has been written: Prescott possesses "a noble nobility without passion," and Cooper creates bald plots and impoverished characters, signs of shallow thought (127–29). Tellingly, Fuller gives her most detailed and approving discussion to works with women at their center and singles out for particular praise "Margaret, or the Real and Ideal." This "harbinger of the new era" (137) presents a fascinating version of the Second Coming with the Messiah as Margaret, who, born in a log cabin and nurtured in the lonely solitude of the wilderness (albeit in Maine), is destined to inspire a new order. Fuller may simply have been writing yet another version of the nineteenth-century "religion of womanhood," with woman functioning "as an all-purpose symbol of the ideals of the culture, the official repository of its acknowledged moral code, . . . [appearing] accordingly as a redemptive figure in the fiction of the era" (*New England Girl* 5). However, she may have been extending the charge she had set for herself when she traveled to the West, making her way to a more radical conception of woman as not redeeming the old, but as creating something altogether new.[10]

In a very real sense, "American Literature" is the last chapter of the tantalizingly incomplete story of Fuller's quest "to woo the mighty meaning" of the American scene. In August 1846, the same year that "American Literature: Its Position in the Present Time, and Prospects for the Future" was published, Fuller sailed for Europe, where she wrote as a foreign correspondent for Greeley's *Tribune,* met the Italian patriot Mazzini in exile, fell in love with Giovanni Angelo, marchese d'Ossoli, and gave birth to their son. Leaving the child in Rieti, Fuller lived with Ossoli in Rome, where she reported on the French siege. When the republic was overthrown in 1850, she fled with her son and husband, first to Florence and later to America. Approaching New York harbor, they encountered a storm, and on 19 July 1850 their ship was wrecked and Fuller, Ossoli, and their son were drowned.

Fuller's death ironically prefigured her literary fate, for her voice soon seemed drowned out by fictional versions of "the woman question" based upon her—Hawthorne's Zenobia in *The Blithedale Romance,* and James's double portrait with Verena Tarrant and Olive Chancellor in *The Bostonians.* And she has seemed submerged, too, if truth be told, under the weight of *Woman in the Nineteenth Century,* the tome that will undoubtedly remain the "monument" to her discovery of an ideal linked to social reform (D. Robinson 96). Fortunately, in *Summer on the Lakes* Fuller also left her account of the discovery itself—immediate, personal, and accessible.

A generation following Fuller's death, Willa Cather was born, the writer for whom Fuller's charge for women to someday "see and do and be more" seems an uncannily prescient benediction. Introduced to the West not with narratives by men but instead with correspondence from the women in her family who preceded her there, upon emigrating with her parents when she was eleven Cather developed the "self-reliance" and "self-impulse" that Fuller knew a woman would need to write a new birth myth for the nation.

2

The Long
Foreground to
Cather's West

Willa Cather was born into ideal conditions to write of the
frontier. The history of the opening of the West coincided perfectly with her personal history. The Homestead Act was passed in 1862,
the transcontinental railroad was completed in 1869, and in 1873—the
same year Willa was born—the Cathers began moving west. Willa's uncle
George married and with his wife, Frances (Franc) Smith, moved to Nebraska, purchased 360 acres from the Burlington Railroad, staked a claim,
and in 1874 moved onto a homestead. In 1874 Willa's grandparents, William and Caroline Cather, left Virginia to join their son George and his
family in a dugout. The next spring William and Caroline returned to Virginia, where they settled their affairs. In 1877 they moved permanently to
Nebraska and Willa's parents, Charles and Mary Virginia Boak (Jennie),
moved into Willow Shade (Willa's home in Virginia from 1874) to oversee
the family sheep operation. Two years later Charles Cather traveled to Nebraska to visit relatives and evaluate the prospects for his own family; in
1882 he returned, and in 1883 he and Jennie moved their family to Webster
County, Nebraska.

"I am convinced that the stereotypes and myths about frontierswomen
must be tested against their own diaries, letters, and memoirs to gain an
understanding of the myriad of questions surrounding their lives," Glenda
Riley wrote in the preface to her 1981 *Frontierswomen: The Iowa Experience,*
stating a position now standard in women's studies as well as in scholarship on the West. Yet we have not read the fiction of Cather, by all accounts

our foremost creator of myths about frontierswomen, against her own family's personal writing. Fortunately, we do have the voices of Cather's relatives speaking for themselves in letters to one another, beginning in 1870 and extending to modern times (unless otherwise noted, all correspondence from Cather family letters). Through them, we can come close to the family story of the West that she inherited.[1]

This story begins when Charles Cather, as if a scout, traveled west in 1870. Writing to his sister Jennie from the Colorado Territory, he adopted the most conventional of poses:

> My Dear Sister
> . . . It was in many respects an exciting trip, as we traveled through the country of the Indian; Mexican; Bear, & Wolf, and had the fun of seeing them all. However we were armed to the teeth which made us feel more secure than if we had been altogether exposed to their mercy.

"The Mexican bandits are worse than the Indians," he writes, then tells of a mail coach robbed and travelers on horseback killed by desperadoes:

> The Prairies here are beautiful beyond description; whilst in full view are the Snow capped peaks of the Rocky Mts. On the prairies the Antelope feed in abundance; they are the most beautiful thing you can imagine. . . . I very often think of you dear Sister; and wonder if your thoughts are oft directed toward your wandering brother in the Western Wilds. . . . Write me at Kansas City Mo. as soon as you receive this.
>
> Affectionately Your brother
> Charles

This is the only letter in the family collection that conforms to conventions of a masculine West; indeed, its humor lies in Charles's self-conscious pose as the single man leaving civilization "armed to the teeth" against the animals and desperadoes he is sure to encounter along the way to adventure and fortune. His eastern manners comically inappropriate to the western setting, the Virginian Charles Cather could be the Tenderfoot in Wister's *The Virginian*—as determinedly standing guard over his gentlemanly bearing as over the mules he feared losing "whilst we were in the midst of these unpleasant surroundings." Significantly, Charles's is also the single description of place or landscape in the conventional sense. His language becomes again a comically self-conscious nod to convention when he writes of the prairies as "beautiful beyond description" and the antelope as "the most beautiful thing you can imagine."[2]

The manner of Charles Cather's letter is as telling as its matter. It is solitary writing with little sense of exchange. Even the closing, "Write me at Kansas City Mo. as soon as you receive this," is expressed as a demand rather than an invitation. In this regard, his manner is characteristic of correspondence by the Cather men. They strain toward public declamation, casting their letters as announcements to an invisible "other" through formal, impersonal, and solitary correspondence. George Cather, for example, writes to his sister that his wife "has left considerable space for me to write & nothing to say. We were visiting in New Hampshire last week. Had a very pleasant time, & passed some very pretty places." Then, with apparent relief upon shifting to more comfortable ground, George writes, "Tell John [his sister's husband] I was at Lebanon N.H. last Monday to see the stock which pass down the Rail Road" and continues to fill the space allotted to him by identifying breeds of sheep, listing market prices, and enumerating types of crops (18 Aug. 1873).

As so often happens in family correspondence, most of the Cather letters were written by women, and they tell their story with different assumptions expressed in a different manner from the Cather men. Rather than straining toward the impersonal, letters by the Cather women are richly detailed about their daily lives and conversationally intimate in tone. Through them emerges the living reality of a family. The matriarch, Caroline Cather, and her husband, William, stand at the center with daughters Jennie plus the twins Alverna and Alfaretta (who is alternately called Alfretta) clustered around them. The women who married into the family are at the next remove, Franc Smith and Jennie Boak, with their husbands, George and Charles Cather. Outside this most immediate circle are aunts, uncles, and cousins, and outside that are more distant relatives and friends. As women describe each other's comings and goings, questions and answers, anticipations and reflections, their letters create a web of correspondence. The result is the multifaceted familiarity of family intimacy: the "double life"—the group life and the life of the individual self—that Cather described as existing within "even . . . harmonious families," ("Katherine Mansfield" 108–10). The double life occurs by a simultaneity of recognitions of the individual as both separate and also a member of the family and makes us aware of how each person sees herself at the same time we are aware of how others view her.

As to live within a family is to be aware of this double life, so in reading the Cather family correspondence we come to identify the distinct person-

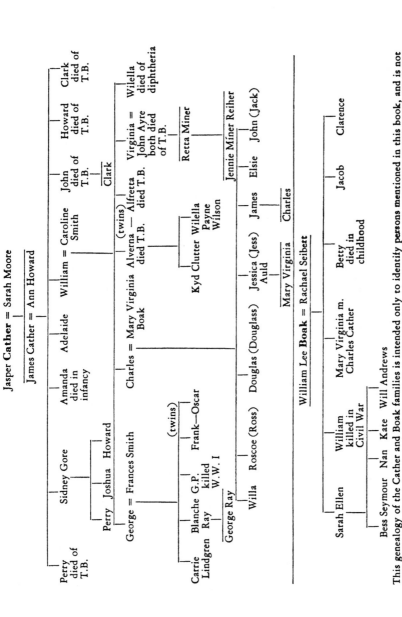

Partial genealogy of the Cather and Boak families.

ality of each voice and then to feel the start of recognition when she flashes before us in another's description. Aunt Sidney Gore's voice, for example, is officious and self-important: "I have been young Gennie and like yourself, flattered. . . . I have traveled over the ground upon which you are now standing, and I know all bout its allurements and fascinations" (10 June 1872); and after hearing it, we recognize her in Caroline Cather's description of preparations for a fair: "your aunty is on the committee of arrangements and I guess she thinks it is verry important that she Should be there" (7 Oct. 1873). Similarly, Willa's mother, Jennie Boak Cather, ostensibly inquiring about her sister-in-law's health, writes of her own with comically transparent self-absorption. Later, when we read Caroline Cather's account of visiting Jennie, we recognize the women we have met before—the pampered and charmingly naive young wife, Jennie; her mother-in-law, Caroline, who describes the younger generation with affectionate wisdom and wit; and (again) the officious Aunt Sidney: "Charleys Jennie has been sick called the Dr in twice I went up to see her & your Aunt Sidney and I think we understand her case as well as the Dr and think he was not needed as much know as he may be after while, but I didnot tel her so for she is so easay insulted I know she would fly right up for she thinks she is awfully sick her mother and Charley has a happy time waiting on her" (17 Apr. 1875). Distinctly individual voices become the constants running through the letters—that much is characteristic of family discourse generally. What is unusual about the Cather correspondence is its extension into Willa Cather's fiction, where, as in the letters, individuals from life remain so distinctly themselves. We again feel, for example, the start of familiarity at recognizing Jennie Boak Cather, newly pregnant and taken to her bed, as the Victoria Templeton of "Old Mrs. Harris."

Thus the letters offer voices of individuals woven together into a family engaged in ongoing conversation. Within the family, the lives of two of Willa's aunts—her father's sister, Jennie Cather Ayre, and her uncle George's wife, Franc Smith Cather, provide contrasting narrative threads. Both married in 1873, but then their lives followed different paths. One remained in Virginia and the other moved to Nebraska. By all accounts, Jennie Cather Ayre was—like Willa's mother Jennie Boak Cather—a favored child. Her aunt Sidney Gore writes "I have no niece that I expect more from than I do from you" (10 June 1872), and her cousin Joshua writes that "there is no cousin or friend of mine that I would tell so much as to you. Nor is there any one who I expect to intrust so much in as you" (13 Oct.

1872). She is, he declares, "my dearest Cousin the one I loved best of all I have" (5 Jan. 1873). Caroline Cather's letters to Jennie reveal a love and devotion to the daughter she has indulged and has "almost made an idle of" (30 Aug. 1873). When Jennie announced her plans to marry John Ayre, the family rallied in the drama of a wedding. Joshua writes of being "very anxious to hear all the proceeding which you promised to tell me, about the ring &c" (13 Oct. 1872), and Franc, preparing to be part of the wedding party, details dress patterns and makes travel plans as if she is part of a military campaign. "What is Miss Ayre's height," she asks about another attendant, "if we are the right and left flanks of the army we want to correspond somewhat" (24 Feb. 1873).

But a subtext darkening their excitement concerns the failing health of Jennie's sister Alfaretta (Rettie), who was suffering from tuberculosis. In some respects the Cathers were typical of their time, when consumption was a threat generally (concentrated efforts against tuberculosis did not begin until the turn of the century). The Cathers were especially susceptible, however, for the spring in the basement of Willow Shade that provided a cool storage room for food also ensured constant dampness throughout the house. References in their letters to colds and chills, hoarseness and coughs, become a code language acknowledging the very real danger of disease hanging over them all.

Once married, Jennie and John Ayre moved to Upperville, Loudoun County, Virginia, and letters followed Jennie from her family and especially from her mother. With their detailed descriptions of the Cathers' days, gossip about friends, inquiries about Jennie's health, and advice about domestic duties, Caroline's letters to Jennie are the love letters of a mother to her daughter: "dear daughter I wonder if you tink of your [mother] as often as She thinks of her darling Jennie you are among my last thought and pryers at night and among my first in the morning" (17 Apr. 1873). This correspondence confirms Carroll Smith-Rosenberg's observation that an intimate mother-daughter relationship lay at the heart of nineteenth-century women's sororal world, a bond that resulted in great sadness when marriage or emigration meant that the daughter left her mother's home (see, e.g., 32, 64).

Along with personal drama, then, we recognize the historical drama, for Caroline Cather's letters are classic examples of an ideology of domesticity threatening to harden into a Cult of True Womanhood. Caroline tells Jennie to honor John: "I hope darling you are striving not in your own stringth but in Christs strength and by his grace to live undr the cross. hope you may be a sourse of comfort and incouragement to John in all the trials of life for you will both no doubt meet with many trials and dis-apointments and need each others simpathys and encouragement" (17 Apr. 1873). In a long letter scolding her daughter, Caroline Cather de-scribes her concern and explains her reasons:

> I was real sorry you kept John waiting so long in town hope he has forgiven my poor little ering daughter. I had a heap to say when you was up and failed to say it Though I would write it all this morning but am so nervous I can scarcely write at all. darling you often say to John he must do so and so now Jennie I hope you will never make use of that expression to him again must and sha[n]t is words you should never use to each other I know you dont mean what you say but it looks bad and hurts Johns feelings and it is not lady like. hope you will make it your studdy to please him regardless of what the world may think of you. I hope if he do or says any thing that hurts your feelings you will not show it in your ex-pression nor any words in the presence of any person it dont matter who but talk the mater over when alone and be sure and not get angry. there is nothing more shameful than for a man and his wife to be speaking of each others faults in the presence of others there is no one in the world with out faults but man and wife should not be on the look out for each others faults but when they cant help but see them they should talk them over in a mild forgiving Spirit when alone. if their is any difference of opinion between you it is your place to yeld woman of-ten think it is verry hard that they are required to obey but I think the man is commanded to do more than that for he is commanded to love his wife as him silf and when that is the case I am sure he will not be hard to obey for no one ever requires unreasonible things of themselves. (31 May 1873)

On the most obvious level, Caroline's letters seem warmly personalized versions of textbook advice about housekeeping: "I thought I would write to you once more before you are of age to give you some more advise hope you may receive it this time and profit by it," Caroline writes to Jennie, then de-tails "simple rules" about tending to the house and keeping herself clean and neat (30 Aug. 1873). Writing supplements conversation when a daugh-ter leaves her parents' home and takes up independent responsibilities. By the act of writing a mother acknowledges her daughter's coming of age:

> now Jennie I ask it of you to do as I advise for one week and if you dont find your hosue in better order and feel happyer and more contented your self and John

more pleasant and better satisfied with you than he ever has been then I will give up and not bother you any more with my advise. commence by asking the blessing of the Lord on all you do and his guidance in every thing. get up early get breakfast over as soon as posible then make up your beds and sweet not wait until evening and have to be told to do it. and when you have attended to every thing you have to do about the house not allowing any thing to go to waste sit down to your sewing or knitting keep on it dont quit and commence beating [?] and kissing John if he wants to kiss you he will do it without your quiting your work and dont put on a dress that will do very well to wear to church and the only clean ribbon you have at home on sunday or a week day eathier. try and keep your self clean and neat all the time unless you should be at some verry dirty work and then if you will do to appear at all dont run of and dress every time a stranger comes in. and never wear a apron that looks much worse than a soiled dress I always thought I was fit to receive company if I could wear a cheerful face & clean colar and apron

now Darling Daughter by observing those simple rules I think you will find you have plenty of time to do every thing you have to do and some time left to read which I fear you are neglecting altogether now. (30 Aug. 1873)

Advice to be domestic, pious, submissive, and pure was nothing new to nineteenth-century women generally, or to Jennie Cather Ayre particularly—for to be favored meant to be indulged by her mother and pampered in a southern tradition. Before her wedding her aunt Sidney Gore had warned her against vanity by advising that "He will expect you to be an *humble, grateful christian*" (10 June 1872). Afterward, she advised Jennie to "forever banish all superfluous *pride*," explaining that "it is my great desire to see you a happy useful wife and *real* ornament in society" (3 May 1873). Aunt Sidney's hortatory and Caroline Cather's loving exchange counsel the common lessons of true womanhood.

Along with the conventional advice about domesticity, concern continues over health. Caroline Cather writes from Willow Shade that Rettie had a very hoarse spell and was growing much worse and that she hoped she "may get better when the Spring comes. The Dr Says it will do her more good to get out in the fresh air when the weather is dry and pleasant than any thing else hope the weather will soon be pleasant and she may be able to go out" (29 Mar. 1873). A letter from Rettie that spring reveals the reality, however. She had gone to her aunt Sidney Gore's, her "first visit," and her anxiety at being exposed pulses through the letter. She feared it was rather late to be out but she was so bundled she didn't think she took cold. "We have had so much gloomy weather for the last three weeks that I very seldom get to go out," she reflects and then concludes, "I think my health has been improving quite as much as could be expected, owing to the gloomy weather we have been having" (7 May 1873). By late November of that year, another letter from Rettie confirms her failing strength: "I will only promise you a short note this morning as I feel but very little like writing, have been sewing some little and feel tired" (26 Nov. 1873). As if a chorus, other correspondents report that Rettie is about the same, or "not so well this morning; think she has taken some fresh cold, by letting the fire get to low" (Alverna [Vernie] Cather Clutter, 14 May 1873), and "not so well as She was when you left this damp weather dont agree with her" (to Jennie Cather Ayre, 18 Aug. 1873).

Meanwhile, a contrasting narrative emerges in the family story. In 1873 Frances (Franc) Smith married George Cather, and in August the couple prepared to go west. The bare facts of their move would seem to support conventions about the pioneer wife: following their marriage she accompanied him to Nebraska as the first homesteaders in the Catherton area. On the frontier they faced devastation by grasshoppers, prairie fires, and drought. George, working outside, left Franc in their dugout, the only woman within miles. Yet Franc's own account of their move confirms more recent recognition by historians of families (see Schlissel, Ruiz, and Monk, introduction to *Western Women*, for a summary of work on this subject).

Educated at Mount Holyoke seminary and a teacher at Winchester Female Institute, Franc Smith Cather was a literate and faithful correspondent, and her letters from Nebraska are significant, generally, as a woman's account of homesteading. They also provide a version of the family story that Willa Cather knew firsthand. Though Franc and George physically left their parents in the East, they maintained family support from the beginning of their move. Franc writes from Vermont of spending time there before moving and reports, "Mother is going west with us, as far as Michigan," where she will visit friends, and "Father thinks he will come and see us next fall when we get located"; they plan to see Niagara Falls on their way West (17 Aug. 1873). En route, she writes from "Uncle Jo's in Iowa" and describes visiting her uncle's parents in Wayne, Illinois (12 Sept. 1873).

In late December Franc writes Jennie Cather Ayre from Nebraska, titling her address "The Grove." Aware of the family's fears whether Rettie (her sister-in-law in Virginia) would survive the winter, by writing "we are wintering well and bid fair to come out in fine condition in the spring" Franc is not making the conventional nod to the weather but is reporting on a life-and-death concern. When she writes that George plans to go hunting on the Little Blue River the next day, Franc corroborates his good health, and when she describes his shooting three times at a buffalo—"but it was with the small revolver & the buffalo went on his way rejoicing"— she makes the frontier accessible. Similarly, she testifies "I am doing very well," then corroborates by enumerating the sewing she has done. "I have made up about 80 yards of cloth this fall & winter," she writes, then numbers the items she made, including "Have made Geo. four shirts & am going to make him some more. I never made any before & so I think it quite an achievement" (28 Dec. 1873).

In the same letter, Franc describes the process of their settling in. She thanks Jennie for the apple seeds, writes that she has seven little trees growing up from seeds she planted earlier, and then comments that "I planted yours in a place by themselves & will write you went they come up." She asks Jennie to send her "anything in the seed line, either garden seeds or trees or anything you may have. I think Geo. will send on to Va. & have a box of acorns, hickory nuts &c. sent out. He has forty acres of timber to set out either this summer or next. I mean to have a big vegetable & flower garden as soon as he can prepare the ground." She describes their plans to take an adjoining 160 acres, making 480, and again she draws a diagram of their land, marking where they are living now and where they intend to move in the spring. "I wish we had it well stocked & our buildings up; but every thing can't be done at once," she reflects.

Finally, she seeks news from Virginia. "I hear from Mrs Willis that the school is doing finely. I saw in the last Winchester Times that the Young Ladies of the Winchester Female Institute held an Apron Fair on the 19th. I am waiting to hear farther particulars. Much love to Joan. Write all the news. Love from Geo. & myself." In a postscript she again crafts a word picture: "I forgot to tell you that to celebrate Christmas Geo. & I cut each others hair. Mine is shingled just as you saw it in those little Ferreotypes. Write soon" (28 Dec. 1873).

More than any other factor, levels of intimacy distinguish the Cather women's letters to one other. Caroline Cather's letters to her daughter Jennie are the most intimate and reveal the expectation of freely exchanged information and feelings; Franc's to her sister-in-law Jennie Cather Ayre request such an exchange both by the fullness of the descriptions of her life and by the repeated request, "write all the news." Yet they acknowledge the privacy of distance, with secrets withheld. Tone, diction, and voice all reflect awareness of an appropriate closeness as made clear in letters surrounding the birth of Jennie Cather Ayre's first child. Caroline Cather writes to her daughter of plans for Jennie's confinement ("dont think I can go over before you are confined I might have to Stay so long but if you can send for me as soon as you get sick I will go over and stay as long as I can" and "hope you will have your mother Ayre over at the time" [27 Mar. 1874]); yet the Nebraska Cathers did not know Jennie was pregnant. Perhaps "heightened language signals heightened feeling" (Hampsten 20); certainly conventional language signals self-consciousness. In one of her most mannered letters, Franc responds to the news that Jennie and John have a daughter: "We were much surprised on the receipt of a letter from Jno' T. [Ayre] a few days ago, to learn of the addition to your family." Puns suggest discomfort ("Expect there will be more putting on airs [heirs] [Ayres] than ever now"), and Franc's labored humor forms a counterpoint to her request that Jennie "tell us all": "This latest development however took us quite by surprise. Write as soon as you are able, and tell us all about the little demoiselle." In a similarly self-conscious manner, Franc asks Jennie to quote her to Mr. Thomas, "& tell him that I resent the imputation cast upon my Virginia sisters and I claim that any true woman no matter where she breat[h] natal air, can not only live unmurmuringly but happily, with the husband of her choice, under difficulties more insuperable than finding a home in a new country & I think there are some Virginia ladies with as much vim & force of character as northern ladies & placed in my situation would be as far from being killed as I am."

As she begins to describe what they are doing, she drops the mannered attempts at wit and writes in a plain style:

A Nursery-man spent the night with us last night and we gave him an order for a nucleus of an orchard to be delivered next fall & planted in the spring. New settlers are coming in quite rapidly. Two new houses have sprung up in sight within a week. I am afraid John [Smith, her brother?] has delayed coming too long to get very near to us. We expect him this week. We will probably go to Lowell next week [to] prove up on the pre-emption and take the homestead. I feel as if it would be quite a trip. I have been at home so long & withal quite a disagreeable one as the accommodation at the hotels are execrable. We were there several days last fall & Geo. had to buy crackers & cheese to subsist upon. He happened to pass through the kitchen & couldn't eat anything after that. I hope to have no occasion to visit the place after this time, as the Land Office will probably be moved before we prove up on the Homestead. Give love to John from Geo. & myself. Havn't any particular news to write, except I was out in the garden today & saw the onions, beets & radishihes were up. I havn't planted those seeds you sent me yet, as Geo. hasn't had time to get the ground ready. Will do so soon. (28 Apr. 1874)

The much discussed loneliness of women on the frontier emerges, but by a wistfulness of tone and submerged details rather than directly. On their first anniversary, for example, Franc writes, "I wonder if anybody has thought of us, on this, the anniversary of our wedding day" and then reports that they celebrated by killing one of "those wonderful chickens of ours &c. Two of our neighbors came to assist in the wonderful feat of eating her. Jno' thought *he* could have eaten her himself. He shot an antelope, so will have fresh meet for several days. Antelope tastes someting like mutton. Jno' is very fond of it" (26 June 1874).

Franc devotes the rest of her letter to taking stock of their first year in Nebraska and describing the process of transforming open plains into farming country:

George is very busy these days. He hardly felt that he would stop today. He has plowed nearly all around the farm forty five ft. wide to keep the fire off this fall; besides he has ten acres on the timber claim & ten on the homestead & one for the orchard broken. I think we will certainly have old ground enough for a garden next yr. Our garden is doing very little good this year, as we had no ground suitable—very few of the seed came up & when up can hardly live. We have a few vines & that is about all. Geo. has some over twenty acres of corn; but we cannot tell yet whether or no it is going to yield. We have some beans also in bloom.

My chickens are doing very well. I think I have between 160 or 170 now and have lost a good many from accidental causes. I do not think I will try to raise over 200. Geo. wishes they were sheep daily. I have only six little ducks. The old drake drowned one, we think, last Sunday while we were over to preaching. We have Methodist preaching two miles from here, every other Sabbath. This seems much better than when there was none. Shall be glad when we can ride tho' I get very tired walking in hot weather & in bad weather I could hardly go at all. It has been very hot here almost all this month. I get almost roasted

I hope you are better than when I heard from you last Kiss the baby for Geo. & me. Expect Geo. would steal it if he had a chance & eat it up kissing it. Its lucky you live no nearer if you want to keep it. The districts here are three miles square there isn't a baby in it, all the residents are bachelors, except us. Small prospect for a school right away. New settlers are coming in quite rapidly. I suppose you have heard that Jno. took 320 acres a mile south of us. There was another man at the Land Office to take it directly after Jno. had entered it, but too late. We were afraid it was taken. Jno. plowed four or five acres with our team & is going to plow some more after Geo. gets his done, which will be in two or three days more. Geo. is going to put a well down soon. You have no idea how bad it is doing without water as we do. I like to go over to our neighbors to get a cool drink of water, but I can't go very often.

And, in a postscript, she notes, "There are three families lately come in here from Rockingham Co. [Va.]. One of the ladies was here today. Smokes &c—(very nice?)" Factual details confirm hardship. Franc is the only woman within miles, they have no water, the garden is producing little, and George is largely occupied outside. Still, Franc's attitude is determinedly optimistic: they had neighbors to help celebrate their wedding anniversary, there is the expectation of a garden next year, she is able to attend church every other week, and settlers are rapidly arriving. Above all, their capacity for hard work confirms their good health.

As if a counterpoint to the Nebraska Cathers' prospects, during the fall of 1874 in Virginia Rettie Cather died, and Jennie and John Ayre's health worsened. Franc wrote to Jennie Cather Ayre:

I was sorry to hear you had been having so serious a time & that Jno's health was so poorly. I hope he is better now. I feel as if he ought to be very careful of himself and give up work entirely for a while. There is no disease concerning which one needs to be more watchful or is more liable to be deceived than lung disease. If you were only able to travel with baby I would think it would be a very good thing for him to come to Nebraska. Our dry winters are just the good thing for people with a tendency to lung troubles, and every body who has come here for that, of whom I have heard, have been cured." "I think I should take alarm on the very first symptoms. I have always feared it for George & that is the principal reason why I chose Nebraska to come to & am willing to stay in spite of grass hoppers or everything else. It is cold and stormy today & I think likely we are having our last storm for the season as we had no rain worth mentioning after we came last year. It has been a drier season than usual this year & the prairie has burned over in some places; but this has stopped everything of that kind for awhile probably.

Geo. has gone to Red Cloud today. We didn't get up so early as usual this morning so I told Geo. I would milk for him. I am learning fast. I milked two cows this morning. Water has been so scarce that he keeps them about a mile & three quarters from the house & it makes a right long walk. We have five cows now; but only two at home now that give milk. I expect to make butter this winter. My butter has been very good since I had two cows & the weather has been cooler—Many thanks for baby's picture. Wish I could see her and give her a squeeze I think she looks like Kyd [Clutter] & they say Kyd looks like Geo. Of course she is good looking & will always be if that's the case. Do you think father & mother will really come out? It seems too nice to believe & I won't hardly let myself think of it for fear I may be disappointed. Hope we shall get moved &c. before they come. It will be pleasanter.

Then in a final paragraph of the same letter she presents a long view: "One year ago today we were traveling in Canada, on our way out here. How many changes since then. We moved on our claim the 9th of Oct. We won't get moved till after that time this yr. Every thing has to stop now till haying is over. Geo. is nearly done" (3 Sept. 1874).

Caroline and William Cather did join their son and daughter-in-law, and in November Franc writes on the day she and George are moving into their own dugout. Like the correspondence generally, this letter offers the immediacy of having been written in the midst of the event it describes. There too is the assumption that Jennie will understand her pleasure over privacy that the new dugout provides. Her comment "just Geo. & I" is both a reminder that conditions have been cramped for the two families and an expression of the happiness of the young couple to have their bed in their own room, even if it is in a hole in the ground. Privacy on the frontier is provided by a location a quarter mile across the prairie. Also in the letter is the ongoing commentary on health:

Mother feels so anxious to hear from you, as we all do since Jno has been sick, that she thinks I had better write a little. We are all in a stir here. Today is the day we had to move on our homestead, so we moved down yesterday, into the new dugout—just Geo. & I. Father and mother are going to stay here until the new one is entirely finished, which I think will be next week sometime. Father & Geo. have been at work on it almost ever since they came tho' Geo. has so much else to do that it takes a good deal of his time. We have only moved our bed, and a few things down & eat & spend most of our time (at least I do) here. It is only a quarter of a mile from here but passing to & fro takes up a great deal of time. We are all going to eat down there tonight for the first time.

Mother wants you to write soon, and tell how Jno' is, & wants to know why he has lost all faith in Fahrney? She sends much love to you both. I hope Jno' will be very careful and not expose himself or do more than he is able. We feel very anxious for him.

We have been having beautiful weather ever since the folks came; but it is quite windy today tho' warm. We have had no prairie fire here yet, tho' have seen the prairie burning six or eight miles from us. We are hoping to escape free this fall, at least on our own land. We have fire breaks fifty ft. wide all around.

Father & mother seem to like the country very well. Father is much better than when he came. They have not been around the country much yet as father has been helping Geo. ever since he came. I hope they will be through soon. We have no well yet. Geo. is going tomorrow to try and engage a man to dig it. It seems a long time to wait. We have been here thirteen months now.

I have so many things to do I must close now. With much love from us all- your sister Franc. (6 Nov. 1874)

"Real isolation was . . . a short-lived phenomenon, usually lasting only two or three years on most parts of the frontier," writes Jeffrey (*Frontier Women* 56). Certainly that was true for the Cathers. By January 1875 Caroline and William Cather were living near George and Franc, Franc was teaching school, and the severe solitude of those first months was rapidly becoming a thing of the past.[3] Caroline Cather now writes to her daughter Jennie from Nebraska. Again, she interprets the weather, the land, and their activities in terms of their health:

It has been along time since I herd from you fear John is worse, but hope I may get a letter tomorrow saying he got intirely well. . . . for health is the greatest blessing on earth. . . . it is beautiful weather now but it has been very cold for the last three weeks. yesterday and to day has been beautiful hope it may continue so. . . . there is snow on the ground now. we dont have any rain in the winter out here it is dry and cold and seems to be verry hlthy. I like it very well. think it suits your Father verry well he is looking much better than when we came here, and that hacking cough he had before he left home has entirely left him. Franc has not been home since she commenced teaching.

George gos over to see her every Saturday and dont get back until Sunday evening. sometimes he forgets he went to the post ofice and brings my letters back with out mailing them. thinks he only goes to see Franc

> your Father keeps buisy fixing up things made Geo a barrom and Franc a table and a loung. partitioned off the bead room this weeke we just had curtains hung, and it took five sheets to hang up and that made a heap of washing I am certainly am glad to have boards in stead of curtains. I gitalong with the work real nicely Geo. does the milking and he and your Father carries the water and wood and I only get two meals a day and I live real nice and cozy. (22 Jan. 1875)

The counterpoint continues. Testifying to possibilities Nebraska holds not for success but for life itself, Caroline and Franc describe all they are doing, then refer back to health. Franc, for example, writes from Batin, Webster County, Nebraska:

> It is perfect bedlam here just now, as I have just let out school; but I will try and write you a few lines. Have been intending to write you ever since I have been over here; but have been so busy have not get about it. This is the seventh week of school I have only three months to teach. Shall be glad when it is over and I am at home again tho' I think they are getting along nicely without me. I do not expect to go home until school is out I give music lessons in the evening—on the organ—so my time is more fulled up than it otherwise would be. I saw George last Tuesday—he said they were all well at home then. Charlie wrote last week that Jerry Orndoff was coming out here next month. he named two others; but I do not remember their names. How is John's health now? I feel very anxious about him. We are having a very severe winter here, tho there has been little snow. The thermometer has been 24 below zero twice. It has been unusually severe all through the west. I believe it has been miled with you. Mother insists that she has seen a colder day in Va.; but I think it is only because our house is so warm that she does not realize how cold it has been.
>
> Father has turned cabinet maker since he has been out here & makes furniture for people, makes tables, lounges, stools, benches &c. &c. People think him a handy man to have around. I got a letter from Aunt Milicent Cather yesterday—all well there. Give love to John and Retta Write me often, & don't be so chary of your home affairs. I like to hear about all that is going on &c. &c. I don't find out everthing that is going on at our home, but expect mother keeps you posted. From your loving sister Franc. (11 Feb. 1875)

In Virginia, Jennie Cather Ayre's health worsened, and her sister Vernie went to Upperville, Loudoun County, to nurse her. From Willow Shade

Charles's wife, Jennie Boak Cather, writes, hoping that her sister-in-law is improved, saying that Charlie would have gone with Vernie to see her had he been able to leave home, and offering to come and stay a short time if Vernie cannot remain until Jennie has recovered. Her daughter "baby Willa" misses her cousin very much, Jennie writes, and "Runs to his cradle, just as soon as she gets out in the dinning room and cries Tid-did Tid-did." She then writes: "Tell Vernie we are all getting along very well. I have a very bad cough and a very sore throat I have been fearful of deptheria but I hope not. I has been so cold that we have not done much work since she left Margery and Ma have not washed altho Margery was crazy to try the new one. I hope Jennie you are really in no serious danger and that soon you will be well and harty My love to Jno. Vernie and yourself kiss the baby and Kyde from Willa Jennie and Charlie" (16 Feb. 1875).

When in the spring or summer of 1875 William and Caroline returned to Virginia, it was to prepare to move to Nebraska. Their preparations were delayed by William's father's death, however (Bennett, *World of Willa Cather* 10), and letters fill the gap. As always, family news provides the reassuring sense that the ordinary continues in Nebraska. Franc reports on sewing completed, hens setting, and gardening done; George tells of acres sowed in barley, wheat, oats, corn, and potatoes and of the stock. The rapidity of settlement is apparent. Less than two years after they arrived in Nebraska, Franc no longer describes settlers coming or houses appearing but instead writes of the variety of opportunities ("we have been protracted meetings of different denominations all around us" [17 Feb. 1876]). As their concern over the health of the Virginia relatives deepens, she and George write more directly of emigration as offering health: "we were truly glad to hear of Jno's improvement in health, and sincerely hope it may be permanent. We have been greatly blessed since we have been out here, having had no permanent ills of body to complain of, and we are learning to look with complacency upon a very lean pocket book in the present, hoping for a full one in the future" (17 Feb. 1876). On the back of the same letter, George writes, "I think if Jno. had have come to Neb. when we did, that he would not have lost his health, for our climate certainly suits persons who are weak lunged. I know I have had much better health here, than I ever had before" (17 Mar. 1876).

Jennie and John Ayre's infant son died that spring in Virginia, and again letters offer the immediacy of events as they are happening. Caroline Cather writes on 3 May while anticipating her grandson's death, then again the next day after having learned of it. Though the fact that she writes on consecutive days indicates her concern, Caroline treats the infant's death as one of the tribulations that await every couple making a life together. In her first letter Caroline expresses the hope that "you and john will not fret over your Dear baby but if it is the Lords will to take him give up knowing and feeling that all things work together for good to them that love the Lord." She then returns to ordinary news of anticipating letters, and to Anna Willa, who "married Alexander and lives in Winchester in Rogers house," and "your father is stil quite lame but is out planting corn" (3 May 1876). In her second letter she offers the solace of Biblical quotation and reflection: "Suffer little Children to come unto me. . . . it is the greatest comfort I have to feel that so many of our children are done with the sorrows and disappointments of this world and are with Jesus Christ which is for better. was sorry to hear John was not so well." (4 May 1876).

As if in response, there is the shortest letter of the collection, begun by Jennie Cather Ayre but not finished. It is eloquent in the simple directness of her grief: "Time flies swiftly and brings many changes Quite a *sad sad change* in our little circle. It seems our Little Jewel was only loaned us a short while I miss him sadly. Seem lost without him. I fear we had set our hearts too much upon him. I had built so many castles in the air, but alas! they are all fallen. John has not been   "(10 May 1876). The play between convention and direct expression tells its own story. The conventional opening sentences give way to the powerfully direct "I miss him sadly" and then the fragment "Seem lost without him." As if to right herself, Jennie returns to convention by writing that she feared "we had set our hearts too much upon him" and "I had built so many castles in the air," followed by "John has not been   " (10 May 1876). Here the letter breaks off, its final silence powerful in expressing what cannot be said—that John has not been well and his own death threatens.

Meanwhile, Franc writes that she is caring for forty hens while George is planting trees and sowing crops. Here as elsewhere she acknowledges the hardships of frontier living: the heat, the difficulty of doing without water, and the uncertainty of crops. But Franc measures such matters in terms of Nebraska's all-important promise for the family's health. Writing in 1876 that they had grasshoppers again, she also writes, "but the small grain was all harvested & they left some of the corn, so it is not as bad as the other time." Continuing, she writes: "we are not discouraged yet. Don't think many people are going to leave the country. We will not have much to eat compared with what you would have at home; but still I think it would be better for you not to defer your visit here too long. I don't feel so much like urging it for fear you would wish you had not come after you got here— still if you both felt better I think maybe you would overlook some inconveniences I am glad to hear you are both improving" (17 Sept. 1876). This is the motif—confirmation of the possibility of health in Nebraska by descriptions of all they are doing and concern over the threat that Virginia holds for those still there. "George has little time for writing because of all he has & has had to do, but he keeps well, which is one good thing" (18 Dec. 1876).

So far as isolation is concerned, travel could be difficult in Virginia too. In January 1877 John Ayre died and Caroline and William (who had returned to Virginia to settle their affairs) write on reverse sides of a single sheet to their daughter, describing their inability to reach her. William writes that they had started for Llangolen in Charlie's sleigh but "found the roads in much worse condition than we expected," so had to turn back. For once, Caroline doesn't turn to the Bible but writes simply of their efforts to reach Jennie. Their shared grief and concern over the hardship ahead for their daughter are raw and immediate: "Da[r]ling Daughter I cant express my feeling or give you any idie of my regret of not getting over to se Dear John I have been trying to go for a week sent for Charley to take me over last thursday but he was not at home got home on friday but was taken with desintary and is not well enough to leave home yet your father and I started this morning he had to get out and tramp the snow before the sley three times and we upset once and both had to get out in the snow before we got in the grade and after geting on the grade we found it very bad sleighing and was compeled to gurn back we will get over Just as son as the roads get so we can go god bles you" (2 Jan. 1877).

In 1877 William and Caroline moved to Nebraska, bringing with them daughter Jennie with her own three-year-old daughter, Alfretta (Retta)—so named after Jennie's sister—and Alverna (who had separated from her husband J. J. Webb Clutter) with her five-year-old son, Kyd (P. Riley 586).[4] By that time Jennie was "so ill that there was some doubt as to whether she could make the trip," writes Mildred R. Bennett. "Her parents put her on a stretcher, and although she survived the journey, she died two weeks later and was buried in an orchard of young apple trees on her brother's farm" (*World of Willa Cather* 10), perhaps among the trees grown from seeds Jennie sent to Franc that first winter they were in Nebraska.

Willa's family was the last of the Cathers to leave Virginia for Nebraska. Her parents, Charles and Mary Virginia (Jennie) Boak Cather, remained at Willow Shade until 1883 with Mrs. Rachel Boak (Jennie's mother) living with them. In 1880 Charles visited his brother and father and "found them flourishing" (Woodress 31), and in April 1883 Charles and Jennie Boak Cather moved to Webster County. When they arrived in Nebraska, Charles and Jennie brought with them four children (Willa, Roscoe, Douglas, and Jessica). They also brought the hired girl Margie Anderson and her brother Enoch plus Rachel Boak "and two of her grandchildren" (Woodress 31). They were met by Willa's grandparents, her aunt and uncle, and her cousins. They were met, too, by frame as well as sod houses, a post office (in Catherton), schools, and church congregations of different dominations that met in the schoolhouses and relied on traveling ministers to preach.

What do we learn from the Cather family letters? They are, as Paul Riley has written, "of interest in themselves" in confirming the importance of the extended family on the frontier. "When thinking of the pioneer," he acknowledges, "we often think of the lone frontiersman, his wife, and perhaps a child or two. And, it is true, this is the way the Cather family began in Nebraska—with George and Franc Cather. Yet, within ten years all surviving members of the William Cather family were living in Nebraska. They were joined by cousins and neighbors until one portion of Catherton Township became known as 'New Virginia,' an appellation still used" (587).

As the letters encourage an expanded view of the pioneer from the individual to the family, so they encourage an expanded view of place and time. The Cather family letters confirm what Elizabeth Hampsten has written of women's concerns—they are much the same from one region to another. Questions posed and advice given about gardening, preserving, sewing, and housekeeping cross geography and join generations, and children's activities provide ongoing drama. In 1873 Franc Smith wrote from Winchester Female Institute in Virginia of preparing for Jennie's wedding, concerned about how her dresses would survive travel and bad weather and asking about the pattern for her dress; two decades later Franc Cather writes from Webster County of preparing to go to church, concerned about how her daughters' dresses will survive travel and bad weather, for "it is going to rain and they will get their new dresses wet." As she had so many years earlier, she again refers to a dress pattern, saying that "Carrie [her daughter] made hers by the pattern Retta gave her and it looks very well indeed" (5 May 1895).[5]

Rettie (originally Alfretta) is the name of William and Caroline Cather's daughter who had died in Virginia of tuberculosis, and Retta is the nickname of Jennie Cather Ayre's daughter who traveled with her and her grandparents to Nebraska in 1877. Reared by her grandparents after her mother died, Retta Ayre would remain in Nebraska and marry Hugh Miner in Red Cloud in 1896, and then she would give her mother's name—Jennie—to her own daughter. Thus names are passed from generation to generation, testifying to ongoing family history. Such is the case with the name Wilella/Willa. William and Caroline Cather named their youngest daughter Wilella but she died in Virginia of diphtheria. The name survived, however, when their son Charles and his wife, Jennie, named their first daughter Wilella also, from infancy shortening the future novelist's name to Willa, and it continued when William and Caroline's daughter Alverna named her daughter Wilella.

In many ways these letters confirm what recent historians have argued after reading other family correspondence from the westering movement: emigration was carried out in families. The Cather letters also confirm much that has been said about the adaptation of domestic ideology to the western frontier. Because of disposition, or circumstance, or a combination of the two, Jennie Cather Ayre is a model of nineteenth-century, middle-class Anglo women in the East, and Franc is a model of adapting those expectations to the West. Caroline Cather's counsel to her daughter conforms classically to what Barbara Welter has called the Cult of True Womanhood, which held four cardinal virtues: piety, purity, submissiveness, and domesticity. Franc translates the idea of true womanhood into cooperation and initiative.[6]

What emerges is a strong sense of class as defined by Hampsten: "the social and cultural 'home' of particular persons, their immediate locale in regard to aspirations" (27). Aware of a letter as performance, Caroline tells her daughter to "do your best when you write" to your grandfather, "for he knows what a good letter is." She then follows with a postscript, "as soo[n] as you read my letters pleas burn them I write so badly I dont want any Strangers to see them" (17 Apr. 1873). Vernie Cather Clutter writes, "excuse the miserable letter as they are all talking around me" (14 May 1873). The self-conscious and conventional language suggests Franc's initial awkwardness of finding herself on the frontier writing back to Virginia friends;

conversely, the emergence of a more direct style suggests that she quickly adapted.

Complementing this sensitivity to the letter as performance, Caroline Cather and Franc Smith Cather reveal a shared assumption that letters within a family maintain connections by sharing ordinary details of daily living. On 18 August 1873 Caroline writes to her daughter Jennie:

I know you and Verna is anxious to hear from home and I will try and give you all the satisfaction I can and tel you all we have been doing since you left. hope you got home safe. Just as soon as you left I commenced sweeping up and never stoped until I Swept the house from top to bottom and Lize finished her ironing Saturday morning She pulled some of her hair out and roled it on curl papers and laid it on the poarch banisters to dry after dinner Taylor and her took the ro-mary [Romney?] stage and started for campmeeting uncle John Started early in the morning went in the wagon with uncle Dick you may think I was glad to get the kitchen cleared of niggers for a few days any how. have been geting along ev-erso nice you Father fetches the cows and helps to milk hunts the eggs and fetches water and wood and makes himself verry use ful and if I could keep him in the house with clean clothes on he would be ornamental but I cant do that he will be out in the mud pulling weeds this wet weather it has been raining most all day. rained all the afternoon yesterday suppose you did not go to campmeet-ing if it rained as much with you as it did here. . . . Dr Baker called on us Satur-day evening looked real nice had the prettiest pair of shoes on I ever saw a man wear. Says he has a verry good practice dont know what he calls a good practice if thepeople was all like me I dont think he would get much to do well enough they are not. Rettie received a letter from Franc this morning they are both well and in fine spirits. I wrote a letter to Franc before I commenced this tel vernie to write so as to give the letter plenty time to come when she wishes to come home for some times they are a long time ond the road if you kow what time the stage gets in winchester let us know so we need not be there waiting so long I will ask Charly perhaps he knows tell Kyd Grandma Shoes has got to behaving better than they did when he was here They allways stay Just where I put them now. give him everysomany kisses for us all and tel him we miss him more than and and his ma both

Rettie is not so well as She was when you left this damp weather dont agree with her hope Vernie has not had any more chills do hope her helth may im-prove Jennie do be careful of your helth dont take any more naps in the daytime take plent of exersize dont mean you have to go horseback or buggy riding to do it for any housekeeper can find plenty oof exersize at home. dont get your feet damp nor change your clothes when you are warm nor sit in the draft for when helth is once gone it isnot easy restored and it takes so little to make any of you Sick. ~~Your Father is~~ Tuesday after dinner your Father is realy going to the association will take the romny sage this afternoon and go as far as winchester to night. Rettie and I will be all alon but I expect John will be over this evening if he is well enough he had a dreadful cold yesterday lvoe to John verna kyd and your self

[Then as a postscript] tel John not to work to hard nor run after stock and over heat himself as he did before he was over God bless you my darling kiss verna Kyd and John for me

Jennie do be careful and not scald yourself or get your clothes afire when you are canning or preserving. (19 Aug. 1873)

Caroline Cather's letter still does what over a century ago she meant it to do, that is, it gives the satisfaction of telling all they were doing that day. Its voice is intimately conversational, its detail generously full. I know of no other document that provides such rich and accessible insight into Willa Cather's Virginia childhood as her grandmother's description of her day, nor do I know of any text that makes the legacy of slavery in that background so painfully personal as her grandmother's casual aside describing relief at getting "the kitchen cleared of niggers for a few days any how."

There is a shared assumption among the Cather women that satisfaction comes from writing not about an impersonal public arena but of their family and friends. There is no reference to politics in these letters; from them we could not learn who was president or state representative. It is not the exceptional or the dramatic that these women strive for, but the fullness of ordinary living. In Nebraska Franc, upon learning of an Apron Fair in Virginia held by the Young Ladies of the Winchester Female Institute, is "waiting to hear further details" (28 Dec. 1873), and we understand that she is writing to her sister-in-law of shared assumptions about the language of a female community. Similarly, when she announces she hasn't "any particular news to write" and then continues, "except I was out in the garden today & saw the onions, beets & radishes were up," we learn that she considers "particular news" an essential part of her letter and that she finds such news by reflecting upon what she observed that day (28 Dec. 1873). Repeatedly, the Cather women affirm the importance of particulars. Their phrases make this clear: "Write all the news" (28 Dec. 1873); "dont write such short letters write me everything" (22 Jan. 1875); "Write me often, & don't be so chary of your home affairs. I like to hear about all that is going on" (11 Feb. 1875). Never in these letters did I find the phrase "nothing happened," that response that Hampsten found to be characteristic of women's private writing and that calls for "a special inventive patience" to interpret "what is not written as well as what is" (4). The Cather women knew that they valued the particulars; they conscientiously provided them to and requested them from one another. With the exception of illness, "what happens" consists of daily events woven together into familiar patterns.

The exception is immense, however, for the threat of disease and death lies behind the Cathers' story of moving west. The Virginia letters tell largely (one might argue exclusively) about that threat. All is reported and interpreted through concern over health, as if it were a lens. Winter threatens death of loved ones; spring promises renewed hope for life; rain brings disease. Nebraska offers not land (though there was that) so much as longevity, and the West's opportunity was not for success so much as for a family to feel secure in its own health.

Indeed, a long view suggests that the move west was a watershed in the Cather family history. Of the eight children born to Willa's great-grandparents, James and Ann (Howard) Cather, four died of tuberculosis and a fifth died in infancy. Of the six children born to her grandparents, William and Caroline (Smith) Cather, the four who remained in Virginia died, three of tuberculosis and one of diphtheria (Bennett, *World of Willa Cather* 228). Susan Parry, the present owner of Willow Shade, wrote me of the children of William and Caroline Cather: "They had *seven* living children (information given me by Helen Cather Southwick); three died in Virginia, two in Nebraska (of tuberculosis), and Charles and George lived their full biblical span. James Howard Cather was born in 1858 between Jennie and Wilella; he died at age 8 in 1867 and is buried in the Gainesboro Cemetery Cather family plot next to sisters Alfaretta and Wilella."

Gender distinctions are as dramatic as geographical ones. The four daughters, who presumably remained more closely indoors, died of lung disease; the two sons, presumably more active in Virginia and certainly the ones to move to Nebraska, lived. In Nebraska George and Frances (Smith) Cather had five children who enjoyed robust health—their son G. P. died at age thirty-five from a war wound, not disease. As for the seven children of Charles and Mary Virginia (Boak) Cather, all enjoyed good health and long lives. "When Grandfather and Grandmother celebrated their Golden Wedding Anniversary" in 1922, their grandson reminisced, "all of their seven children were alive (there had been no infant, etc. deaths) and all except Douglass were there for the occasion" (qtd. in Bennett, "What Happened" 621).

What difference does this background make to our reading of Cather's fiction? For me it has meant a revisioning in the manner of Adrienne Rich, a return to familiar texts to see and hear them fresh. I now hear in Cather's storytelling manner not only the tradition of oral storytelling but also the conversational style of the letters. When in *My Ántonia* and "Neighbour Rosicky" characters appear or come forward to tell their own stories, each voice is individual yet becomes woven into the larger narrative of the novel just as the distinctly personal voices in the Cather letters combine to create the ongoing correspondence of a family.

I am more sensitive to how Cather's accounts of moving west—autobiographical and fictional (the two are closely linked for her)—are accounts of family emigration. In quoting Cather's description of coming to Nebraska as being thrown onto a piece of sheet iron, we too readily read by a Turnerian premise of confrontation while ignoring the fact that the quote is preceded by paragraphs that describe the feelings of Cather's family and is followed by others that describe her visits to neighboring families. Similarly, I am now more sensitive to the structure of *My Ántonia*, which by opening with the Shimerdas and closing with the Cuzaks establishes itself as a narrative of families merging.

When I read Cather's western fiction against a background of the Cather family letters, I also recognize metaphors of health and disease that I had previously overlooked. The air may be at least as important as the land in Cather's idea of the West, and breathing freely may be a defining feature of her frontier. In *O Pioneers!* Cather describes the Divide as where "the dry, bracing climate" is. She writes that it has a "strong clean smell" and "the power of growth and fertility." There the wind "often blows from one week's end to another," and "You feel in the atmosphere the same tonic, puissant quality that is in the tilth, the same strength and resoluteness." Balanced sentence structures suggest the rhythm of inhalation and exhalation. Their sounds are not the vibrations of voice but the exhalations of breath—telephone wires "hum," windmills "vibrate," and the earth rolls away from the shear with "a soft, deep sigh of happiness." As if drawing increasingly freer and broader breaths, the passage expands until it celebrates all of nature when "the great, free spirit . . . *breathes across*" such a country, and "the air and the earth are curiously mated and intermingled, *as if one were the breath of the other*" (73–74; emphasis mine). Ántonia's children are another testimony to good health; she hasn't lost one, and their robust vitality is unshadowed by a threat of disease. "We'd never have got through if I had n't been so strong," Ántonia reflects about the hard early years of their marriage: "I've always had good health, thank God" (332).

With the family letters in mind I recognize how dramatically the Peter and Pavel story brings onto the frontier the horror of death by consumption, and remembering that to die of consumption is to drown, I am newly sensitive to the fear of death by drowning that runs through Cather's fiction. By offering a release from that threat, Cather's frontier offers the natural and easeful death that her archbishop enjoys, when after visiting France he returns to the Southwest, for only there had he found "this peculiar quality in the air of new countries [that] vanished after they were tamed by man and made to bear harvests. . . . The moisture of plowed land . . . utterly destroyed it; one could breathe that only on the bright edges of the world, on the great grass plains or the sage-brush desert" (*Death Comes for the Archbishop* 275). Cather's positive treatment of the unpeopled western landscape suggests that we deepen the foreground of Cather's idea of the West to include the land behind it. To understand Cather's celebration of good health in the West, one might read her Nebraska fiction against the claustrophobic, disease-ridden *Sapphira and the Slave Girl*, Cather's last book and her single novel set in the Virginia of her childhood. Reading her western fiction in this manner has meant becoming newly sensitive to the attention that Cather gives to *voice* in distinguishing her characters and to *conversation* in structuring her stories. For Cather the birth of a nation had to do with drawing breath freely and awakening life's desire to free the human spirit—momentarily, at least—from death's long shadow.

3

Cather's

Western

Stories

As the Nebraska Cathers were sending accounts of the West to their Virginia relatives, Willa was growing up with an eastern landscape and established traditions. In 1874 when Willa's grandparents went to Nebraska to visit her aunt and uncle, her parents moved into Willow Shade to oversee the farm and tend its sheep. Cather's earliest experiences were of gentle hills covered with trees, winding roads, fields cleared for farming and grazing, a house of classical proportions and elegant grace, and a community of neighbors and relatives. By the time she was nine, Cather had a firm sense of a landscape long settled and of rituals long practiced, an ideal preparation for being "thrown out into a country as bare as a piece of sheet iron" (qtd. in Bohlke 10).

When Charles and Mary Virginia (Boak) Cather emigrated to Nebraska in 1883, Cather found herself witness to the historic changes taking place in the West. Red Cloud, organized in 1871, was serving as a division point for the Burlington and Missouri Railroads by 1885, when the Cathers moved into town. By the time Cather began writing of it, the state was settled—its population increased from slightly over 120,000 in 1870 to more than a million in 1890 (Dale 7). She could with personal assurance write that though the first generation may have consisted of poor exiles, they were merely "the advance guard of a mighty civilization to be" (*Collected Short Fiction* 360).

The most striking difference between Cather and both her predecessor, Margaret Fuller, and her successor, Jean Stafford, is her positioning of herself in terms of these changes. Whereas Fuller had realized that the frontier was closed before her and Jean Stafford was to realize that it had closed behind her, Cather saw that for her it was wide open. Not surprisingly, of the three only Cather was comfortable with threshold or boundary experiences, and only she identified herself as an artist by them. For her physical West, Cather chose the Divide, that high country separating the Republican from the Little Blue Rivers; for her temporal West, she wrote of the frontier, that pause between past and present. And for her western plots, Cather wrote of last men and first women, of a search for origins, and of an awakening of desire.[1] In the process Cather discarded the gendered West that history had bequeathed to her and prepared to write her own birth of a nation.

Locations of desire in narrative involve unstable boundaries and yield threshold experiences such as the metamorphosis of participants in a creative act—writer and reader, character and (for Cather) country—that occurs by the freeing of energy. Desire in this sense has become, writes Patricia Meyer Spacks, "an indispensable term for late-twentieth-century critics investigating psychological intricacies of narrative." Continuing, Spacks explains: "The word suggests the emotional force implicit in the acts of reading and writing fiction; it provides a means of linking the energies of characters within a text to those involved in creative and in responding to that text; it calls attention to latent as well as overt erotic elements in fiction" (1).

Cather's early western stories trace ways in which she freed herself from the "codes (mores and social contracts)" that, according to Julia Kristeva, "must be shattered in order to give way to the free play of negativity, need, desire, pleasure, and jouissance" (*Desire in Language* 23).[2] Cather began with last men, basing her first published fiction, "Peter" (1892), upon Francis Sadelik, the father in an immigrant family who lived near the Cathers and who on the Nebraska frontier was so lonely for the fine music and good friendships of Bohemia that he committed suicide. Cather followed Peter with a long line of men on the frontier who die, disappear, or retreat, each having realized that, as Peter said, "it was all different now" (*Collected Short Fiction* 542; hereafter all page references for stories are from *Collected Short Fiction*). Lou the Prophet receives a vision of the end of the world, then disappears; Canute Canuteson loses himself in drink because "it is not easy . . . to change the habits and conditions of his life" ("On the Divide" 496); Eric Hermannson suffers because to be "transplanted in an arid soil" meant "toil and isolation sobered him" ("Eric Hermannson's Soul" 369); and Harvey Merrick decamps for the East after realizing that childhood in Nebraska meant being caught in a "frontier warfare" between the new and old in this "borderland between ruffianism and civilization" ("The Sculptor's Funeral" 184). Cather was clearing the stage, as it were, of the frontier for her own play of imagination.

Frederick Jackson Turner's writings are useful here as they exemplify the notion of historic genesis from which Cather was freeing herself.[3] At first glance her stories of the West seem akin to the frontier hypothesis so widely identified with the new generation of historians that Turner "ordained" (Vorpahl 283): like him Cather described a reversion to primitive conditions. But where Turner wrote of the primitive as an early stage in the evolution of human civilization, Cather wrote of the primitive as an original or archetypal nature. Where Turner's primitive is overcome by the progress of western expansion, Cather's primitive is revealed by an awakening of desire.

A radical experience of emptiness or lack is the wellspring of desire and is precisely the experience that Cather associated so consistently with the West. She described her own entry into Nebraska by her feeling that "we had come to the end of everything—it was a kind of erasure of personality" (qtd. in Bohlke 10), and she wrote variations upon that feeling in her earliest stories. The loneliness of Cather's early characters is that of the mute who is unable to give voice to what lies within, and the desolation of her early landscapes is that of material seeking form. "[N]orth, east, south stretched the level Nebraska plain of long rust-red grass that undulated constantly in the wind" ("On the Divide" 493), Cather writes of this landscape, and "The flat plains rolled to the unbroken horizon vacant and void, forever reaching in empty yearning toward something they never attained" ("El Dorado" 294). From such an experience of silence, vacancy, and void springs desire as an energy animating life or the "power which had kindled the world" ("A Wagner Matinee" 240).

"[T]he activity of desiring, in its purest form, involves an undisturbed use of the world as the theater for our fantasies," writes Leo Bersani (286). Cather claimed the West as her theater and thus distinguished the rationalist discourse of history from the activity of desiring in literature. "A Wagner Matinee" (1904) illustrates this distinction through its treatment of two ideas of the primitive. Georgiana's elopement with young Howard Carpenter took her from Boston to the Nebraska frontier, where he had filed on a homestead. Cather describes those early years in precise, realistic detail. Entering the open frontier, the couple measured their quarter section by counting the revolutions of a cloth tied to their wagon wheel. After locating that section they "built a dugout in the red hillside, one of those cave dwellings whose inmates so often reverted to primitive conditions. They got their water from the lagoons where the buffalo drank, and their slender stock of provisions was always at the mercy of bands of roving Indians" (236).

The description could be out of Frederick Jackson Turner's essay "The Significance of the Frontier in American History"; it is what Cather does with it that distinguishes her from him. Whereas his subject describes a precivilized stage of history, hers concerns a woman responding to an experience of lack. Silence has been Georgiana Carpenter's lot for thirty years, and she has become as passive, inert, and mute as the country in which she has been living. While visiting her nephew in Boston, however, she attends a Wagner matinee, and the Pilgrim's Chorus "broke a silence of thirty years; the inconceivable silence of the plains" (239).

Acknowledging lack releases the energy of desire, and when after the matinee Aunt Georgiana turns to her nephew and through him to the reader, she challenges him/us to recognize that. Watching the members of the orchestra depart, "leaving the stage to the chairs and music stands, empty as a winter cornfield," Aunt Georgiana cries, "I don't want to go," for outside the concert stage lies a return to the emptiness of the Nebraska landscape. Significantly, she doesn't suffer *from* the country so much as she embodies the suffering *of* the country: "the world there was the flat world of the ancients; to the east, a cornfield that stretched to daybreak; to the west, a corral that reached to sunset" (241–42). In this moment Aunt Georgiana is an early version of Alexandra Bergson, who would embody pure desire by taking into herself the Genius (or spirit) of the Divide, pouring her personality into her "enterprise" and metamorphosing so fully that (as Bersani writes of other narratives of desire) "we no longer have coherent, individuated, intelligible structures of personality" in the narrative. "In a sense," he writes, " we no longer even have a locatable self" (190). As if affirming the deconstructed self that Bersani describes, in 1913 Cather concludes her narrative with a benediction upon that metamorphosis: "Fortunate country, that is one day to receive hearts like Alexandra's into its bosom, to give them out again in the yellow wheat, in the rustling corn, in the shining eyes of youth!" (*O Pioneers!* 274).

During the two decades that passed between "Peter" and *O Pioneers!*, Cather prepared for her metamorphosis of woman by writing a series of stories with interlocking themes. "El Dorado: A Kansas Recessional" (1901) illustrates the basic plot that reappears as variations upon claiming desire. In that story, Cather writes of Colonel Bywaters, who, enticed from Virginia to invest in western Kansas by Apollo Gump, remains in Kansas when the wave of speculative emigration recedes. As so often in Cather's stories, names are symbolic, here of a history that would recognize only men. On the American frontier, Apollo, the classical god of prophecy, is joined to the Americanized Gump to produce a salesman whose announcement rolls off his tongue with the rhythm of a circus barker: "Eldorado, the Queen City of the Plains, the Metropolis of Western Kansas, the coming Commercial Center of the West" (294). Such names provide their own indictment of the commercialization of the West. Promoters named this desolate part of Kansas "the Solomon Valley" in the same spirit that Gump's parents named their sons Apollo, Isaiah, De Witt, Chesterfield, Aristotle, Hezekiah, and Ezekiel. The sons, in turn, promote their interests with discourses "upon the builders of great cities from Menes, Ninrod and Romulus down" (298), which culminate with themselves as the builders of El Dorado.

It was all a great swindle, of course, this dream of fortune and, implicitly, this version of history; and when the Gumps decamp, Colonel Bywaters finds himself utterly ruined, staying on as "a sort of 'Last Man.' The tide of emigration has gone out and left him high and dry, stranded on a Kansas bluff" (295). There he has time and opportunity to reflect upon what lay ahead for the West: "Often as he sat watching those barren bluffs, he wondered whether some day the whole grand delusion would not pass away, and this great West . . . would become panic-stricken and disappear, vanish utterly and completely, as a bubble that bursts, as a dream that is done" (303).

What remains when the false prophecy of the West vanishes? Cather's answer takes the form of a voice whispering that a myth of origins and a promise of plenitude lie at nature's source. "Sometimes, in the dusk of night, when the winds were not quite so hot as usual and only the stars could hear, the dry little corn leaves whispered to echo that once, long ago, real yellow ears grew in the Solomon Valley" (294). In responding to that voice Cather begins to give play to the rhythm and tone of the poetic language characteristic of desire.[4] In contrast to the barrenness of human lives, images of gemlike richness ornament the Solomon Valley after a night storm when "all the land was washed fresh and clean from the dust of the desert summer. It was a day of opal lights, a day set in a heaven of gold and turquoise and bathed in sapphrine airs; one of those rare and perfect days that happen only in desert countries, where Nature seems sometimes to repent of her own pitilessness and by the glory of her skies seems trying to compensate for the desolation of the lands that stretch beneath them" (308). As if assisting Nature in compensating for the desolation of her materials, Cather uses language to confirm that the wealth of Solomon Valley was there all along, revealed to the writer who, in seeing it with compassion, released its meaning.

The human story in "El Dorado: A Kansas Recessional" ends melodramatically when Apollo returns to unearth a woman's picture he had buried, is struck by a rattlesnake, and dies, leaving behind not only his body but, on it, money to repay the colonel and thus enable him to return to Virginia. When the colonel departs, Nature's story continues. She receives Apollo's body, "ready to . . . make him again a part of the clean and fruitful earth" (309), and Cather—continuing—reflects: "In the spring the sunflowers grew tall and fair over every street and house site; and they grew just as fair over the mound beside the oak tree on the bluff. For if Nature forgets, she also forgives. She at least holds no grudge, up in her high place, where she watches the poles of the heavens. The tree itself has stopped growing altogether. It has concluded that it is not worth the effort. The river creeps lazily through the mud; it knows that the sea would be only a great, dirty, salty pond if it should reach it. Year by year it buries itself deeper in the black mud, and burrows among the rotting roots of the dead willows, wondering why a river should ever have been put there at all" (310). Remaining after the last man has retreated, Cather's narrative voice speaks with an inhabitant's sympathy for the land: "There was a sort of mysterious kinship between those trees and the men who lived, or tried to live, there" (293), she reflects. And though Colonel Bywaters hated western Kansas, "in a way he pitied this poor brown country, which seemed as lonely as himself and as unhappy. No one cared for it, for its soil or its river" (303). Indeed, God, as though a schemer himself, seemed to have made it only for the purpose of speculation and, now tired of the deal, was trying to get it off his hands. The schemers—men and God—abandoned their creation, leaving it in the writer's care.

Cather's early fiction tells of seeking ways to save the West from the literary speculators—the writers of the Western as America's masculine romance—by shattering their codes and freeing herself from them. Doing so meant negotiating a response to the revival of the romance fiction that began in Victorian England. "While women writers after George Eliot saw themselves as writing especially for other women, the romance novelists determined to write for boys" (77), observes Elaine Showalter of the men who at the turn of the century were trying to make a place for themselves in the wake of the matriarchal legacy of "Queen George" (78). "The revival of 'romance' in the 1880s was a men's literary revolution intended to reclaim the kingdom of the English novel for male writers, male readers, and men's stories"; it excluded women by valorizing the creative generation of celibate males and denigrating female creation and reproduction (78–79). Male writers imagined fantastic plots with "alternative forms of male reproduction or self-replication: splitting or cloning, as in *Dr. Jekyll and Mr. Hyde*; reincarnation, as in H. Rider Haggard's *She*; transfusion, as in *Dracula*; aesthetic duplication, as in *The Picture of Dorian Gray*; or vivisection, as in *The Island of Dr. Moreau*" (77–78). These were the stories Cather grew up reading, and Robert Louis Stevenson was (in Cather's words) "the King and Father of them All" (*Kingdom of Art* 232).

Complications are worth exploring. Stevenson was attempting to revive romance against, in Cather's words, "the advancement of encroaching realism and 'veritism' and all other literary unpleasantness" (*Kingdom of Art* 312). Revival of romance was the cause in which Cather enlisted her own literary aspirations. She was writing against cultural forces in America that were strikingly similar to those of the English male quest romance as male writers of the American Western were also attempting to reclaim the novel for men. Indeed, the affinities between them and their English cousins are so close that Showalter's description of the English version could, with only slight modification, apply to the American Western:

> The literary genre which these writers created is called the male quest romance. In various ways, these stories represent a yearning for escape from a confining society, rigidly structured in terms of gender, class, and race, to a mythologized place elsewhere where men can be freed from the constraints of Victorian morality. In the caves, or jungles, or mountains of this other place, the heroes of romance explore their secret selves in an archaic space which can be safely called the 'primitive.' Quest narratives all involve a penetration into the imagined cen-

ter of an exotic civilization, the core, Kor, *coeur,* or heart of darkness which is a blank place on the map, a realm of the unexplored and unknown. For fin-de-siecle [English] writers, this free space is usually Africa. (81)

We need add only that for American writers this free space is usually the West and that Showalter's remarks might include the classic American quest romance—the Western—where narratives of male self-reproduction and self-replication have entered American literary criticism as variations upon the American Adam (R. W. B. Lewis) and as a double for the emerging American industrial order (Helen Fiddlymont Levy).[5]

How was Cather to participate in a quest romance revolution designed to exclude women? Characteristically, she proceeded by taking on the "great master and chief" of the genre in her title "The Treasure of Far Island" (1903), setting her sights on Stevenson himself.[6] Douglass Burnham, world-famous playwright, returns to his childhood home in Nebraska where he seeks his childhood friend Margie (a combination of Muse and girl Friday). Following a map they had once inscribed with the promise that whoever followed it would find "great treasure and his heart's desire," together they go to a sandbar (their treasure island) where they had long ago buried a chest. Digging up the moldy container, they find within it a glass jar and, perfectly preserved within that, a "manuscript written in blood" telling of fantastic deeds.

The basics of Stevenson's quest romance are in Cather's plot: the escape from adult constraints, the exploration of secret selves, the penetration into a blank place. But whereas Stevenson's manuscript is a map leading to a treasure of gold, Cather's manuscript *is* the treasure; and whereas Stevenson made from such materials "a primer of empire" (Showalter 81), Cather put empire to the cause of art. In the manner of Emerson, Cather wrote that the children in her story were privileged "because they were of that favored race whom a New England sage called the true land-lords and sea-lords of the world" (265). The sandbar was hardly a place at all but instead a vehicle for their desire: "Long before they had set foot upon it the island was the goal of their loftiest ambitions and most delightful imaginings," and once upon it they planned "the conquest of the world" (276). By such imaginings a child was an explorer and a creator, a "trail-breaker and world-finder" (278). Anticipating the linking of the imagination, art, memory, epic, and empire of *My Ántonia,* Cather explained: "To people who live by imagination at all, that is the only life that goes deep enough to leave memories. [These children] were artists in those days, creating . . . making epics . . . building empires" (280).

By adding a girl to her band in no-man's-land, Cather laid the groundwork for a woman to succeed in the previously male art of "creating . . . making epics." She made it clear in "The Treasure of Far Island" that Margie was one among equals when she was a girl. Becoming a beautiful woman was, however, a fate as restrictive to her in its gender expectations as Douglass's success was to him. The childhood secret self that the story reveals is Margie's as well as Douglass's, and as the story unfolds she emerges as more companion than Muse.[7]

When Cather tried her hand at the all-boys story, she wrote a comic subversion of the quest romance adventure. Cather's characters in "The Enchanted Bluff" (1909) are reminiscent of the boys' fiction Showalter calls "Clubland" (81), and Cather's language of empire again signals the male quest romance. Busy with their own affairs, adults leave a group of boys "in undisputed possession" (69) of a sandbar, the unknown country that they find and claim—with their imaginations, of course. Sitting around their last watch fire of the year, the boys dream of the other explorers who had been there—Mound Builders and Aztecs, Spaniards, including Coronado and his men who "were all over the country once," as well as Mormons, who went through it in search of freedom (73). By dreaming, the boys ascend the Enchanted Bluff, a lone red rock in the Southwest, and discover there its extinct people. Whereas male writers of the quest romance told of journeys into exotic places, Cather undercut any such illusion. Her boys sitting on a sandbar in Nebraska are destined to live ordinary lives. They are Huck's brothers in their everlasting return to childhood, and they are among a long line of Cather's men, linked to the East and ill-suited for the West, repeating their nostalgic, elegiac stories into the night. Eventually, they leaven into Bartley Alexander's frenzied journey toward death and Jim Burden's gentler return to childhood.

Back in town Cather's girls, Tommy and Eliza Jane, who appear in lighthearted stories that subvert the Western by parody, are shattering the social code of the Western plot simply by appropriating it. Cather takes on the standard plot by which the hero restores order to the community and blesses the young lovers who will replenish it in "Tommy, the Unsentimental" (1896). Tommy saves the bank by riding to the rescue (on a bicycle rather than a horse) and then sanctions the union of the bank president's son (who is rather a weakling) with Miss Jessica (a most discreet "though pale and languid maiden" [476]). And in "The Way of the World" (1898) Cather writes a parody of the empire-building at the heart of the Western. Excluded because she's a girl from the community of packing boxes that Speckle Burnam organized for his band of boys, Eliza Jane flourishes as an outlaw. She waylays Speckle while he (milkmaid-like) takes his cow to pasture, and she ambushes him when he takes his milk home in the evening. Not content with the role of outlaw, she opens a store in one of Speckle-ville's boxes and from it sells cookies, cream puffs, and candy. Eliza Jane is, Cather reflects, one of those "girls who would make the best boys in the world—if they were not girls" (401), and as such, she continues her rise to power. She "deposed Speckle and made herself sole imperatrix of Speckle-ville" (400), reigning unchallenged until a New Boy arrives to pay currency instead of pins in a shop he opens in a piano box across the street, and the deserted Speckleville residents disband, leaving Speckle "in his deserted town, as Caius Marius once sat among the ruins of Carthage" (404). Both stories are slight, of interest here primarily because in them Cather grants to girls the raw power of competition. Girls who can ride faster and think more quickly than boys defy conventions and assume authority, and as such they play a role in shattering the Western code and in liberating Cather's narrative for the play of desire.

Shattering inherited codes is one thing; liberating desire is another, and it was in liberating desire that Cather (who was at heart neither a rebel nor an innovator) found her voice as a writer. Acknowledging the romance traditions of prose narrative, she neither revolted against nor broke with these traditions; rather she passed beyond them, reinventing the idea of the heroic and revisioning creativity as desire. Read in sequence, "On the Divide" (1896), "Eric Hermannson's Soul" (1900), "The Bohemian Girl" (1912), and O Pioneers! (1913) tell of that liberation. In a sense these are different versions of the same story. Their common theme is an awakening of desire. In their retelling, however, Cather was to shift her focus and redefine her terms. Beginning with a man seizing a woman to claim that which he lacks, Cather moved from male to female protagonist, from conventional man to natural woman, and from an untamed nature to be conquered to a wildness within to be freed.

In "On the Divide" Cather presents a stark picture of "a country as flat and gray and as naked as the sea" (496) and of Canute Canuteson, the giant Norwegian immigrant who "was the wreck of ten winters" (495). Onto the scene flashes Lena Yensen, the pretty daughter of a family on the next eighty and the first appearance in Cather's fiction of the natural woman who eventually will displace the conventional man. "Not afraid of man nor devil" (497), Lena diverts herself by teasing Canute until she is tempted by "stories of ten cent theatres, firemen's dances, and all the other esthetic delights of metropolitan life," and goes "to town to seek her fortune at the ironing board. From the time she came home on her first visit she began to treat Canute with contempt. She had bought a plush cloak and kid gloves, had her clothes made by the dressmaker, and assumed airs and graces that made the other women of the neighborhood cordially detest her" (498).

Herein lies the genesis of Lena Lingard and Ántonia Shimerda Cuzak, for in time Cather was to fulfill the promise of this aside by focusing upon women who defy convention by being true to their own natures. In 1896, however, she returned to a script she had read about in classical mythology. Canute abducts Lena and takes her to his shanty, "even as his bearded barbarian ancestors took the fair frivolous women of the South in their hairy arms and bore them down to their war ships" (501). Yet Lena momentarily broke through the type, and as if in tribute to her, Cather resolves Canute's barbarism into sympathy. The story ends with melodramatic sentimentality: Lena, moved by Canute's loneliness, asks him to come to her, and Canute, moved by Lena's request, sobs at her feet.

As if dissatisfied with the sentimental direction her plot had taken, Cather returned to the theme of awakening in "Eric Hermannson's Soul." Nominally this is the story of an eighteen-year-old youth who came to the Divide as "handsome as young Siegfried," loving life and thereby evoking warnings from the Free Gospellers that he was damning his soul. Eventually Eric Hermannson submitted to the gospellers' admonition that "one must live without pleasure to die without fear" (369). He stopped playing his fiddle for the prostitute Lena Hanson, then broke his violin, his only bridge into "the kingdom of the soul" (361). When the cultured and beautiful Margaret Elliot visits, however, she awakens in him desire, and he dances with her in defiance of the gospellers' damnation.

So much for the nominal subject. Despite its title, the story turns out to be Margaret's. Through her Cather appropriated for a woman the idea of claiming a wilderness. By doing so, she extended the idea of female sexuality previously limited to marginalized women (immigrant Lena Yensen and prostitute Lena Hanson) to the custodian of culture, Margaret Elliot.

Cather brings Margaret to the West by using a twinned protagonist.[8]

Rather self-consciously casting her story as a variation of western convention, Cather explains that Margaret's brother, Wyllis (a variation upon Willa?), came to Nebraska when he was graduated from Harvard and "it was still customary for moneyed gentlemen to send their scapegrace sons to rough it on ranches in the wilds of Nebraska or Dakota." Having sowed their wild oats, young men became fit to take their place in society, or having fallen to wild ways, they remained in the West. Wyllis Elliot, however, "had not married a half-breed, nor been shot in a cowpunchers' brawl, nor wrecked by bad whisky, nor appropriated by a smirched adventuress." Instead, "he had been saved from these things by a girl, his sister, who had been very near to his life ever since the days when they read fairy tales together and dreamed the dreams that never come true" (363).

By shifting her attention to Wyllis's sister-savior Cather begins her revision of creativity, transforming her story from a male initiation into a female awakening. Margaret's story is not about saving her brother at all; it is about releasing her own desire. Like "all women of her type," Margaret feels "that desire to taste the unknown which allures and terrifies, to run one's whole soul's length out to the wind—just once" (363), and it is because she is "restless and filled with a desire to see something of the wild country" that she comes to the West. Once there, the wilderness she discovers lies within herself.

With the merest pretense of being grounded in realistic action, the story builds to two scenes that explode with a woman's passion. In the first, Margaret and her mare (*not* stallion) "are tempted by the great open spaces and try to outride the horizon, to get to the end of something" (369–70). The physical landscape dissolves into a dreamlike sequence in which "down the gulch in front of them and over the steep clay banks thundered a herd of wild ponies, nimble as monkeys and wild as rabbits, such as horse-traders drive east from the plains of Montana to sell in the farming country. Margaret's pony made a shrill sound, a neigh that was almost a scream, and started up the clay bank to meet them, all the wild blood of the range breaking out in an instant" (372).

The wild blood stirring in Margaret culminates in a dance where "the girls were all boisterous with delight," for "something seemed struggling for freedom in them tonight, something of the joyous childhood of the nations which exile had not killed" (374–75). Dancing, Margaret feels "strength . . . like an all-prefacing fluid, stealing through her veins, awakening under her heart some nameless, unsuspected existence that had slumbered there all these years" (375). It is an awakening to "wealth before undiscovered," Cather writes—the quest romance adventure again, but with a difference, for here the seeker is a woman and the treasure she discovers is Eros, not in the romantic sense of passion in love but in the classic sense of passion underlying creativity, akin to what we would now call *jouissance.*

The struggle within the artist as a maturing woman, Hélène Cixous writes, "is between two types of knowing, the pleasurable and the symbolic." She could have been writing about Cather, who contrasts (in Cixous's words) "the highest education," which is "knowing through pleasure," to the knowledge that one learns in a university, "which is the knowledge of knowing, which has to do with mastering" (2). Interrupting Margaret's pleasure in the West is "a strange love letter" from her fiancé in the East, the man who would possess her in the name of love. The letter begins "My Dearest Margaret" (373), revealing the voice of a civilized man at odds with nature and suspicious of woman's ties to it, a voice that could be called "emotionless (objective, detached and bodiless)" (Griffin xv).[9] He assumes control in describing the plays he has managed and the pictures he has purchased, and he censors independence, particularly in women, in describing their responses. He criticizes, for example, an acquaintance playing Rosalind in *As You Like It,* who "insists on reading into the part all sorts of deeper meanings and highly colored suggestions wholly out of harmony with the pastoral setting" (373).

For his version of the pastoral to which he would have women conform, this male critic describes the *Puvis de Chavannes* he purchased, in which, all hint of the physical removed, "a pale dream-maiden sits by a pale dream-cow and a stream of anemic water flows at her feet" (373). By contrast he indirectly disparages the painting by Constant he acquired because Margaret admired it: "The drapery of the female figure is as wonderful as you said; the fabric all barbaric pearl and gold, painted with an easy, effortless voluptuousness" (373). The false praise is only his prelude, however, to his "irritation" against the Constant, which he attacks under the guise of objectivity. Admitting that he "cannot prove the charge against" Constant, he nevertheless "suspects him of cheapness," the very charge leveled against women who would live in the splendor of their glowing sensuosity and with an easy voluptuousness.

In writing of Margaret's escape from the censorious voice of the male critic, Cather positioned herself firmly in a long line of writers of awakening. She reacted against Flaubert's *Madame Bovary* and Chopin's *The Awakening* and anticipated Susan Griffin's *Woman and Nature*. Cather knew precisely what she was doing, having surveyed her territory well when she reviewed Chopin's novel the year before she wrote "Eric Hermannson's Soul." In that review Cather grouped Edna Pontellier with Emma Bovary as "the same feminine type," calling them "the victims of the over-idealization of love," then explaining that

> They receive impressions through the fancy. With them everything begins with fancy, and passions rise in the brain rather than in the blood, the poor, neglected, limited one-sided brain that might do so much better things than badgering itself into frantic endeavors to love. . . . Then 'the awakening' comes. Sometimes it comes in the form of arsenic, as it came to Emma Bovary, sometimes it is carbolic acid taken covertly in the police station, a goal to which unbalanced idealism not infrequently leads. Edna Pontellier, fanciful and romantic to the last, chose the sea on a summer night and went down with the sound of her first lover's spurs in her ears, and the scent of pinks about her. And next time I hope that Miss Chopin will devote that flexible, iridescent style of hers to a better cause." (*World and the Parish* 2:697–99)

As if an extension of her review, in "Eric Hermannson's Soul" Cather claimed the West as her arena for a woman's awakening and then described that awakening in direct, even polemical terms as an awakening of the blood to better things than abstract ideals. Atop a windmill Margaret sees the open country stretching about her, and she realizes that her destiny links her not to a man (she never imagined herself in love with Eric) but to nature: "She belonged to an ultrarefined civilization which tries to cheat nature with elegant sophistries. Cheat nature? Bah! One generation may do it, perhaps two, but the third—Can we ever rise above nature or sink below her. . . . Does she not always cry in brutal triumph: 'I am here still, at the bottom of things, warming the roots of life; you cannot starve me nor tame me nor thwart me; I made the world, I rule it, and I am its destiny" (377).[10]

Thus the story reaches its climax with Margaret liberated and reveling in her own desire. It is, Cather writes, nature's "cry in brutal triumph" that "This woman . . . heard that cry tonight, and she was afraid!" Cather goes on to explain that this is not the shrinking fear conventional to women but "the terror and delight of that moment *when first we fear ourselves! Until then we have not lived*" (377; emphasis mine). As Susan Griffin wrote of women's awakenings generations later, "we are nature seeing nature," which allows a woman's "I" to be the defiantly, triumphantly female voice of woman *and* nature, releasing "the roaring inside her" (*Woman and Nature* 226).

Margaret Elliot is an unlikely western hero, however. She can adequately articulate ideas atop a windmill in Nebraska, but she is decidedly unsuited to take up action once she descends. "But was it a curse, this awakening. . . ?" (375), Cather asks, challenging the reader to move beyond the end of her story to realize that Margaret's inevitable return to her fiancé in New York made Edna Pontellier's drowning in the sea seem a blessing. A woman's awakening to her confinement within the marriage plot is hardly a satisfactory revisioning of romance. To further inscribe a woman into the western quest romance, Cather needed to find a way to separate gender and sexuality, to grant a woman independence from culture, and to develop her kinship with nature. She found it in the Gypsy.

In "The Bohemian Girl" Cather refined Eros into the Gypsy as her alternative to Dionysus, her link between woman and nature. For her plot she wrote female creativity into the western quest romance, making its treasure the nature of a Bohemian girl that has been hidden behind the facade of her marriage. In the story's opening scene, Nils Ericson arrives with his flute, a modern-day Orpheus to sing Eurydice from the netherworld. His Hades is the country of his childhood; with its "rank, resinous smell of sunflowers and ironweed, which the night damp brought up from the draws and low places" (6), the details used to describe it are evocative of death. Nature itself has fallen into decay, it would seem. Hiding behind some wild plum bushes when he hears the tramp of a horse coming down the hill, Eric voyeuristically watches a woman appear on her horse, hears her exclaim angrily in Bohemian, and then watches her move on: "Once in the main road, she let him out into a lope, and they soon emerged upon the crest of high land, where they moved along the skyline, silhouetted against the band of faint color that lingered in the west. This horse and rider, with their free, rhythmical gallop, were the only moving things to be seen on the face of the flat country. They seemed, in the last sad light of evening, not to be there accidentally, but as an inevitable detail of the landscape" (6-7).

The scene is that of the classic Western, but the rider who seems so inevitably part of it is a woman for whom Cather appropriates qualities of the male hero: she is tall, dark, and brooding, possessed of a wild spirit that is forever restless within the confines of domesticity: "Mrs. Olaf Ericson—Clara Vavrika, as many people still called her—was moving restlessly about her big bare house that morning. . . . She was a tall, dark woman of thirty, with a rather sallow complexion and touch of dull salmon red in her cheeks, where the blood seemed to burn under the brown skin. Her hair, parted evenly above her low forehead, was so black that there were distinctly blue lights in it. Her black eyebrows were delicate half-moons and her lashes were long and heavy. Her eyes slanted a little, as if she had a strain of Tartar or gypsy blood" (13–14).

In claiming the female Gypsy for her western hero, Cather drew upon a tradition ideally suited for her purposes. The Gypsy offered a distinct, positive identity that was independent from and subversive of the dominant culture. The Gypsy "does not consider himself as belonging to the same race as the native, and would rather be judged by a different standard. The life which he leads is not that of the lowest class of the country in which he dwells, but the primitive, original state of a people of great antiquity, proscribed by law and society; himself an enemy of, and an enemy to, all around him" (Wedeck 77). Sympathy with the Gypsies implies both sympathy with nature and mystery in nature, "the witchery of wood and wold" (Wedeck 436). These are precisely the qualities that Cather needed to forge her link between woman and the West.

Historical circumstances and literary connotations of the type fit Cather's purposes well. Because Bohemians were the name of the Gypsies who settled in Bohemia, Cather could readily imagine Gypsy antecedents for her Bohemian neighbors in Webster County, and literature provided the catalyst for doing so. Included in *The Dictionary of Gypsy Life and Lore* as an illustration of the Gypsy-Slavic nature, for example, Charles Leland's poem "The Bohemian" (446) includes classic elements from Gypsy lore that reappear in Cather's story—the sympathy with nature, the witchery of the dance, even the name Klara/Clara.

The awakening of "The Bohemian Girl" is of a woman's desire shattering and freeing itself from gendered codes. As the Ericsons have "run over this here country like bindweed" (5), so marriage to Olaf Ericson has bound Clara Vavrika in gender expectations that she both recognizes and chafs against. Clara explains that she married "to oblige the neighbors," having discovered "that most girls marry out of consideration for the neighbors. . . . You see, they have it on you, Nils; that is, if you're a woman. They say you're beginning to go off. That's what makes us get married; we can't stand the laugh" (22–23). Her rebellion is a secret, subversive activity, however. Clara conforms in public (she doesn't go to her father's saloon anymore because "Olaf doesn't like it. I must live up to my position, you know" [21]), while she remains privately defiant, which means tormenting the Ericsons. Her sad and self-defeating rebellion means that Clara is depleting her energy, becoming bitter, and (worse) losing the "wild delight" (36) of her Bohemian blood—her nerve. Clara's awakening means reviving the courage to "tear loose" (37) from convention, and as it evolves, chrysalis-like, Cather's Gypsy emerges: Mrs. Olaf Ericson—Clara Vavrika—the Bohemian girl.

Whereas the plot of "The Bohemian Girl" concerns gender (will Clara cut loose from a role defined by her marriage?), its major scenes concern sexuality, and they are the gems of this story. In its easy voluptuousness, the garden of Clara's father is a pastoral in the manner of Bohemie. When Varika pours glasses of Tokai (the classic drink of Gypsy lore) for the lovers and then explains that it "costs its weight in gold," his invocation is to the sensuality slumbering within all of nature: "an' now he wake up; and maybe he wake us up, too!" (25). At a barn raising, the awakening continues when the lovers drink the French brandy given to Clara upon her marriage. Through these scenes Clara, at the outset spinsterlike with her severe black dress, cold hands, and severe expression, comes to life: she dons white, her hands grow warm, "the deep salmon color in her cheeks burned vividly, and her eyes were full of life" as she dances (30).

As suggested by the recurrent image of rootedness, kinship with nature informs the desire behind these awakenings. Talking with his younger brother, Nils recalls that "we always said the leaves were whispering when they rustled at night? . . . In a high wind they had a desperate sound, like something trying to tear loose" (11). Explaining to Nils her hesitation to leave with him, Clara says that "something seems to hold me. I'm afraid to pull against it. It comes out of the ground, I think." For their climactic scene, Nils and Clara ascend no water tower (as Eric Hermannson and Margaret Elliot did) but instead meet in the country where as they talked Clara "sank down on a sheaf of wheat": "The great, silent country seemed to lay a spell upon her. The ground seemed to hold her as if by the roots. Her knees were soft under her. She felt as if she could not bear separation from her own sorrows, from her old discontent. They were dear to her, they had kept her alive, they were a part of her. There would be nothing left of her if she were wrenched away from them. Never could she pass beyond that skyline against which her restlessness had beat so many times. She felt as if her soul had built itself a nest there on that horizon at which she looked every morning and every evening, and it was dear to her, inexpressibly dear" (37).

The language of enchantment was by now familiar in Cather's western fiction, but in "The Bohemian Girl" Cather eschews the devices of an imported plot. No longer about buried chests and hidden manuscripts, the secret of Clara's awakening is the country itself that casts the spell upon her by its very vastness and silence. The horizon "was dear to her, inexpressibly dear," Clara realizes; against it her restlessness had beat, and "She felt as if her soul had built itself a nest on that horizon."

Metamorphosis is at work dissolving dichotomies: pleasure/pain, self/other, woman/nature. Awakening of desire springs from woman *and* nature, sexuality *and* fertility. The earth that seemed inert matter in Olaf, whose stubbornness was "like the unyielding stickiness of wet loam against the plow" (20), is by women's stewardship awakened in a barn dance tableau. As if a treasure chest opened to admit light glittering on gold, barn doors open to admit golden light shining on the scene within:

> The barn faced the west, and the sun, pouring in at the big doors, filled the whole interior with a golden light, through which filtered fine particles of dust from the haymow, where the children were romping. There was a great chattering from the stall where Johanna Vavrika exhibited to the admiring women her platters heaped with fried chicken, her roasts of beef, boiled tongues, and baked hams with cloves stuck in the crisp brown fat and garnished with tansy and parsley. The older women, having assured themselves that there were twenty kinds of cake, not counting cookies, and three dozen fat pies, repaired to the corner behind the pile of watermelons, put on their white aprons, and fell to their knitting and fancywork. They were a fine company of old women, and a Dutch painter would have loved to find them there together, where the sun made bright patches on the floor and sent long, quivering shafts of gold through the dusky shade up among the rafters.
>
> "Look at them over there," [Nils] whispered, detaining Clara as she passed him. "Aren't they the Old Guard? . . . In reality he fell into amazement when he thought of the Herculean labors those fifteen pairs of hands had performed: of the cows they had milked, the butter they had made, the gardens they had planted, the children and grandchildren they had tended, the brooms they had worn out, the mountains of food they had cooked. It made him dizzy. (28–29)

The language of empire celebrates the domestic work of women as art, an epic effort put not to conquest but to nourishment, creating not pyramids of self-aggrandizement but "mountains of food." The scene anticipates the explosion of life from Ántonia's fruit cellar, where Cather further undermines sexual hierarchies and erases boundaries by joining woman and nature in sexuality/fecundity/fertility.

Along with claiming wilderness and nature for her women, Cather claimed materiality; that is, she wrote of women's relationships with nature as a kinship with a vital and animate physical world.[11] In *O Pioneers!* she created Alexandra Bergson, who, returning to the Divide after visiting farms along the river, "had a new consciousness of the country, felt almost a new relation to it. . . . She had felt as if her heart were hiding down there, somewhere, with the quail and the plover and all the little wild things that crooned or buzzed in the sun. Under the long shaggy ridges, she felt the future stirring" (68–69). She felt "close to the flat, fallow world about her, and felt, as it were, in her own body the joyous germination in the soil" (183–84).

"Desire exists beyond need," writes Eugene Goodheart in *Desire and Its Discontents* (3), and as such desire is distinct from romantic love, which demands an object. The two plots that make up *O Pioneers!* develop this distinction: Alexandra's love for the land is the desire of creative passion, while Marie's love for Emil is romantic love for another person. Similarities between the plots are as interesting as their more obvious differences, however. As different as Marie Shabata's plot is from Alexandra Bergson's, the women are alike in feeling a kinship for the physical world that a parent feels for a child and that a sister feels for a brother—the feeling that they are one nature inside different skins. Though inside sewing or crocheting, Marie Shabata "was always thinking about the wide fields outside, where the snow was drifting over the fences; and about the orchard, where the snow was falling and packing, crust over crust. When she went out into the dark kitchen to fix her plants for the night, she used to stand by the window and look out at the white fields, or watch the currents of snow whirling over the orchard. She seemed to feel the weight of all the snow that lay down there. The branches had become so hard that they wounded your hand if you but tried to break a twig. And yet, down under the frozen crusts, at the roots of the trees, the secret of life was still safe, warm as the blood in one's heart" (*O Pioneers!* 202). Walking along the path Marie feels that "the years seemed to stretch before her like the land; spring, summer, autumn, winter, spring; always the same patient fields, the pa-tient little trees, the patient lives; always the same yearning, the same pull-ing at the chain" (248). Paradoxically, everlasting desire is everlasting suf-fering. It is the positive life force protecting one from annihilation. Passing a pond, Marie considers, then rejects, suicide, for "she wanted to live and dream—a hundred years, forever! As long as this sweetness welled up in her heart, as long as her breast could hold this treasure of pain! She felt as the pond must feel when it held the moon like that; when it encircled and swelled with that image of gold" (250). "From the writer's point of view, the modernist narrative can be the acting out of desire, the courting of suffering and death," writes Goodheart (8).[12] The hunt for treasure that began in Cather's adaptation of Stevenson's quest romance has led to this: her affirmation that desire springs from "this treasure of pain."

Cather's early stories tell of finding her way toward her version of the West. In them she contrasted two ideas of primitive: crudity to be over-come by progress and original nature to be revealed by awakening. Her sto-ries begin conventionally enough with a man's attempt to possess the fe-male nature that has been lost to him: Canute Canuteson abducts Lena Yensen, and Apollo Gump digs toward a woman's picture that lies buried. In her retellings, however, Cather shifted her focus from male quest and conquest to female awakening and freedom. She gave to her women a pas-sionate nature that she identified with the Bohemian girl or Gypsy, and she made women's own nature the motive of her stories. As a motivating force, desire appears in various ways. It is Aunt Georgiana's yearning that lies behind her experience of lack at a Wagner matinee, Margaret Elliot's Gypsy blood that sends her to the West, and Clara Vavrika's restless spirit that gives her the courage to cut loose from her childhood home.

The woman whose image lay buried in Kansas has come to life and be-gun to dance, it would seem, and thus I return to one of those asides that we recognize in retrospect as a site of origins. In "El Dorado: A Kansas Re-cessional," Apollo Gump attempted to dig up a picture of "a handsome, smiling woman, in short skirts and spangles. She stood on the toe of her left foot, her right foot raised, her arms lifted, her body thrown back in a pose of easy abandon. She was just beginning to dance, and there was something of lassitude in the movement of the picture" (299). With fine irony, Cather included a snake to protect her Eve in this western garden, and poisoned by its venom, Apollo dies, leaving the image of the Gypsy to slumber in nature until it would come to life as desire in the Bohemian figures of her later fiction: Clara Vavrika, Marie Tovesky, Ántonia Shimerda Cuzak, and Lucy Gayheart. Each is memorable from those scenes in which her Gypsy nature shines through: Marie in her Bohemian dress telling fortunes at the church fair; Ántonia dancing at the Vannis's tent; and Lucy Gayheart, that "slight figure always in motion: dancing, skating" (3) through the novel that bears her name. "There was something in her nature that was like her movements," Cather wrote of Lucy Gayheart, but she could have been writing of Marie Tovesky or of the West itself. Among this gallery of women, Ántonia is preeminent, *the* figure that gives resonance to the rest. For it was through Ántonia Shimerda Cuzak that Cather realized her version of the birth of a nation.

4

Pro/Creativity
and a Kinship
Aesthetic

In *The Land before Her* Annette Kolodny begins her account
of women's historical responses to American frontiers and
the West with a chapter titled "Dispossessed of Paradise." "By the time
European women began to arrive on the Atlantic shores of what is now
the United States," Kolodny writes, "the New World had long been given
over to the fantasies of men." Before explorers lay "the virgin land," "a
country that hath yet her maydenhead," a *"Paradise* with all her Virgin
beauties." But, as Kolodny continues, "the psychosexual dynamic of a vir-
ginal paradise meant, however, that real flesh-and-blood women—at least
metaphorically—were dispossessed of paradise." English-speaking women
struggled to find an alternate set of images by creating "gardens in the wilderness" (3).

Willa Cather accepted no such dispossession. Instead, she sent Adam
packing and claimed paradise for women, restoring to them a psychosexual
identification with nature and appropriating for them the promise of nature's wildness. Rather than writing about a virgin land waiting to be de-
spoiled, Cather conceived of the West as female nature slumbering, awakening, and roaring its independence. In her stories, and culminating in
O Pioneers!, she gave women's fantasies to the West and cast their domestic
materials on an epic scale; in doing so she reclaimed materiality for wom-
en, rewrote the captivity myth into a story of liberation, and divorced the
plot of sexuality from its gendered confinements. It was all in preparation,
as it turned out, to return a flesh-and-blood woman to paradise by writing

about Annie Sadelik, the Bohemian hired girl of one of Cather's neighbors, celebrating her as "one of the truest artists I ever knew" (qtd. in Bohlke 44), and through her, revising the idea of creativity that she had inherited.

As Marta Weigle writes in *Creation and Procreation,* in this cosmogonical tradition procreation existed as an antithesis to creation. "Procreation is relegated to elemental or physical or biological status, while spiritual or metaphysical or symbolic creation becomes the valued paradigm for ritual custom, art, narrative, and belief systems" (xi). Women have babies; men write books. Definitions from *The Oxford English Dictionary* (1933) illustrate the difference:

> Create: Transitive. Said of the divine agent. To bring into being, cause to exist; *esp.* to produce where nothing was before, "to form out of nothing."
> Procreate. To beget, engender, generate (offspring). To produce offspring . . . to give rise to, occasion.

By structuring her novel around images of birth, Cather evoked traditional mythologies of cosmogony and parturition, then revised those traditions as she created her birth of a nation. Her descriptions of the Shimerdas living in a dugout on an unbroken frontier evoke Native American emergence mythologies; Ántonia's emerging sexuality is set within the Judeo-Christian culture of Black Hawk, and Jim Burden's awakening to ideas at the university recalls classical mythologies of creativity. Cather revised these traditions, however, by refiguring into them the Muse, the midwife, and the Earth Mother. Read sequentially, *My Ántonia* provides a historical survey of myths about and attitudes toward birth; read incrementally, Cather's narrative creates a new myth for America.

Childhood scenes in *My Ántonia* revolve around two visits to the Shimerdas in their dugout. Each visit suggests both an emergence mythology of a people's "journeying through lower or other worlds, domains, or wombs" (Weigle 7) and a people's origin in their mother, the earth. In his first visit, Jim witnesses the Shimerdas emerge from a hole in the bank as if the earth was giving birth to life itself; in the second visit, during winter and amid the apparent absence of life, Jim enters that dugout hole as if descending into an underworld to discover its secrets. To Jim, "The air in the cave was stifling, and it was very dark, too" (71). Only gradually, as his eyes adjust to the darkness, does he realize that "In the rear wall was another little cave; a round hole, not much bigger than an oil barrel, scooped out in the black earth," where Ántonia and her sister sleep (72).

Earth caves may suggest to Jim a frightening descent into a secret, sealed womblike space closely associated with death,[1] but Ántonia presents another view: "I like for sleep there," she insists, "this is warm like the badger hole" (73). Her description echoes not only emergence myths generally but the Acoma Pueblo origin myth specifically, a myth Cather likely knew from her family's copy of John M. Gunn's *Schat-Chen: History, Traditions and Narratives of the Queres Indians of Laguna and Acoma* (1917). Here she would have read of two sisters who were born underground and remained in the dark as they slowly and patiently grew until they finally emerged through a hole made by a badger.[2]

For her second stage of revisioning, Cather set Ántonia within the Judeo-Christian tradition of the Fall. Whereas the childhood scenes concerned Ántonia's genesis and birth, the Black Hawk scenes concern her awakening to a sexuality that is complicated for Western civilization because of its polarized treatment in the book of Genesis. Adam and Eve gained sexual knowledge by eating fruit from the tree of knowledge of good and evil, and as Gerda Lerner has written, "Once and forever, creativity (and with it the secret of immortality) is severed from procreativity. Creativity is reserved to God; procreativity of human beings is the lot of women. The curse on Eve makes it a painful and subordinate lot" (197). Plot lines in *My Ántonia* separate to reflect this polarized tradition when Jim aligns himself with the world of ideas while Ántonia aligns herself with that of human relationships.[3] He prepares for a creative life of the mind by excelling in high school and by studying trigonometry and beginning Virgil alone the following summer. He then leaves his family and friends to attend the university in Lincoln. During the same period Ántonia follows her script for procreativity by entering domestic service with the Harlings, going with the hired girls to the dances, and loving railway conductor Larry Donovan. Tension is inevitable when a fertility goddess from emergence myth is transplanted into Protestant Black Hawk, and Black Hawk responds by tightening its constrictions upon Ántonia until, following her lover to Denver, she disappears from the text.

Two books and two decades later, Jim returns to Ántonia, now settled with her husband and many children on a Nebraska farm. His visit builds to the most famous birth scene in American literature: "Why don't we show Mr. Burden our new fruit cave?" Ántonia's daughter asks, prompting a gathering of the family as children emerge from the house, join with other children from the yard, and run ahead to open the cellar door, so that "When we descended, they all came down after us" (326–27). The scene reaches its climax when, as Jim describes it: "We turned to leave the cave; Ántonia and I went up the stairs first, and the children waited. We were standing outside talking, when they all came running up the steps together; big and little, tow heads and gold heads and brown, and flashing little naked legs; a veritable explosion of life out of the dark cave into the sunlight. It made me dizzy for a moment" (328). Making explicit that this scene is Cather's version of the birth of America, Jim reflects that Ántonia is "a rich mine of life, like the founders of early nations" (342), and thus brings the succession of birth myths to the present. The power of the scene lies in our reading not only sequentially, but incrementally, to recognize that the Cuzaks' fruit cave is reminiscent of the dugout cave that first held Ántonia in the New World, and from which she emerged as if in a first birth, and that Ántonia has fulfilled her destiny as a natural born mother—undeniably, an Earth Mother.

Ántonia as Earth Mother? The description has become so standard that it is easy to pass over how revolutionary is Cather's revisioning of western myths that depict women. As Simone de Beauvoir wrote of the Earth Mother tradition that Cather inherited, the connection of woman with nature is decidedly ambivalent. Though praises may be sung to a fecund nature, "more often man is in revolt against his carnal state; he sees himself as a fallen god: his curse is to be fallen from a bright and ordered heaven into the chaotic shadows of his mother's womb. . . . This quivering jelly which is elaborated in the womb (the womb, secret and sealed like the tomb) evokes too clearly the soft viscosity of carrion for him not to turn shuddering away. . . . The Earth Mother engulfs the bones of her children" (144–47).[4] By Cather's account, however, the Earth Mother tradition is no imprisonment to earth, no secret and sealed space. Instead the nurturing womb is liberated and celebrated, fertility goddess and Earth Mother restored into a birth myth for the New World.

Celebration takes the form of perception made finer. Having witnessed the explosion of life out of a fruit cave, Jim now sees womblike enclosures replicated in the larger scene, as if Ántonia's body has regenerated itself in his perception of space. The Cuzaks' house is encircled by a roof so steep that the eaves almost touch "the forest of tall hollyhocks" growing alongside it, and its front yard is "enclosed by a thorny locust hedge" (328–29). Behind the house a cherry orchard and an apple orchard are "surrounded by a triple enclosure; the wire fence, then the hedge of thorny locusts, then the mulberry hedge. . . . The hedges were so tall that we could see nothing but the blue sky above them. . . . The orchard seemed full of sun, like a cup" (330–31). Movement of descent and ascent and of in and out creates a feeling of freedom in each enclosure, and colors establish the inestimable value of contents protected therein: the gemlike glow of fruit preserved within the cave and the flash of gold from bodies tumbling out of it; the silvery trees flashing from the yard and the purple-red crabs in the orchard that have "a thin silvery glaze over them"; the handsome drakes "with pinkish gray bodies, their heads and necks covered with iridescent green feathers which grew close and full, changing like a peacock's neck" (331). Through it all, the afternoon sun pours down in a shower of gold as if in granting grace.

Female space, liberated from the dark confines of secrecy and shame associated with birth, becomes the central and ongoing metaphor through which the world's fertility and fecundity are experienced. There is no *I* here (to refer to Ántonia's fruit cellar is to miss the point). Instead there is the *we* of family and, by implication, community and nation. "Why don't *we* show Mr. Burden *our* new fruit cellar," Anna asks; "in winter there are nearly always *some of us* around to come out and get things" Ambrosch explains; and Ántonia describes "the bread *we* bake" and the sugar it takes "for *us* to preserve with" (326–27; emphases mine).

Enlightenment is all the more powerful because it is a release from confinement, which is so closely associated with birth as to be considered its necessary condition. Mores and laws defining and legislating procreativity undergird Black Hawk's "respect for respectability" (195), another form of confinement when, under its guise, women, bound by both class and gender, are denied sexual knowledge. "[P]hysical exercise was thought rather inelegant for the daughters of well-to-do families," Jim observes of Black Hawk society; "When one danced with them their bodies never moved inside their clothes; their muscles seemed to ask but one thing—not to be disturbed" (192–93). Country girls, on the other hand, were "physically . . . almost a race apart," for their "out-of-door work had given them a vigor which . . . developed into a positive carriage and freedom of movement," in contrast to the town girls (192).

The cultural tensions of Black Hawk reflect tensions of mythic appropriations. By moving to Black Hawk and becoming one of "The Hired Girls" (the title of book 2) Ántonia confronts a Judeo-Christian ethos by which the sexuality of the fertility goddess "was so defined as to serve her motherly function, and it was limited by two conditions: she was to be sub-ordinate to her husband, and she would bring forth her children in pain" (Lerner 196). With Genesis in the background, a fall is inevitable—appar-ently Ántonia's as she suffers the cultural confinements imposed upon her and the assumptions behind those confinements.

As Ántonia develops into adolescence, the circumstances of frontier liv-ing provide her knowledge: "Ambrosch put upon her some chores a girl ought not to do, . . . and the farm-hands around the country joked in a nasty way about it" (121). The strength of her body results in hunger (eat-ing is a metaphor for lust), and her emerging beauty attracts attention. Maturing as robustly physical and vibrantly sexual, Ántonia defies expec-tations that a woman be either physical *or* spiritual, sexual *or* maternal. In Black Hawk she continues going to the summer tent dances despite her employer's ultimatum that she stop because she was getting "a reputation for being free and easy." "Stop going to the tent?" Ántonia retorts; "I wouldn't think of it for a minute! My own father couldn't make me stop! Mr. Harling ain't my boss outside my work. I won't give up my friends, ei-ther!" (200). She goes to work for Wick Cutter even though she knows that previous hired girls who worked for him were ruined, and she goes to Denver to join Larry Donovan even though they are as yet unmarried.

From Fielding's Tom Jones to Fitzgerald's Nick Carroway, countless young men have left the country for the city, where they gain the knowl-edge of the world they will need to take their place in it; the analogous script for women is the cautionary one played out in Theodore Dreiser's *Sister Carrie*. Young women moving to the city support themselves by en-tering "service" and becoming "hired girls," language that doubles for prostitution and signifies the sanctions against them. Cather evokes these sanctions in "The Hired Girls," revisiting the literary version of a woman's fall into knowledge in which a young woman moves from country to city, learns sexuality, and is punished by "the nothingness that surrounds the . . . prostitute" (Michie 73).

In Black Hawk an undercurrent of gossip links a woman's indepen-dence with female sexuality and prostitution. Wick Cutter "was noto-riously dissolute with women," and two Swedish girls "were the worse for the experience" of living in his house—he had taken one to Omaha "and established [her] in the business for which he had fitted her. He still visited her" (203). Lena Lingard is suspect by becoming a seamstress,[5] and Tiny

Soderball by running a lodging house for sailors. "This, every one said, would be the end of Tiny" (291). Everyone knows also, one might add, that such gossip follows Ántonia.

Her punishment takes the form of silencing. Ántonia's own voice grows distant and then silent when from Denver she writes a letter, then a post-card, and then nothing. More powerfully, Jim's narrative voice erases Ántonia's presence when he admits that he scarcely thinks of her while he is at the university in Lincoln and recalls how grudging and painful references to her are in Black Hawk. "You know, of course, about poor Ánto-nia," Mrs. Harling says to Jim, upon which he bitterly thinks, "Poor Ánto-nia! Every one would be saying that now" (289). She has become a subject to be avoided, acknowledged only when necessary and then with the barest of details. Jim reports that "grandmother had written me how Ántonia went away to marry Larry Donovan at some place where he was working; that he had deserted her, and that there was now a baby" but cuts short his recollection with "This was all I knew" (289–90). When Jim remembers Frances Harling telling him tersely that "He never married her" and ad-mitting that "I have n't seen her since she came back," Jim cuts off that reminiscence too by acknowledging flatly, "I tried to shut Ántonia out of my mind" (290).

Whereas the first half of My Ántonia tells of circumstances surrounding Ántonia that narrow into confinements, the second half tells of those cir-cumstances widening into liberation. Between the two lies Jim's (and the reader's) education—not by the formal instruction of the university but by his friendship with Lena Lingard, through whom Cather rewrites the clas-sical tradition of the Muse. Whereas allusions to Judeo-Christian tradi-tions undergird procreativity in the Black Hawk section, classical tradi-tions undergird the emphasis on creativity in the Lincoln section. While living in Lincoln and attending the university, Jim awakens to the world of ideas under the influence of Gaston Cleric, "a brilliant and inspiring" young classical scholar (249). The furnishings in Jim's boarding-house room reflect his teacher's influence, as do the conversations that take place there. Jim covers his wall with a map of ancient Rome ordered by Cleric, hangs over his bookcase a photograph of the Tragic Theatre at Pompeii that Cleric had given him, and buys a comfortable chair for Cleric to sit in, hoping to entice his teacher to visit and linger. Cleric "could bring the drama of antique life before one out of the shadows" (253), and with it a literary legacy held together by an authority of influence. Entranced, his forgotten cigarette burning unheeded, Cleric would speak lines of Statius who spoke for Dante of his veneration for Virgil.

Jim distinguishes himself from that tradition, however. He recognizes that, unlike Cleric, he should "never lose himself in impersonal things," and he acknowledges an alternative idea of memory for which he uses language of conception, gestation, and quickening. "I begrudged the room that Jake and Otto and Russian Peter took up in my memory," Jim reflects, "But whenever my consciousness was quickened, all those early friends were quickened within it, and in some strange way they accompanied me through all my new experiences" (254). The reflection moves him to question the separation of creativity (forming something out of nothing with an assumption of absolute, godlike authority) from procreativity (generating offspring with an assumption of giving rise to or occasioning independent life): "They were so much alive in me that I scarcely stopped to wonder whether they were alive anywhere else, or how" (254). By stopping to wonder, Jim prepares for his invocation of the Muse.

Alone, staring listlessly at the *Georgics,* Jim reads, "for I shall be the first, if I live, to bring the Muse into my country." As if invoking a spell, he repeats the phrase "bring the Muse," and then he recalls the phrase yet again—the magical third utterance (256–57). Thereupon he hears a knock at his door and, opening it, sees Lena Lingard standing in the dark hall. Admitting her, Jim leads her to the chair he had purchased for Cleric, and once she is seated he "confusedly" questions her.

Answering Jim's summons and sitting in Cleric's chair, Lena displaces Cleric as Jim's teacher and embodies Cather's answer to one of the most telling of silences, that of the Muses. Excluded by conventions that authorize the poet in creativity as the father is authorized in procreativity, Muses are to creativity as the mother is to procreativity. As standard handbooks demonstrate, the Muses are given short shrift. According to *Crowell's Handbook of Classical Mythology* there are few myths specifically given to the Muses, who were "little worshiped, though often invoked." *The Concise Oxford Dictionary of Literary Terms* notes succinctly that the Muses are "usually represented by a female deity," and Holman and Harman's *Handbook to Literature* specifies that "In literature, their traditional significance is that of inspiring and helping POETS." In short, the Muse is the female inspiration to the male poet, and as Mary Carruthers has written in "The Re-Vision of the Muse," "he addresses her in terms of sexual rapture, desiring to be possessed in order to possess, to be ravished in order to be fruit-ful." Though the poet is dependent upon her, Carruthers continues, "she speaks only through him. She is wholly Other and strange, . . . an ethere-ally beautiful young girl in the tradition of romance." Whatever guise she assumes, however, "the basic relationship of dominance and possession is constant between her and her poet" (295).

Cather's Muse is another matter altogether. Her authority is an-nounced by the title of book 3, "Lena Lingard." Rather than speaking only through a man, Lena speaks for herself, and rather than submitting to a relationship of dominance and possession, she invites equality in friend-ship. Jim's expectations are the familiar ones of the male poet to "his" Muse: he feels himself possessed, perceives the encounter as sexual, and assumes her dependency upon him. What Lena offers to him, however, is an alternative to such conventional notions of creativity. Her self-posses-sion contrasts comically to Jim's assumptions that because she lives alone, she is lonely; that by visiting her in her room, he will compromise her; and that because she is unattached to a man, she wishes to marry.

Cather's Muse speaks for herself when she explains that men pay court to her because "It makes them feel important to think they're in love with somebody" (281) and that "men are all right for friends, but as soon as you marry them they turn into cranky old fathers. . . . I prefer to . . . be accountable to nobody" (282). Rejecting the relationship traditional to the Muse, Lena offers instead the kindness of mutual respect. When she sees Jim's hurt at hearing her say she is not dependent upon him, for ex-ample, she softens his pain by saying, "I've always been a little foolish about you" (284).

By instructing Jim in the mutuality of friendship as an alternative to dominance and possession, Lena prepares him for his return to Ántonia. Whereas the early books in My Ántonia depict others' attempts to control Ántonia by narrowing her confinements until she disappeared, the later ones tell of Ántonia reasserting herself into the text. "[S]uch entries for women into textuality and into language are always painful in that they al-ways involve a shattering of the silence which enshrouds women's physical presence," observes Helena R. Michie, who in The Flesh Made Word (74–75) could have been describing Ántonia returning pregnant and unwed. No-body visits her. She was "crushed and quiet," "never went anywhere," and "always looked dead weary" (306). Though afflicted with toothache, she "wouldn't go to Black Hawk to a dentist for fear of meeting people she knew" (306), and after her daughter was born, she "almost never comes to town" (290).

The power granted to birth is apparent when Ántonia asserts her daughter against cultural erasure. Ántonia's reentry into textuality is indirect at first, accomplished by the stories that Jim hears of her. Though nobody visits Ántonia, she brings her daughter to Black Hawk to show to Mrs. Harling, and though others expect her to keep "her baby out of sight," she has the child's "picture on exhibition at the town photographer's, in a great gilt frame" (295–96). A character asserting herself against the discomfort of her own novel is the effect Cather creates when the photographer speaks of Ántonia with "a constrained, apologetic laugh" and when Jim Burden reflects, selfishly, that "I could forgive her, I told myself, if she had n't thrown herself away on such a cheap sort of fellow" (295–96).

The stories that Jim hears are powerful, however. They work against the cultural discomfort of the text to create in Jim the "feeling that [he] must see Ántonia again" (295). Seeing again is re-visioning, and—appropriately—Jim goes to see a midwife for the re-visioning necessary to break the silence surrounding birth. Rhetoric and ritual signal that this is no ordinary visit. To reach the Widow Steavens, Jim journeys to the high country, reflecting as he travels upon the "growth of . . . a great idea" apparent in the changing face of the country, where human lives were "coming to a fortunate issue" and the flat tableland was responding by "long, sweeping lines of fertility" (298). Jim's meeting with the midwife has the ceremonial greeting of gravity: he "drew up," and the Widow Steavens "came out to meet [him]. She was . . . tall, and very strong . . . her massive head . . . like a Roman senator's. I told her at once why I had come" (299). This scene is the ritual supplication of youth to age, quester to oracle.

Further ritual, the sharing of food and withdrawing to a solemn setting, prepares for a transfer of knowledge. By such rituals Jim and the midwife eat supper and then retire to the sitting room where the moon shining outside the open windows recalls Great Goddess belief systems.[6] The Widow Steavens turns the lamp low, settles into her favorite rocking chair, then "crossed her hands in her lap and sat as if she were at a meeting of some kind" (299). As Cather proposed her version of the Muse in Lena, so she now proposes her oracle by drawing upon the ancient female tradition of a gossip/midwife serving as godparent and witness, figures "who think and act strongly about childbirth . . . [and who] must be counted among the enablers of powerful symbolic processes" (Weigle 145).

In telling a woman's version of procreativity, Cather's midwife releases birth from the secrecy that had enshrouded it, thereby setting in motion the powerful symbolic processes by which a birth story will become a national epic. By the Widow Steavens's account, rather than suffering the punishment inherited from a fallen Eve, Ántonia gave birth without confinement and apparently without pain ("without calling to anybody, without a groan, she lay down on the bed and bore her child"); rather than affirming a male line, she gave birth to a daughter; and rather than suffering shame over her child, "She loved it from the first as dearly as if she'd had a ring on her finger." "Ántonia is a natural-born mother," the Widow Steavens concludes, contradicting conventions governing the "rights" of motherhood (308–10).

As she offers a woman's version of birth, the midwife also establishes a woman's way of telling. Jim's authorial *I* that assumes possession ("*my* Ántonia") is replaced by the compassionate *I* of the Widow Steavens, and Jim's terse report of withdrawing from Ántonia contrasts with Widow Steavens's description of visiting Ántonia the morning after she returned home. Taking Ántonia in her arms and asking her to come out of doors where they could talk freely, the Widow Steavens said "'Oh, my child,' . . . 'what's happened to you? Don't be afraid to tell me'" (304); after hearing Ántonia's reply, she "sat right down on that back beside her and made lament" (305). Drawing Ántonia near, inviting her open and free speech, and then responding with compassion is the mutuality of friendship, the effect of which is suggested by the W. T. Benda drawings that Cather commissioned to accompany her text. Whereas Ántonia was previously depicted from a distance with her face averted, she now turns toward the viewer as if in response to the Widow Steavens's voice. We see her face as she walks forward, her body swelling with new life beneath her black overcoat.

In this manner expectations are reversed and conventions are overturned. Whereas the other hired girls have, like Ántonia, made places for themselves, the men have been displaced by various narrative devices. The introduction to *My Ántonia* complicates Jim's authority in matters of both procreation (he has no children) and creativity (rather than inventing the story, he wrote down stories as they returned to him in memory). Other men are killed or marginalized: Mr. Shimerda commits suicide, Peter and Pavel become outcasts, the tramp jumps into a thrashing machine, Jake and Otto vanish into the West, Mr. Harling disappears on business, and the Widow Steavens's husband is as absent as the vestigial "Mrs." from her name. Most interesting, there is Larry Donovan. Scarcely a character in his own right, he is instead a foil to Ántonia. Never pictured or described directly, Larry Donovan remains voiceless and faceless, as expendable to Ántonia's plot as the bride was to Peter and Pavel's plot.

Stories within the novel celebrate the New World as a site of miraculous births. Fuchs tells of the woman he accompanied on the boat crossing who in mid-ocean "proceeded to have not one baby, but three!" (67), and on Christmas Mr. Burden reads "the chapters from St. Matthew about the birth of Christ, and as we listened it all seemed like something that had happened lately, and near at hand. He thanked the Lord for the first Christmas, and for all it had meant to the world ever since" (81).[7]

As she releases her narrator from the desire to frame (or confine) Ántonia, Cather also liberates the reader from the desire to frame (or confine) the text. In Western paradigms, birth—like reading—is gendered and individualized. "What is it?" is the first question after birth that, once answered, determines responses to that child. Similarly, "who wrote it?" is the first question of a book that, once answered, determines our reading. As Susan Stanford Friedman has observed, "We seldom read any text without knowledge of the author's sex. The title page itself initiates a series of expectations that influence our reading throughout" (55).

From the outset Cather undermined her readers' reliance upon gender distinctions. The appearance of her name on the novel's title page initiates gender expectations that the introduction unsettles when, by appearing as the reader of Jim Burden's manuscript, Cather contradicts the most basic separation between self and other, writer and reader. Having evoked the question, "Where is the author in this text?" Cather complicates answers with a series of disclaimers. First her fictional narrator states that he didn't "arrange or rearrange" but instead "simply wrote down what of herself and myself and other people Ántonia's name recalls to me" (xiii). Then Cather herself renounces authority by writing that "my own story was never written," saying that "the following narrative is Jim's manuscript, substantially as he brought it to me" (xiii). The effect is to undermine the premise that authority is basic to creativity.[8] This is a manuscript conceived not by a distinction between creator and created, author and subject; instead, it is conceived by the mutuality of long friendship. "We grew up together in the same Nebraska town," "we had much to say to each other," "we were talking," and "we agreed" (ix)—the exchange of conversation establishes that this text is a collaboration that grew out of continuities of life into art, of past into present, of childhood retrieved by adults, of female author and male narrator *in agreement*.

As the metaphor of birth had expanded into enlightenment, so the mutuality of friendship expands into an aesthetics of kinship in the novel's final scenes when Jim witnesses storytelling within the Cuzak family. "The distinction between female and male discourse lies not in the [childbirth] metaphor itself but rather in the way its final meaning is constituted in the process of reading," writes Friedman (61). Though she was not, Friedman could have been writing of *My Ántonia,* where Cather reconstitutes the process of reading to provide an alternative aesthetic based on an "emphasis on birth leading to a lifetime of maternal nurturance" (Friedman 62).[9]

Far from previous assumptions of possession and dominance, storytelling now proceeds by cooperation and inclusion. Ántonia's daughter Anna, for example, reveals sensitivity to her youngest brother by recognizing his need to tell his story to Ántonia: Jan "wants to tell you about the dog, mother," Anna says, whereupon Ántonia beckons her son to her and listens to him while he tells her about the dog's death, resting his elbows upon her knees as he does so (326). Ántonia then whispers to Jan, who then slips away and whispers, in turn, to his sister Nina. The principle is now of repetition. Jan repeats his mother's words to his sister, and the younger children ask Ántonia to tell the story of "how the teacher has the school picnic in the orchard every year" (330). Contrary to the convention of male author(ity) and female subject, Ántonia is at the center of storytelling by which, like the metaphor of birth, language returns to its source.

As the metaphor of birth has expanded, so does that of language's return. Coming home from a street fair in a nearby town, Cuzak says, "very many send word to you, Ántonia," then asks Jim to excuse him while he delivers their messages in Bohemian (346). As the birth scenes build to the explosion of bodies from the fruit cellar, so now storytelling builds to the reminiscences and exchanges of family stories as the Cuzaks and Jim look at photographs and then to reminiscences and exchanges at dinner. Here again storytelling is a cooperative enterprise. When at dinner Rudolph asks if Jim has heard about the Cutters, Ántonia (upon hearing that Jim hasn't), says "then you must tell him, son. . . . Now, all you children be quiet, Rudolph is going to tell about the murder." "Hurrah," they murmur, then are quiet as Rudolph tells his story "in great detail, with occasional promptings from his mother or father" (349–50).

The younger children, Anna, Jan, and Nina, the older son, Rudolph, and the parents, Cuzak and Ántonia herself—all have a voice in the family's ongoing story. What is the principle of narrative here and of the use of the word? Clearly, Ántonia is not using language in the tradition of creation (i.e., to produce where nothing was before, to form out of nothing). Instead, she is a source of the family legend in the sense that she begets, engenders, generates, produces, gives rise to, and occasions. These—the definitions of *procreate* with which I began—come together in the pro/ creativity of a kinship aesthetic. In Cather's version of the Fall, Ántonia disappeared from Jim Burden's text only to return independently to claim her language and to demonstrate its power. She speaks Bohemian with her children, and around the dinner table she teaches them not only the mother tongue but also a reciprocal and communal use of language.

Cather's birth of a nation is significant for what it is not as well as for what it is. It is not a separation from or casting off of other cultures. It does not set a New World against an Old World, an American future against a European past or a Native American mythology. Instead, it offers a national identity affirming analogies and continuities. As Virgil brought the Muse to Rome by writing of his neighborhood in Mantua, so Cather would bring the Muse to the United States by writing of her neighborhood in Nebraska. By drawing upon emergence mythologies, Cather renewed familiar figures so that the Muse inspires collaboration and the midwife sets in motion powerful symbolic processes of language and metaphor. Through Cather's revisioning, an immigrant girl she knew in Nebraska gives birth to a nation.

5

Stafford's
Inherited
West

Margaret Fuller, Willa Cather, and Jean Stafford each continued the commitment of and fulfilled the prophecy of her predecessor. Like Fuller and Cather, Stafford looked to the West as her literary
Muse, and like them, Stafford approached that Muse in terms of a tradition that would exclude her from it. Stafford's link to Cather is especially
close. Like Cather, Stafford devoted much of her literary life to negotiating
her relationship with a West that was, to paraphrase Cather, the curse and
blessing of her life. As Cather had moved from Nebraska to the East, so
Stafford transplanted herself from Colorado; and as Cather, even while remaining in New York, was to return in her fiction to Nebraska, so Stafford
wrote again and again of her own western roots. Along with these similarities in circumstance, a common credo joins the two women. To each, literature—which they distinguished from propaganda and preaching—
meant an arduous commitment to refining language as truth-telling. As
Cather had declared that "an artist's life is . . . ceaseless and unremitting
labor" (*Kingdom of Art* 413), so Stafford declared that "writing is the most
backbreaking of all professions." Both believed that the writer must have
"the courage to go on without compromise," not succumbing to jargon
and rhetoric (Cather, "Katherine Mansfield" 103; Stafford, "Psychological
Novel" 225). Finally, both had a natural ear for language, writing with a
"virtuosity, a love for the medium" they chose (Cather, "Katherine Mansfield" 107). When in reviewing the 1973 reissue of *A Lost Lady* Stafford paid
tribute to Cather for having created fiction "as controlled and graceful, as

sinuous and luminous as any in American literature" (7), she was describing those qualities she admired in literature of the highest order as well as the standard that she set for herself.

But such similarities only make more dramatic the differences that come with Stafford having been born almost four decades after Cather, and on the opposite side of the literary West. Again, Stafford's review of *A Lost Lady* is revealing, for in describing loss in Cather's novel Stafford could have been writing of herself: "Marian Forrester is not lost in the frivolous way of Emma Bovary or in the neurasthenic way of Anna Karenina or in the petulant and irresponsible way of Kate Chopin's Edna Pontellier. . . . But she is lost in a deeper sense, in a historical sense: she lives in the wrong place at the wrong time, during 'the end of an era, the sunset of the pioneer'" (1, 6–7). Like Cather's character, Jean Stafford was lost in the deeper sense of living "in the wrong place at the wrong time." The decades separating the writers (Cather, 1873–1947; Stafford, 1915–79) were ones of transformation. The year Cather was born her family began emigrating to free land on the frontier in Nebraska. By then the 1848 California gold rush was long past, agriculture had developed in California's Central Valley during the 1860s, the completion of the first transcontinental railroad in 1869 linked Sacramento with the rest of the nation, and by the late 1880s citrus groves around Los Angeles had begun to produce large quantities of fruit. In California, promises of the West had been succeeded by collapses, devastations, betrayals, and riots. In 1882 federal legislation was passed against further Chinese immigration, and by the turn of the century Theodore Roosevelt expressed the view of much of the nation when he remarked, "When I am in California, I am not in the west, I am west of the west" (qtd. in Haslam 1).

The literary landscape was as transformed as the geographical one. Whereas Cather positioned herself as a pioneer in art who was "the first to bring the Muse to her country," Stafford wrote from within a West fictionalized as a cultural code. Frank Norris's *McTeague, A Story of San Francisco* (1899) made the West a shorthand for the inability to escape one's past, and his book about the railroad, *The Octopus: A Story of California* (1901), made the West synonymous with the strangling effect of concentrated power; similarly, Jack London's *Call of the Wild* (1903) was a shorthand for an identification with nature. It was a code made personal by two facts of Stafford's childhood. First, the West in which she had her roots was a fictional one bequeathed to her by her father, and second, the experience of writing the West was colored by her father's failures.

The last of the Staffords' four children, Jean had the distinction of being the only one who was a 'native daughter' of California (the preceding three were born in Missouri) (Goodman, *Jean Stafford* 1–2). To be a native daughter of California was not to be a native westerner, however, by John Stafford's version of things. Jean grew up hearing her father tell stories of the West as the territory they had passed over (his West lay east of California), the life they had left behind, and a reality that never existed. In *The Collected Stories* Stafford wrote: "By the time I knew him, my father was writing Western stories under the *nom de plum* Jack Wonder or, occasionally, Ben Delight. But before that, before I was born, he wrote under his own name and he published a novel called *When Cattle Kingdom Fell*" (author's note).

Jean was a precocious child who by the age of six had written a poem she would later include in *The Mountain Lion* (1947) and who by the age of seven had begun her first novel. As the writing child of a writing father, Jean had a bit part as Jack Wonder's sidekick and one summer spent several weeks with her father "in a cabin in the mountains that a friend allowed them to use. There, on separate typewriters, they worked side by side on their stories" (Goodman, *Jean Stafford* 26). The scene represents well a childhood in which fiction and fact have not merely interpenetrated (as Jane Tompkins sees happening in the work of Western writers Owen Wister, Zane Grey, and Louis L'Amour)[1] but in which fiction actually displaced fact. As Stafford reflected in middle age, her heritage consisted not of real people and places but of pseudonyms and types, so that "when my cacoëthes scribendi set in, I wrote about twisters on the plains, stampedes when herds of longhorns were being driven up from the Panhandle to Dodge, and bloody incidents south of the border. All the foremen of the ranches had steely blue eyes to match the barrels of their Colt .45's" (*Collected Stories* author's note).

The second experience that colored Jean's childhood concerned her father's failures. John Stafford's youthful promise (his early novel sold well, and he inherited stocks, bonds, and property worth well over $270,000) only made more dramatic his subsequent inability to provide for his family. Seeking new starts from financial disasters, John Stafford moved his family to Colorado and, after a series of relocations, to Boulder, where Jean's mother opened a boarding house in which Jean worked serving tables and cleaning. As devastating as his financial insolvency, the failure of John Stafford's creative promise was a constant, pervasive factor that colored Jean's childhood. Though he found no publishers interested in his work, he continued to write, compulsively and bitterly descending to his study in the basement of their house from where his oaths could be heard through the heating ducts.

Not surprisingly, Stafford left home with relief. "As soon as I could, I hotfooted it across the Rocky Mountains and across the Atlantic Ocean," she recalled from the distance of middle age. After establishing a brilliant record at the University of Colorado, Stafford graduated in 1936 with both an A.B. and an A.M. and then went to Heidelberg on a fellowship. For the rest of her life she traveled in mainstream eastern literary circles. She was encouraged by influential writers and critics—Howard Mumford Jones, John Crowe Ransom, Randall Jarrell, Peter Taylor, Edward Davison, Caroline Gordon, and Allen Tate. Following her marriage to Robert Lowell in 1940, she worked as a secretary for *Southern Review* (while Lowell attended graduate school on a fellowship) and then at Sheed and Ward in New York. Stafford and Lowell lived for a year with Caroline Gordon and Allen Tate in Tennessee, where Stafford worked on her first novel, and she completed her manuscript at Yaddo. Upon its publication, *Boston Adventure* was reviewed by several journals and greeted as "the most interesting novel of the season" (rev. of *Boston Adventure, Commonweal* 20) and the "outstanding first-novel of 1944" (rev. of *Boston Adventure, Catholic World* 283). As for Stafford, she was hailed by Howard Mumford Jones as "a commanding talent, who writes in the great tradition of the English novel" (10).

But the years leading to the critical acclaim and financial success of Stafford's first novel included episodes of dreadful violence. At Boulder, Lucy McKee, the friend with whom Stafford lived, shot herself in the temple while her husband and Stafford looked on. Before her marriage to Lowell, Stafford was in a car accident that occurred while Lowell, intoxicated, was driving. She emerged with a smashed nose and a fractured jaw and skull; the painful effects of these injuries plagued her the rest of her life. During their marriage, violence and potential madness continued to play a part in the creative ferment of her life, assuming the form of Lowell's emotional as well as physical abuse of his wife and his obsessive Catholicism.

Throughout these years, Stafford tried to juggle what she saw as incompatible parts of her life—human relationships versus solitude, domestic responsibilities (which were solely hers) versus the desire to write, her nature as a woman versus her need to create. Why can't a woman write like a man, she wondered, and then explained in a 1938 letter to her friend James Robert Hightower: "Yesterday I began my novel over again with an idea that has been working in my mind for a long time: the question why is it that a woman cannot write a book like A Portrait of the Artist. I mean, why is it that her experiences cannot be those of a man. The main character, Gretchen Marburg, will make an attempt to live such a life, that is with a male mind in which there is such and such a compartment for literature and such a one for love, but in the end she will be faced with the realization that a woman's mind can never be neatly ordered and every experience is tinged by every other one" (qtd. in Goodman, *Jean Stafford* 81–82). When Stafford died in 1979, she had come to be known primarily for her stint as Lowell's first wife, for her short stories published in the *New Yorker,* and for her tragic personal life (she was hospitalized repeatedly for various physical problems, mental collapse, and alcoholism).

I begin not with her stories or her life, however, but with her three novels. Superficially they seem very different from one another, yet they make up three versions of Stafford's Portrait of the Artist as a Young Woman. In *Boston Adventure* (1944) Stafford tells of Sonia Marburg's attempts to authorize herself in an eastern society of women abandoned by men who have lit out for the territory; in *The Mountain Lion* (1947) Stafford takes her adolescent would-be-writer Molly Fawcett into the male preserve of the West; and in *The Catherine Wheel* (1952) she writes of the final summer of middle-aged Katherine Congreve, who in her diary releases a personal voice she never uses publicly.

"Because we were very poor." With the opening words of *Boston Adventure* Stafford announces an American version of a fairy tale, as recognizable in its desire for money as "Once upon a time there lived a king and queen" is in its desire for class. As a brief synopsis demonstrates, the plot of *Boston Adventure* provides variations on the myth of rags to riches. The daughter of a poor German cobbler and his Russian immigrant wife, Sonia Marburg is born in America, only to be abandoned first by her father, who disappears into the West, and then by her mother, who escapes into madness. Just when it would seem that there is no hope for her, Sonia is discovered by the wealthy and cultured Bostonian lady Lucy Pride. After committing her mother to an insane asylum, Sonia joins the household of her benefactress, where she is trained as a secretary-companion and where she acquires a reputation as a promising writer. There Sonia meets various members of Boston society, including young and idealistic Doctor Philip McAllister, who marries Hopestill Mather, Miss Pride's beautiful and high-spirited niece and heir. The initial blush of happiness fades from their marriage when Philip realizes that his wife is pregnant from a liaison with another man, and Hopestill causes a riding accident in which she and her unborn child die. In the end Sonia is left alone with Miss Pride in the large Boston house.

Fantastic, melodramatic, and unbelievable? Of course. If the book is to work at all, a reader must accept at the outset that Stafford is writing with an "imagined removal from the everyday and active world" ("Psychological Novel" 214); here Stafford describes the psychological novel, which works by a "method that is not inhibited by the restrictions of traditional rules" and which makes possible the subjective scrutiny of "the author's own heart and mind" (214-15). At an imagined remove an author is ideally positioned to see the everyday; lack of inhibition allows her to reflect upon rules. Writing a fantasy frees an author to explore the conventional plots of literature and culture. Our culture deposits in us our fantasies, and our fantasies release us to explore that culture. But as Marcia Westkott argues, "Fantasy not only opposes real conditions, but also reflects them. The opposition that fantasy expresses is not abstract, but is rooted in the real conditions themselves, in concrete social relations. As a negation, fantasy suggests an alternative to these concrete conditions," the "reality that a person encounters, experiences, and interprets" (qtd. in Habegger 7–8). The situation is complicated for women in that "this means that fantasy is rooted in a situation that is already a negation." When a culture identifies woman as not-man and as Other, for "women fantasy is not a negation of reality per se, but a negation of the reality that women experience. . . . a negation of a negation, a protest against being the negative" (2).[2]

Stafford explores this tension between reality and fantasy by exploring its consequences. Release from traditional rules may give way to fantasy, but to what end? If fantasy is so powerful that it actually creates reality, what would it be to live that created reality? These are the questions that Stafford poses in *Boston Adventure* by granting to Sonia Marburg the power to create something by dreaming it. Before dreaming creatively, however, Sonia must free herself from the myths she has inherited—that of the western hero as an American version of the savior-prince and that of the angel in the house. The western hero who seeks adventure beyond the frontier is the legacy of Sonia's father, who shapes his imagination by perpetually reading *Riders of the Purple Sage*. But told by the daughter who is left behind, this story is one of abandonment rather than adventure:

> Probably from his frequent readings of this book, my father longed to see the west and one time, some years before, when he had made a little extra money carrying trunks at the Hotel, he bought a fine yellow hide and made a pair of cowboy boots which he sometimes wore on Sunday. As he read, I could tell by the pleasure that illuminated his face and caused him now and then to chuckle deeply in his throat, that he was far away from me and that the world in which he rode a pinto cow-pony or a roan mare contained no blubbering, angry child nor any sullen, pregnant woman. Once he paused and swung an invisible lariat over his head, leaned forward on his horse's neck as to its flanks he pressed spurs with tied rowels. A little later, he whipped a revolver from his holster and aimed at the empty caviar can. Then, conscious once more of where he was, he kicked the stove in vexation and scratched his head. (46)

While crouching in the corner watching her father's pleasure in dreaming himself far away from her, Sonia realizes that to be the daughter of a western hero is a contradiction in terms. Sonia cries, and her father's attempts to console her only dramatize the abyss between them. He imitates "the friendly rancher of the Saturday night movies by saying 'Put 'er there, pardner!'" (47) and awkwardly offers her his hand. Though troubled by Sonia's lack of ambition when she wishes only to live in Boston someday, her father is unable to imagine a future for her beyond the roles cast by the western scripts. "I thought you wanted to be a school teacher at least," he says to her; "you should want to be a school teacher" (48). When he offers to her his dream of traveling west, it is a dream so remote that Sonia can only translate it into drawing-room conversation:

> "I'll tell you what we'll do, Sonie, we'll go west some day to Cheyenne, Wyoming. Wouldn't you like to ride a little wild horse?"
>
> I said I would in much sincerity, but because I was unschooled in both the scenery and the customs of the west, I did not immediately seat myself astride a horse or envisage Cheyenne, but instead, heard Miss Pride say to a friend, as I entered the drawing room "*Here* is our cow girl. You know she and her father own several thousand wild roan stallions." (48–49)

When Sonia's father actually goes west his vanishing creates a sense of loss that informs the rest of the novel; his departure provides a literary version of a black hole.

Rejecting the bit part of the daughter seeking her father her "whole life through, as [she] had seen daughters do at the Bijou, missing by a few minutes a reunion in a South American cabaret, a Peking tea house, an English garden party" (56), Sonia begins to explore the female legacy remaining to her, one as clearly drawn from literary type as her father's western hero. Sonia's mother, Shura, is a descendent of the angel in the house, with a beauty so holy that upon seeing her others would say, "She is the image of a saint" (50). At first glance, Shura's life in Russia does indeed seem the stuff of which fairy tales are made. After Shura's mother died when she was nine or ten, she was reared by a kind witch and grew into a radiantly beautiful young woman. At seventeen she set off for the New World, on the boat meeting a handsome young German who was filled with dreams of becoming rich in America. They married, she soon gave birth to Sonia, and she settled in to live happily ever after—or so the formula would suggest.

Shura's telling, however, presents a dark underside of the tale: her father locked her out of the house and her surrogate mother was called a witch because, "for a price, she mutilated men who wished to escape military service" (8). The men drawn to Shura's beauty abused her, and her marriage to the handsome German meant a life of poverty and disappointment. Far from living happily ever after, Sonia grows up watching her mother obsessively embroidering birds without tails and doggedly believing in a golden egg long since spent, living out her life in frustrated pursuit of fairy-tale plots from which men have departed. Disabused of any faith in men as protectors, Shura "had fortified herself, long, long before, with the conviction that men were all villains and women were their innocent victims" (153). Recognizing that the script her mother has followed has led to the bitter madness of a victim, Sonia frees herself from it by committing her mother to an asylum.

Rejecting her father's westering myth and her mother's fairy tale is the necessary preamble to Sonia's quest to originate her own material. To accomplish such a quest, as every daughter of Virginia Woolf knows, a woman needs a room of her own, and while sleeping on her pallet in her parents' room Sonia begins to dream of just that: "when I played wishing games or said 'Star light, star bright,' my first wish always was that I might have a room of my own" (3). Thus Sonia's fantasy begins to take shape, adjusted as necessary to accommodate the most intractable aspects of her own life. She reads stories about girls at boarding schools, for example, dressed by their mothers to be presentable in society; then, recognizing that her unstable mother is decidedly unsuited for such a role, she inserts into their plots the real-life Lucy Pride, the elderly and very proper Bostonian lady she has observed at the hotel where she serves tables.

The novel works by taking Sonia inside the plots she has imagined, allowing her to dismiss one and imagine another. Its structure resembles envelopes within envelopes. Beginning with the outermost narrative's simple wish fulfillment, it proceeds to other narratives that are increasingly internal and psychological.[3] When Miss Pride invites her to Boston as her secretary, Sonia finds herself living her daydream. She is sent to a business college, dressed in fine clothes, coached in the ways of society, and finally told by Miss Pride to "never . . . leave me until I die!" (481). Most important, in Miss Pride's house Sonia has her own room, containing a writing desk that Sonia describes in loving detail: "[It had] deep drawers on either side which had been filled with watermarked paper, yellow second sheets, onion skin and carbon paper. Its surface was furnished with silver tools: letter openers, pen-knives, scissors, boxes of paper clips and rubber bands, and postage stamps. In a small upper drawer, there was pale green stationery with our address embossed in small white letters. The typewriter on which I practiced my home-work had its own stand at the right corner of the desk so that I had only to turn my chair to be facing it" (236).

The promise of writing is a charade, however, for the lessons that Sonia learns from her mentor are ones of negation rather than possibility. Far from being the independent woman Sonia had believed her to be, Miss Pride inhabits her father's house as a living memorial to his authority. As Sonia soon realizes, Miss Pride intends not to write her own memoirs (the life of a woman is not interesting enough, she believes) but "to preserve certain things, certain recollections of my father, a most praiseworthy man" (168–69), and rather than looking to Sonia to help her find her voice, she trains the girl to act as "a caretaker to silence her" in her old age, lest she "dodder into half-crazed and ludicrous senility" (238). Most telling, "Miss Pride, shrewd, witty, and fluent in conversation, was inarticulate when she began to write" (347). From her Sonia learns that language itself is gendered. For a woman, publication means a wrenching translation from the personal discourse of conversation with other women to the public discourse of men, and though her letters to Sonia "had been as elegant as her speech," Miss Pride's diction for her father's memoirs was juvenile and her syntax was crude.

After the two women flounder for months without success, they "hit upon a plan. She would write me a letter, very carefully in the style of Horace Walpole, of whom she was an assiduous student, which begged me to set down in 'sound English' the anecdote which she then wrote out in her tumid language" (347–48). As Sonia realizes, under such constraints any writing is painful and the task of creating a woman's story is hopeless: "As her calligraphy was obscure (not intentionally . . . but because she wrote in the heat of passion), it often took me a full morning to decipher a single sentence and in a short time my desk bore a formidable sheath of manuscript which I had not transcribed or edited. Thus, all morning we worked facing one another at two long desks which had been pushed together" (348). Women transcribing experience received secondhand according to standards set by men long since dead—the scene presents the dilemma of Boston Adventure as women living in plots from which men have long since departed.

"I had got my wish and could find no other," Sonia realizes (315). Her realization is the turn of the story that enables Stafford to address the questions with which Woolf ends "Professions for Women": "You have won rooms of your own in the house hitherto exclusively owned by men. . . . You are earning your five hundred pounds a year. But this freedom is only a beginning; the room is your own, but it is still bare. It has to be furnished; it has to be decorated; it has to be shared. How are you going to furnish it, how are you going to decorate it?" (289).

The rest of Boston Adventure explores the dilemma for women who, having discarded inherited myths and tales, must create their own. Any pretense at realism drops away, and Sonia's quest for a room of her own becomes purely internal and fully psychological. While visiting her mother in the common room of the asylum, Sonia frees repressed memories of what it means to be female. Sitting beside the mute older woman, Sonia enjoys a "cataleptic tranquillity," and her mind, released from anxieties, roams "through favorite daydreams" and follows "a string of associated memories" until, abruptly, she reaches "a single, clear-cut image . . . a room which I had never before seen, but a room in which there was hardly an object that was unfamiliar" (390–91). By free association, Sonia has reached the room of her own, the signifier of creativity that lies at the center of Stafford's novel.

Imagining herself upon the threshold of what she calls the red room, Sonia initially responds to it as familiar and welcoming. It was a dark room with open windows, all of which were red, reflecting a sunset; the full bookshelves along one wall contained well-worn volumes; and as the climax of the description, "between the two windows stood a little Victorian writing desk, open, and revealing a portfolio" on which rested a letter opener (392). Looking onto the room, Sonia feels that time is suspended, and she experiences happiness. Only later would she actually identify the furnishings her memory has supplied; for now, Sonia enjoys a dreamlike state of creative bliss strikingly reminiscent of the characters created by her literary grandmothers.

In *The Song of the Lark,* for example, Cather's Thea Kronborg descended into "the sanctuary" of "a dead city" (370) where she claimed for herself a rock-room that was once inhabited by Cliff Dwellers; there, daily living dropped away and her imagination was freed. Warmed by the sun, she sometimes slept and sometimes lay "for half a day undistracted, holding pleasant and incomplete conceptions in her mind . . . like a pleasant sensation indefinitely prolonged" (373). In this state of lethargy, "everything was simple and definite, as things had been in childhood" (380). Woolf too wrote of a novelist's bliss within the room of her own as "a state of trance"; for her it was "to be as unconscious as possible," to induce "a state of perpetual lethargy," "so that nothing may break the illusion in which [she] is living—so that nothing may disturb or disquiet the mysterious nosing about, feelings round, darts, dashes and sudden discoveries of that very shy and illusive spirit, the imagination" ("Professions for Women" 287).

Perhaps Stafford was drawing specifically upon Cather and Woolf—she knew their writing well—or perhaps she was describing creativity in terms common to women writers. In any case, she echoes them when she describes Sonia's room as "a sanctuary" and "a dead . . . city" (414) where Sonia experiences a "lulling, soporific warmth" in which "my mind was blank, or, rather, was occupied by certain abstractions such as 'warmth' or 'absence of pain' or 'motion'" (390). Cather or Woolf could have written— as Stafford did for Sonia—of fancying that "I could sense in my tired muscles the slow vertigo of the earth. When I emerged from this ethereal baptism, I was more than ever at ease, and I was so freed of any anxieties, in this isolated place and in this parenthetical time, that my mind could roam like an innocent child, at will, through grouped reflection and through favorite daydreams" (390–91).

Thea Kronborg's solitary reveries in Panther Canyon end upon the arrival of her patron-lover Fred Ottenburg, and Woolf's dreamer is stopped short by a male critic's imagined voice. When Sonia Marburg's creative trance is similarly cut short, however, it is not by a man but by a woman. "I'm in the crazy house," Sonia's mother says, and Sonia sees that her mother's "eyes blazed with the anger of a terrified animal as she was forsaken by the merciful anesthesia which for these months had made her live burial tolerable to both of us" (393). As Jane Eyre awakens from her red room to see bars outlined against the red of a fire, Sonia wakens to see bars of imprisonment through her mother's eyes: "Those powerful eyes now saw the barred windows behind the coy, concealing blinds, saw the inimical, impassive strength of the attendants, saw the moonstruck women grinning and gurgling like babies and they saw, completing the circuit, wider with each new revelation, that I was not a little girl just home from school but was a grown woman whose fine tailored suit and costly shoes cried aloud my treachery" (393).

It is yet another example of what I have elsewhere described as the novel of awakening—the female version of the Bildungsroman, by which a woman's growth is measured not by her readiness to take her place in the world (as in the male Bildungsroman) but by her awakening to limitations. For Sonia Marburg, creativity means claiming a female legacy of victimization, and independence means betraying her nurturing instincts. Dramatizing her dilemma, Sonia attempts to make the red room (that is, creativity) hers by identifying its furnishings as those *she* had provided, but she recognizes that doing so ties her to the women's roles from which she has tried to escape. The lobster-claw letter opener belonged to a very old woman who had "rendered some service" to her mother when she was about five (422); the bottle of red wine is from a hostess's music room; the writing desk once belonged to the creator of little women, Louisa May Alcott. Inevitably, Sonia's imaginative journey to the sources of her own creativity takes her to her mother and to the feeling "that my mother's idiosyncrasies were already cropping up in me, for as I listened to her, I lost my identity" (314). "Matrophobia" is, according to Adrienne Rich, the fear "of becoming one's mother . . . the splitting of the self, in the desire to become purged once and for all of our mother's bondage" (237–38). Stafford's Sonia Marburg is like the many daughters whose mothers stand "for the victim in ourselves," as "the one through whom the restrictions and degradations of a female existence" are passed on (Rich 238, 237).

Whereas Sonia's desire toward creation is strong, her fear of becoming her mother is stronger. Instead of confronting her genesis by entering her red room, she turns away from its threshold and then seldom visits it because she is "loath to make my seclusion there a habit" (422). Most painful, she cannot imagine working there, "for I was never actually in the room and could not visualize myself taking a book out of the shelves or sitting at the desk" (422). Recalling her fear, Sonia makes the connections explicit between the loss of her self, the room, and her mother: "I heard my mother's voice and experienced the now familiar sensation that it was actually she who was speaking. Instantaneously, upon my image of her which accompanied the sound of her voice through my lips she vanished like the will-o'-the-wisp and what stood before me was the red room" (464).

What—or who—is the mother at the heart of this novel? She is the witch from Europe who, transported to America, becomes the shrew who drives men into the wilderness. She speaks for the women left behind in the movement west. To imagine her is to experience passivity and pain, rage and madness, victimization and violence; to see through her eyes is to create effigies for her hatred; to claim her means acknowledging that creativity is fatal for a woman.

Her influence is everywhere evident in the nightmarish landscape of births and abortions of Sonia's childhood, during which Sonia was counseled by a chorus of warnings against procreativity. She hears, for example, her father solemnly pronounce that she "should never have been born" (10), and she also hears her mother hiss "I hate you," then curse the baby she is carrying (91). When she goes to a doctor for help, he suspects her of seeking an abortion; the friend to whom she might turn dies in childbirth; her first employer gives birth to a stillborn child; and her second employer kills the kittens her cat has borne. In *Boston Adventure* pregnancy is a curse and birth is a tragedy.

The novel extends lessons against a woman's procreativity to her creativity with the relentless logic of a syllogism. When victims create, they project their anger onto effigies. Women are victims; therefore, when women create, they do so to punish and destroy. Trapped in their scripts as victims without victors and women without men, women turn against women, even (especially) against those women whom they have wished to resemble. By such a projection, Miss Pride's beautiful, wealthy, and privileged niece is destined to be admired, then envied, then hated, and finally destroyed by Sonia. "Do you believe in supernatural things?" Hopestill asks Sonia before she dies. "I mean, do you think hate can kill? There is a story about a woman who makes a doll in the image of another woman and burns it and the woman comes to some dire end, I think. It's been so long ago that I can't remember, but lately it's been haunting me" (489). As if in response, Sonia recalls feeling such intense jealousy and hatred of Hopestill that she had wished (i.e., willed) her dead: "All the time she had lain in the hospital dying, I had been able to think only of her bare feet and of the green slippers which I had defaced and slashed and of her recollection, that night in the studio, of the effigy-burning in *The Return of the Native*. Reason told me I was laughable and self-important in feeling myself an element in her death, but superstition rebuked me" (492).

If by our superstitions we acknowledge the power of fantasy once it is released from the constraints of reason, then in this novel of unleashed fantasy it is only natural—perhaps inevitable—that Sonia turns to superstition to account for her feeling of responsibility. As Sonia had first imagined Hopestill Mather and then destroyed her by envy, so others in *Boston Adventure* create effigies to punish and destroy. In giving birth to a son Sonia's mother imagined him to be an image of his father, then punished him for his father's sins and omissions by fixing her gaze on him and willing in him seizures until "the beastliness" in him erupted (116);[4] and in imagining her mother, Sonia willed her insane so that she might dispose of her.

The parable of Mercy, the cat that Miss Pride confines to her bedroom and a storeroom, serves as a gloss upon the idea that characters are effigies. Recognizing it as a "potentially sinister fact" that she heard the cat's call only when she, too, "was virtually a prisoner" (425) in that house, Sonia makes explicit that the cat's tale is a cautionary one. "I had been told that she was jumpy and unfriendly because her kittens, begot by an unauthorized tomcat . . . had been chloroformed as soon as they were born," Sonia says, and the mother, "her instincts baffled, hunted them with piteous persistence" (424). Her understanding awakened, Sonia recognizes the muffled sobs of Miss Pride's niece and her imagined double, Hopestill Mather, who is preparing for marriage to a man she does not love as a result of a pregnancy she does not want. Thus the madwoman in the attic metamorphoses into the mother Sonia confines to an asylum, the cat imprisoned in Miss Pride's house, the niece trapped in custom, and women bound by convention.[5]

Going to the asylum a final time, Sonia learns that her mother had gone from manic depression (the condition that Freud associated with creativity) to catatonia. Upon hearing that her mother has been moved from the common room to a private room, Sonia leaves without visiting her. Back at Miss Pride's she recognizes that "The red room, now that I needed it, would not come. . . . For the time being, I had walled up my mother into the farthest recess of my mind, knowing that the time would come when I must let her out again" (484).

The last scene presents to Sonia the consequences of her actions. In another of the novel's symbolic settings, Sonia visits Authors' Ridge in Concord cemetery, where Emerson, Alcott, Thoreau, and Hawthorne are buried. There Sonia seeks to exorcise Hopestill by imagining her, but she can feel only the most conventional emotion. In the end, Sonia returns, to be met by Miss Pride: "Under the lamplight, she appeared vigorous and even youthful, as if her age which she had passed on to her niece were buried along with Hopestill in New Hampshire. She looked again as she had done when I was five years old in Chichester; her flat, omniscient eyes seized mine, grappled with my brain, extracted what was there, and her meager lips said, 'Sonie, my dear, come out of the cold. You'll never get to be an old lady if you don't take care of yourself'" (496).

Gothicism is appropriate as the final narrative envelope in this novel of possession. As her father's imagination had been possessed by *Riders of the Purple Sage,* Sonia's is possessed by fictional plots—the western plot of Sonia's father, the fairy tale of her mother, Virginia Woolf's room of her own, and beyond that, by other plots suggested by a myriad of allusions. Sonia's vision of the red room echoes the red room of *Jane Eyre*; she compares the power of her imaginings to the effigy-burning in *The Return of the Native*; and her search for a room of her own comes to have the surreal quality suggested by the title of Tsao Hsueh-Chin's *Dream of the Red Chamber*.

Having willed herself into various roles for women in the world's classic plots, Sonia finds each of them empty; yet she is unable to create an alternative for herself, and her attempts to imagine stories demonstrate how limited her options are. She recalls one such attempt when, "under the influence of the cook from Idaho, Maudie's western magazines, which I pored over far into the night after my mother had gone to bed, I began to tell a story"—compositions "all upon the subject, that is, the heroism of the young sheriff, Sonny Marburn" (79). Sonia must transform herself into Sonny to enter the heroic spaces of the Western. Exploring the domestic interiors of her own world is equally unsatisfactory, for to do so Sonia must become furtive. She must steal along hallways, lurk outside doors, listen by windows, and peer through the narrow openings that yield dark secrets of women's lives. Creeping along the wall to peer between bedroom-door hinges, Sonia sees her mother lying in bed doing needlework while her doctor pulls down her gown to examine her lungs (177). Hiding in the shadows of her mother's bedroom, she sees that same doctor, vampire-like, attempting to kiss her mother's neck. Standing in the hall of Miss Pride's house, listening to the murmur of voices, she hears her benefactress claiming rights to her exactly as she would claim rights to her other property (317).

Positioned outside the spaces that contain action, Sonia can only imagine plots that she will never write; denied a language of her own, she can reveal her desires for and fears of authorship only covertly through the metaphors by which she in-forms her consciousness into her text. A subtext runs through *Boston Adventure,* in which Sonia, using metaphors of author/authorize/authority, acknowledges that creativity and power converge to exclude her. Because they were "begot by an unauthorized tomcat," Mercy's kittens were chloroformed (425); because her "signature" is on the room assigned to her by Miss Pride, Sonia is unable to imagine an alternative (315–16); because she "could not demonstrate the external *authorship*" of herself (424), Sonia fears she does not exist. Language again carries the relentless logic of a syllogism: an author is the originator or maker of anything; to authorize is to give a right to act, and authority is rightful power. But to be a girl is to be without power, and to be without power is to be unauthorized/excluded/erased—inescapably, it would seem. When she is asked to tell a story, Sonia replies, "I'm afraid all I can do is read" (302).

Men are the actors, women the observers; men are the authors, women the readers. The distinctions seem familiar, yet Stafford turns them around. In *Boston Adventure* (where the men have died or departed and the only writers are buried on Author's Ridge) *it is reading that is powerful.* By imagining the myths she has read, Sonia Marburg becomes a reading of those myths; she takes them in, comprehends them, renders their significance, and ascertains their intent. In a similar manner, through her character Stafford has read her own life and that of her culture

Stafford drew upon her own life—that much is, as her biographer Charlotte Goodman writes, "transparently apparent" (*Jean Stafford* 140). She gave to Mr. Marburg her father's obsession with western fiction; to Hopestill Mather she gave her friend Lucy Stone's beauty, recklessness, and suicide; her friend Hightower appears as Sonia's friend Nathan; her husband's mother, Mrs. Lowell, appears as the Boston grand lady, Miss Pride; to Sonia Marburg she gave not only her own meeting with Boston society but also her temperament. As was Stafford, the young Sonia is eager, intelligent, quick, a voracious reader, and an avid storyteller. Like Stafford's, Sonia's imagination is shaped by cultural myths, particularly those from literature, and as did Stafford, so Sonia questions what it means to live by those myths, particularly as configured by Freud into a cultural unconscious. Freud's psychoanalysis "has created what W. H. Auden calls 'a whole climate of opinion', and, no matter whether we are aware of it or not, the way we think and the way we feel is coloured by its discoveries" (Klein 71).[6] In other words, Freud has taught us how to read.

Stafford, who read Freud throughout her life, incorporated his principles into *Boston Adventure*.[7] To reveal Sonia's repressed desire to write, Stafford employed the free association of dreams; to explore Sonia's unconscious, she employed dream interpretation; and to develop Sonia as a character, she proceeded by transference and countertransference. Indeed, Freud's writing on creativity could serve as a gloss on Stafford's characterization: "The psychological novel . . . owes its special nature to the inclination of the modern writer to split up his ego, by self-observation, into many part-egos, and, in consequence, to personify the conflicting currents of his own mental life in several heroes," Freud wrote (23:145), as if describing characters in *Boston Adventure*. Sonia's struggle invites the familiar Freudian gloss as that of the ego to negotiate between the id (her mother, who represents "that which is inherited . . . the instincts" [23:145] and that which is primitive, emotional, illogical) and the superego (Miss Pride and parental prohibitions that merge into society's standards and are incorporated as the conscience). Sonia's red room is a site akin to the couch where, by the psychoanalyst's principle of free association, she enunciates her fears and desires.

Where would such principles take her? To the impasse of gender and the constitutively misogynist discourse of Freud, of course. In "Creative

Writers and Day-Dreaming," Freud describes the creative writer as doing "the same as the child at play. He creates a world of phantasy which he takes very seriously—that is, which he invests with large amounts of emotion—while separating it sharply from reality" (9:144). When the growing child stops playing, "instead of *playing,* he now *phantasies.* He builds castles in the air and creates what are called *daydreams*" (145). "The motive forces of phantasies are unsatisfied wishes, and every single phantasy is the fulfillment of a wish, a correction of unsatisfying reality" (146). Stafford incorporates this principle in the structure of her novel as a succession of daydreams, each becoming "a picture of the future" (148), and explores the implications of each by granting it to her character, who, upon testing it in reality, awakens to its limitations.

Sonia's visit to her mother imprisoned in a madhouse is Stafford's fictional confrontation with Freud's division of creative play into erotic wishes (which "predominate almost exclusively" in young women, whose "ambition is as a rule absorbed by erotic trends" [9:147]) and ambitious wishes ("in young men egoistic and ambitious wishes come to the fore clearly enough alongside of erotic ones" [9:147]). That is, whereas men repress the Oedipus complex and sublimate it into creative and cultural activities, women, not needing to overcome an Oedipus complex, have a correspondingly minimal urge for sublimation.

In placing the mother at the irretrievable center of her female Bildungsroman, Stafford anticipated feminist discussions of Freud's place in reading Western patriarchal culture. "If it is true," Madelon Sprengnether writes in *The Spectral Mother,* "as Juliet Mitchell in *Psychoanalysis and Feminism* and Nancy Chodorow in *The Reproduction of Mothering* maintain, that the unconscious of any given social order is culture specific, then we may be genuinely indebted to Freud for illuminating the psychological underpinnings of Western patriarchal society" (227). We may be similarly indebted to Stafford for illuminating the psychological underpinnings of a Western literary culture in its more patriarchal forms:

> In this system, it appears that the subordination of women manifests itself in the inability adequately to theorize the position of the preoedipal mother and hence in the psychocultural understanding of femininity as subversion. While this configuration allows of a certain romanticization of the position of subversion, it does not permit an alteration of the structure as a whole. In psychoanalytic terms, it thus becomes difficult to imagine any significant change of atti-

tude toward the mother as, on the one hand, providing the ground for subjectivity and, on the other, lacking in subjectivity herself. As long as the Oedipus complex remains identified with the stage of mastery in masculine development which acts as a prerequisite for civilization, moreover, the mother will continue to represent a threat to both. (Sprengnether 227)

Sonia learns her lessons well. She resolves never to marry for fear of reproducing her mother's madness (314); she accepts her position in the cultural background; and she assumes the passive, masochistic, and narcissistic role that nature (according to Freud) has fitted her for and that the sentimental plot represents. The final plot that she imagines presents the cost of that repression: "Although I envied the fortunate creatures, my own life which I plotted in a variety of patterns was richer. My hair became blond; my name was Antoinette de la Mar. 'Soon after Antoniette or Toni, as her chums called her, went to live in the Pride mansion on Pickney street, a handsome Harvard student named Andrew Eliot Cabot Lodge fell passionately in love with her. But as she had already decided not to marry anybody, she spurned him with a few kind but firm words. That night he shot himself, but he did not die and she nursed him back to health. She had many suitors but she lived only for Miss Pride who adored her and often had her do a toe-dance for her visitors who were often kings and queens'" (31).

In imagining herself as Antoinette, or Toni (as her friends call her), Stafford's Sonia Marburg recalls Cather's Ántonia, or Tony (as her friends call her), American literature's prototypical mother. Cather claimed biological motherhood for a woman's creativity when in Ántonia she celebrated the preoedipal mother and presented femininity as subversion. In psychoanalytic terms, Cather imaged the mother as, on the one hand, providing the ground for subjectivity *and, on the other, having subjectivity herself.*[8] Denied sexuality, procreativity, and motherhood, Ántonia becomes Antoniette, stranded within the sentimental script that Sonia is plotting by the principles she inherited from Freud.

Thus *Boston Adventure* confirms a pattern that is as endlessly confining in the Western as it is in Freudian thought, where the destiny of anatomy prescribes women to the narcissistic, masochistic, and passive roles of sentimentalism. Left behind when her father lit out for the territory, Sonia comprehends and renders in her own life the plot that as a girl she inherited. The plot is familiar as the staple of the Western, for which sentimen-

talism provides a backdrop and subtext (and with few exceptions, it is un-
fortunately also the staple of criticism about the literary West). Over two
decades after Stafford's novel was published, Leslie Fiedler acknowledged
Freud as the source of his basic vocabulary in *Love and Death in the American Novel* and then explained that "I cannot imagine myself beginning the
kind of investigation I have undertaken without the concepts of the conscious and the unconscious, the Oedipus complex . . . etc." (xiii). What *is*
it to grow up female in a culture that cannot imagine a girl in concepts
other than those supplied by Freud? That is the question of *Boston Adventure,* where Stafford empowered reading as the activity open to a girl and
confirmed circularity as the pattern of her life. Breaking out of that circle
would mean redrawing boundaries for the female Bildungsroman, giving
to a girl the destiny of creativity, and moving her story to the West—which
is precisely what Stafford did in her short stories and *The Mountain Lion.*

6

Stafford's

Western

Stories

In 1970 Jean Stafford won the Pulitzer Prize for *The Collected Stories of Jean Stafford.* An author's note established her literary inspiration as western, and her roots as remaining in the "semi-fictitious town" of Adams, Colorado. The following year Houghton Mifflin published *The Literature of the American West,* an anthology edited by J. Golden Taylor planned as a basic textbook following criteria of quality and representativity. The single entry by a woman writer is Willa Cather's "Neighbour Rosicky," which is described as "charming" (245). Stafford, who wrote some of her most important stories about Taylor's own state of Colorado, is not mentioned.

The anthology represents well the conventions against which Stafford wrote. It is introduced by a symposium of western writers, all male, who addressed defining questions, among them, "What are the characteristics of the American West, especially the chief motivating force on fiction?" (25). For Frederick Manfred space to wander, "time to brood on things," and "enough left of wild nature to subdue" are factors, "but it all still comes down to . . . men who are ruggedly individualistic" (25); and for Frank Waters the West represents "a boundless realm of individual freedom; a psychological realm where men are men, and women like it" (27). As in the past, so today the distinguishing criterion of the West is, in Walter Van Tilburg Clark's words, "that it is a vast land with a relatively small population, so that other aspects of nature than man must count for more than they usually do elsewhere. Nature, we might say, must become actor, not backdrop" (32). The West is a male legacy, as these writers emphasize: "I have thought of myself as a mountain man," Vardis Fisher writes, "as my father was and his father was. I suppose some characteristics of mountain men . . . are self-reliance, abhorrence of cities and of crowded humanity anywhere, passionate devotion to the beauty of great mountains and mountain valleys, unpolluted streams, vast spaces, and all the marvelous colors and scents of clean mountain country" (34). For Forrester Blake "The American West is space: time: motion. The West is tension: the picaresque, seeking freedom to wander, contends against set unities of time, place, and action" (38). Behind it all, however, the appropriation of nature for the heroic soul is, as Paul Horgan writes, the "single pervasive theme in writing about *west* . . . as the theme of man, alone, against the grand immensity of nature—the nature of the land, reflected in his own soul" (41).

Stafford was intimately familiar with these conventions. They were behind the "Western prototype, daring, dashing, tall in the saddle and easy on the eye, [that] figured as the hero in all the short stories and novels I wrote between the ages of eight and ten" ("Heroes and Villains" 196), and they are the conventions she wrote against as an adult. Stafford's idea of the West begins not with vast spaces and untrammeled wilderness but in Adams, Colorado, the "semi-fictitious town" of her roots. Adams is located fifty miles north of Denver. To the west, the mountains stretch upward beyond vision; to the east, the plains stretch out beyond the horizon.

The geography of the town is notable mostly because it is so ordinary. Adams features a park with picnic tables and a small bandstand, a courthouse with the jail in its basement, various churches, a high school, and Nevilles College, near which are boarding houses for college students. Stores include a Safeway and a Piggly Wiggly, the Comanche Cafe, the Nelson Dry, plus (located next to each other) Kresge's and Woolworth's. At the northern end of Adams on a high hill stands the Gold Palace Hotel, built by Mr. Norman Ferris who came from the East and who has a private polo field. At the west side of town Arapahoe Creek runs by a settlement of poor cottages and a tourist camp, where tents are sometimes pitched and trailers sometimes parked. Tuberculosis, not gold fever or pioneer adventure, is the reason most people come to this high western town, seeking relief or a cure for themselves or a member of their family. The old men who are permanent residents of the downtown hotel, the Goldmoore, sit in the lobby each day, talking. Men out of work because of the depression cluster in the park during the day, and each afternoon landladies meet for tea in one of their kitchens.

Stafford grounds her short fiction in realism that she sets in an adversarial and corrective dialectic to the Western formula.[1] Formulas of pioneer courage linger in Adams as romantic cliché: descendants of the Bays (who were among the founders of Adams) have inherited a popularized version of history in which the early Bays "had toiled in . . . peril and with . . . fortitude across the plains in a covered wagon and who with such perseverance had put down the roots for their traditions in this town that they had virtually made" ("The Liberation" 305; unless otherwise indicated, references to Stafford's short stories are to Stafford's *Collected Stories*). The claustrophobic realism of Adams seems a world apart from the great mountains and plains on either side of it, yet the presence of such expanses recalls formula Western stories of escape into the wilderness. Each spring children go from the park into the foothills looking for flowers, for the past four summers one of the landladies' daughters has worked in the mountains at the Caribou Ranch, and throughout the year the German teacher at Nevilles College can see the mountains from her upstairs bedroom window. Nature isn't the actor here that Walter Van Tilburg Clark says it must be in literature of the West. Instead, Stafford's West is where people struggle with the traditions they have inherited.

To populate Adams, Stafford created a cast of characters among whom Emily Vanderpool was her favorite. In "The Violet Rock," Stafford introduces Emily through the eyes of her very good, very polite, and very compliant younger sister, Tess. A model product of society, Tess is the ideal narrator to describe Emily as nature's child, for Tess is sufficiently awed: "Emily's temper tantrums, like her ghost stories and her tales of mutilation and kidnapping, entranced while they horrified. They came on with as little warning as an electric storm, and they were as dramatic and incomprehensible. Her whole being participated in them—not just her oratorical big eyes and her lopsided mouth and her rich, wide-ranged voice but her hands and her elbows and her knees and her feet, which articulated just as clearly as any vile words could the fury that had bedevilled her since she was born" (35). Power results in such a performance; "our bamboozled, bullied parents enjoined Jack and Stella and me never to cross her and never to bait her and never to disagree; Emily might die of apoplexy, they said" (35–36), and once their brother "Jack had been sincerely carried away by her performance and had cried 'Bravo!'" (36).

Stafford gives to Tess qualities expected of a girl, and then with Emily as her vehicle explores their absurd consequences. Together the sisters leave town for the foothills to look for pasqueflowers, the earliest to bloom after a Colorado winter and the occasion to win a prize, for the first student to return with a flower receives a pencil box. When Tess, always conventionally feminine, becomes fearful as night is approaching, her timidity gives Emily the opportunity to create some excitement by scaring her. Emily tells her sister "the dooming story of the Violet Rock and why it was that I, and I alone, must never go near it after the sun had set" (38). The rock belonged to Mr. Norman Ferris, multimillionaire owner of the Gold Palace Hotel in Adams, who had once told Tess and her brother to dismantle the popcorn stand they had set up on his polo field. Tess had "sassed" him ("Here, Reddy! Get away from those dudes!" she had called to their dog). In revenge Mr. Ferris had bought a large violet rock in the foothills and had his scientists imbue it "with a special kind of lethal gas that was released only at twilight and would kill only me" (40). Then, because he was very angry indeed, he saw to it that boulders in the Adams park were treated also, with the result that Tess felt safe only in her house.

A spell cast by a powerful man that makes rocks personally and specifically lethal to a girl—Emily's story is a comic version of the western tradition that would forbid nature to women. Tess's response is that expected of girls: she fearfully avoids open spaces and remains indoors reading instead of playing in the park after school. Manners motivated by fear win release for Tess. When she goes to Mr. Ferris and apologizes for calling him a dude, he listens with amusement, then gives her a silver dollar as "the sign that the Violet Rock is now the safe way for you" (42) More importantly though, the story of the Violet Rock wins respect for Emily. As Mr. Ferris mounts his horse, he turns and, in the best manner of the Western, delivers his parting words: "I'll be interested to know what ever becomes of Emily" (42).

What became of Emily was that Stafford gave her life in three subsequent stories. By making Emily the narrator in each, Stafford gave her voice, and by placing Emily in familiar western plots, Stafford used her to defy their conventions.[2] "A Reading Problem" (1956) begins with Emily's desire for a place to read where she wouldn't be disturbed. Pestered by people in her living room and distracted by her sister in their bedroom, evicted from the library for popping her gum and cracking her knuckles, teased by old men when she tried the lobby of the downtown hotel, turned out of the waiting room of the jail when the sheriff brings in moonshiners, Emily leaves town. The classic westering impulse can be seen in precisely this action—the individual seeking solitude leaves civilization for nature. However, Emily is a girl, and the landscape she enters brilliantly symbolizes warnings familiar to every female reader: unspeakably bad things happen to girls who venture out on their own:

> I walked down the length of the main street, going toward the mountains, over whose summits hung a pale heat haze; the pavement was soft, and when it and the shimmering sidewalk ended, I had to walk in the red dirt road, which was so dusty that after a few steps my legs, above the tops of my socks, looked burned— not sunburned, *burned*.
>
> At the outskirts of town, beside the creek, there was a tourist camp where funny-looking people pitched tents and filled up the wire trash baskets with tin cans. . . . Today there was only one tent up in the grounds, a sagging, ragged white one. . . . There wasn't a soul in sight, and there wasn't a sound nearby except for a couple of magpies ranting at each other in the trees and the occasional digestive croak of a bullfrog. Along the creek, there was a line of shady cottonwoods, and I decided to rest there for a while and cool off my feet in the water. (328–29)

Sitting under a tree, Emily closes her eyes to practice reciting the books of the Bible (an inveterate seeker of prizes, she is now trying to win a New Testament at Sunday school); when she opens them she "looked up into the bearded face of a tall man in black clothes . . . and into the small brown eyes of a girl about Stella's age, who wore . . . a long, dirty thing that looked like her nightgown" (329). It is a western version of Little Red Riding Hood meeting the wolf, but here the wolf masquerades as a traveling evangelist: "Evangelist Gerlash was immensely tall, and his bones had only the barest wrapper of flesh; he made me think of a tree with the leaves off, he was so angular and gnarled, and even his skin was something like bark, rough and pitted and scarred. His wild beard was the color of a sorrel horse, but his long hair was black, and so were the whiskers on the backs of his hands that imperfectly concealed, on the right one, a tattoo of a peacock. His intense and watchful brown eyes were flecked with green" (331). Wild, natural, dark—Gerlash caricatures the primitive violence that girls are warned against in men and nature. Imagining how she would taste, it would seem, "The Gerlashes complacently scrutinized me, as if I were the very thing they had been looking for" (330). Practicing how he would subdue her, perhaps, while he looked at her Gerlash squeezed his beard, "as if he were strangling it," and when he greets her, he gave her "an alarming smile that showed a set of sharp, efficient teeth" (331).

"Don't you doubt me, sister Vanderpool . . . when I tell you your innocent life is in danger" (340), Gerlash ends up telling Emily, yet by this time Stafford has transformed him into a quack preacher. Violence anticipated and then diffused creates the humor here. Gerlash's fumbling chicanery and Emily's unwavering manners are wildly incongruous to the western traditions against which the story is drawn. Setting her up for the sting, he hands her an ad for gastro-pep, then tells of locating hell in the nearby town of Mongol. Never considering that she "didn't have to answer questions put to me by adults" (333), she provides a history of her family and an inventory of their home. Following the formula, the encounter ends with an abduction (Gerlash proposes that he drive Emily to her father's Safeway so she can get them groceries), the heroine's resistance ("But I can't get into a car with strangers"), and rescue ("just then, like the Mounties to the rescue, up came Mr. Starbird's official car, tearing into the campgrounds and stopping, with a scream from the brakes, right in front of me and the Gerlashes" [341]).

The evangelist and his daughter are run out of town, and Emily is the neighborhood hero. All this attention means, however, that Emily is banned from reading in the jail, for copycats made such a nuisance in the waiting room that the sheriff had to forbid anyone there except on business:

> He was as sorry, he said, as he could be.
>
> He wasn't half as sorry as I was. The snake season was still on in the mountain; Mrs. Looby hated me; Aunt Joey was visiting, and she and Mother were using the living room to cut out Butterick patterns in; Stella had just got on to pig Latin and never shut her mouth for a minute. All the same, I memorized the books of the Bible and I won the New Testament, and I'll tell you where I did my work—in the cemetery, under a shady tree, sitting beside the grave of an infant kinswoman of the sheriff, a late-nineteenth-century baby called Primrose Starbird. (344)

This scene symbolizes Stafford's challenge to literary tradition. Abandoning the house where her mother cuts out patterns she will follow and her sister babbles in a parody of language, Emily goes to a cemetery (nature is often reduced to parks and cemeteries in Stafford's writing). By choosing to work beside the grave of the sheriff's kinswoman, Emily introduces the idea of relationships—that of those who survived (the sheriff, who is a descendant of nineteenth-century western tradition) and those who did not (his kinswoman, the female child who did not live to take her place in that tradition). Reading beside the grave of the infant Primrose Starbird, Emily aligns herself with voices denied to her, as if claiming herself a kinswoman to that child who was buried before she could speak for herself.

"The Scarlet Letter" (1959) tells of Emily's experience with courtship, western style, when after she had insulted everyone and didn't have a friend, she accepts Virgil Meade as her "fellow." He offers her a glimpse into a boy's world by sharing his stories, all of which are on the single theme of showing "who was boss" (64). He tells of walloping cows when he visited his uncle's ranch, bagging an eight-point buck and giving it away to bootleggers, and escaping from Big Red, the desperado who had kidnapped him. Usually he and Emily sit in his father's den, and Emily so loves the dark room and his sporty talk that she allows him to tease her cat, agrees to watch him mistreat donkeys she loves, and laughs when he slaps her dog on the nose. "Ever his slave" (67), Emily agrees to help him draw up a petition against geography homework and to sew on her sock rather than her sleeve the scarlet letter she received for reading. Virgil disappears when it is time to present the petition and Emily ends up in a heap of trouble: the principal lectures her, the geography teacher assigns her extra homework, and her mother sends her to her room. What is worse, her classmates ostracize her, believing that she betrayed school spirit by sewing the letter on her sock. Virgil's bravado undoes him, however, and once he reveals he was behind the sock episode, "I was in and Virgil was out. . . . In time I took pity on him; indeed, some months later, we again became boon companions, but I saw to it that he never hoodwinked me again: I ruled him with an iron glove and . . . ever after that Virgil Meade was the most tractable boon companion I had" (101).

Again, the theme is power cast in terms of gender convention, this time with Stafford exploring the danger to a girl of betraying herself in her eagerness to be part of a boy's world. Again, too, struggle over power is worked out by the use of language. Emily's opening salvo against a teacher who "abhorred children and loved hard words" was to read the dictionary at night and then ask her what "palimpsest" meant (63), she and Virgil campaigned by writing a petition modeled on a bounty land grant signed by Lincoln, and Emily clinched her rule over Virgil by climbing on a boulder and telling him to kneel, "Then, like Moses on Mount Sinai," laying down the law.

In the last Emily story, Stafford writes of the power of words as a girl's means of defending herself. "Bad Characters" (1964) is about Emily Vanderpool's "tongue," which was "awful" in all the complex ways the word suggests—"extremely bad or unpleasant; terrible; horrible" but also "dreadful; appalling; fearsome" and, sometimes, "great" (*American Heritage Dictionary*). The dilemma of determining one's allegiance with language—whether to others or to oneself—appears here in Emily's dilemma in reconciling her wish for friends and her passion to be by herself:

> Up until I learned my lesson in a very bitter way, I never had more than one friend at a time, and my friendships, though ardent, were short. When they ended and I was sent packing in unforgetting indignation, it was always my fault; I would swear vilely in front of a girl I knew to be pious and prim (by the time I was eight, the most grandiloquent gangster could have added nothing to my vocabulary—I had an awful tongue), or I would call a Tenderfoot Scout a sissy or make fun of athletics to the daughter of the high school coach. These outbursts came without plan: I would simply one day, in the middle of a game of Russian bank or a hike or a conversation, be possessed with a passion to be by myself, and my lips instantly and without warning would accommodate me. My friend was never more surprised than I was when this irrevocable slander, this terrible, talented invective, came boiling out of my mouth. (263)

When Emily meets a strange girl with uncombed hair preparing to steal a cake cooling in the Vanderpool kitchen, she meets her double, for Lottie Jump is as irreverent and independent as the tongue that gets Emily into such trouble. As polite as she was with the Gerlashes, Emily shows Lottie through the house, pledges friendship, and agrees to meet her at the five-and-dime to serve as her accomplice in robbery. As Lottie's sidekick Emily finds herself once more conforming. Following Lottie's instructions, she distracts the clerk by pretending interest in hairpins and rickrack while Lottie lifts a tea strainer, a box of all-purpose nails, rubber gloves, and packages of mixed seeds. Emily's independence cuts their heist short. Getting tired and wanting nothing Lottie was taking, Emily is suddenly struck by a desire to be alone, and instead of diverting attention from Lottie directs attention to her. "Your brother isn't the only one with no brains" (280), she says, startling the clerk, who then sees Lottie putting pearls under her hat. Lottie, who pretends to be deaf and dumb, is sent away with a sack of candy; Emily, blamed for it all, is sent home with her father, who arranges for his friend, Judge Bays, to lecture her about the dangers of vice. Emily learned her lesson, she reflects in the end. Thereafter when she wants to be alone she says she has a headache and must go home to take an aspirin or that she just remembered she has to go to the dentist. "After the scandal died down, I got into the Camp Fire Girls" (282).

As in all the Emily stories, in "Bad Characters" Stafford explored a girl's badness in the same way a pioneer explores uncharted territory. Emily's adventures result from her independence, straight talk, and passion to be alone, qualities that would show glimmers of greatness in a boy but that are strictly off-limits to a girl. Like Huck Finn, Emily confirms her good heart by believing in her badness: "I had a bad character, I know that, but my badness never gave me half the enjoyment Jack and Stella thought it did" (274). And like Huck, Emily has no talent for iniquity. She suffers from having stolen from her widow fund for church, and she feels mean when she resists staying with Tess while her mother visits Mrs. Rogers in a sanitarium, "for Mrs. Rogers was a kind old lady" (274).

Unlike Huck's, however, Emily's goodness is a passive virtue. Here is no resolve to go to hell to help a friend. Though Emily feels guilty hearing poor people cough themselves to death, she doesn't bring them relief; and while she recognizes that the Gerlashes are hungry, she agrees to get them food only when instructed to do so. The effect is complex: Stafford protects Emily from the compulsive do-goodism that plagues fictional little women and at the same time suggests restrictive gender distinctions. As Mary Ellen Williams Walsh has noted, Stafford's male children at least dream of escape and do take action, though it may lead to nothing (see, e.g., *Jean Stafford* 28).

Nevertheless, of Stafford's western characters, Emily Vanderpool comes closest to successfully negotiating the tensions of childhood. She claims qualities denied to children generally and girls particularly—anger, solitude, independence, and power; and at the same time, she not only keeps but makes more honest that which has long been considered the province of children—friendship. Emily receives a tribute for her story of the Violet Rock, and she gains the respect of her classmates as well as the "boon companionship" of Virgil Meade—this time on her terms. She becomes a neighborhood hero *and* finds the solitude to read, and she finds ways to be alone without slandering her friends.

To make possible such negotiations, Stafford surrounds Emily Vander-

pool with a charmed circle of stability. Her traditional family comprises a
father who manages the local Safeway, a mother who bakes cakes that cool
on the counter, sisters and a brother to tease and be teased by, a dog and a
cat to befriend her when she is lonely. From this security Emily ventures
with her sister into the mountains and alone into the camp of transients,
tries robbing the five-and-dime, and challenges her teacher, all the while
safe from the dangers she glimpses. Economic stability insulates the dra-
mas of her childhood, with its agonies of friendships broken and joys of
others begun, and she is free also to test the power of her temper and the
possibilities of her vocabulary. Her father is there to drive her home, the
sheriff to rescue her, and a friend of her mother's to admit her into
the Camp Fire Girls. Most of all, Emily is protected by Stafford from growing up.

For the narrator of "The Healthiest Girl in Town" Stafford seems to
have reincarnated Emily Vanderpool, then tightened the circumstances
around her. Jessie (she has neither a father nor a surname) has Emily's
spunk, intelligence, and energy but none of the Vanderpools' stability. Her
father's death meant that she moved to Adams with her mother, a practical nurse who was assured employment among the tuberculars. The plot is
a twist on a classic formula wherein a westerner uses a tall tale to turn the
tables on a tenderfoot from the East. Jessie's mother is employed by the
bluestocking Mrs. Butler, who "had an orthodox aversion to the West, and
although almost no one was native to our town, she looked down her
pointed nose at the entire population, as if it consisted of nothing but
rubes" (205). Because she cannot refuse invitations from her mother's
employer, Jesse finds herself the unwilling playmate of Mrs. Butler's
daughters. Delicate of constitution, pale of complexion, and refined of
habit, they would prefer to sit primly and "converse" than to play crack-
the-whip. Reminiscent of the nineteenth century's glorification of the delicacy of consumptive women, Laura and Ada Butler are femininity in its
most perverse form. Their effect was to make Jesse feel "bovine in the
midst of nymphs" (207) and believe "that my health was a disgrace"
(206). Jessie began to have fantasies of mortal illnesses that would align
her with Laura and Ada.

Jessie's opportunity comes when she is asked for details surrounding
her father's death. "'Leprosy,' I said, and watched the Bostonians freeze"
(208–09). The tall tale backfires, however, for rather than being welcomed

into the family of the ailing, Jesse finds herself a pariah as the sisters back out of the room, then prepare for her a cure containing the "slithering, opalescent intestines" of a chicken. Emboldened by her distaste, Jesse speaks out: her father was "shot out hunting, if you want to know. . . . My father was as tall as this room. The district nurse told Ma that I am the healthiest girl in town. Also I have the best teeth" (216).

Jessie's robust good health is belied by the death, disease, and poverty that are shaping her life, however. Jessie cannot afford the temper tantrums of Emily Vanderpool, nor can she afford to have an "awful tongue." Instead she visits "that tomb-still house" (203), filled with its "vaguely medicinal fragrance" (202), where in listening to Laura and Ada talk of the infirmities "that victimized them" (205) she is herself victimized. As often in Stafford's writing, victimization is played out in language. Because her mother's job is at stake, Jessie "could not talk back" (202). Though Jessie feels momentarily liberated by proclaiming herself healthy, she must still visit the Butlers' house, where "we talked steadily and solely of the girls' grave illnesses" (216–17). And though she always says, "Take care of yourselves" with "snide solicitude" when she leaves (217), the Butler girls always have the final word. When the story ends with Jessie's statement that she "invariably cut an affronting caper on the Butlers' lawn and ran off fast, letting the good mountain air plunge deep into my sterling lungs," her defiance seems as precarious as childhood itself (217).

Stafford does recognize that children grow up; as she writes of their doing so, her tone becomes bitter, her vision dark. In "The Tea Time of Stouthearted Ladies" the college-aged Kitty Winstanley presents a female version of another western mainstay—a flight to nature. The point of view is from inside a series of enclosures—a perspective Stafford often uses. From her upstairs bedroom, Kitty hears her mother in the kitchen entertaining the other landladies from the block. United in the profession of running boarding houses for college students, "and united more deeply but less admissibly in hardship and fatigue and in eternal worry over 'making ends meet,'" they behaved at this hour each day "like urban ladies of leisure gossiping after a matinee" (220). Protecting themselves from intimacy that might shatter them, "they mouthed their sweet clichés like caramels": "Anything you work hard for means so much more than something just handed to you on a silver platter," and "our children's characters will be all the better for their having gone to the School of Hard Knocks" (223). Their

already clichéd civilized banality from which men and boys have so noto-
riously fled is made doubly clichéd when they describe their own desire to
flee to the mountains:

> "What wouldn't *I* give to be up there in the mountains away from the hurly-
> burly of this town. . . ."
>
> "Oh, I'm by no means partial to summer on the plains. And all those pesky
> grasshoppers spitting tobacco juice through the screens onto your clean glass
> curtains, to say nothing of the fuss-budget old schoolmarms—give me a dude
> any day of the week." (219)

Not surprisingly, the nature to which they would flee is indeed tame,
now called Caribou Ranch and run by two women for dudes, a place Mrs.
Winstanley has never seen but where Kitty has worked as a waitress and
chambermaid each summer since she was fourteen. Hearing Mrs. Winstanley describe "this summer job of hers [as] really more a vacation with
pay than work" (219), Kitty reflects on the reality. The servants' lake was
cold and abounding in mud puppies, and only one spooked, spavined old
cow pony was available for the help—the "lambent green pool" and lively
blooded bays and palominos were for the exclusive use of the dudes (225).
Separation between the classes was as absolute as their living quarters,
with the waitress-chambermaids staying a mile from the main lodge, in a
filthy, converted chicken coop.

"All the same, each spring for the past four years Kitty had been wild
with impatience to get to the Caribou," pulled not by the call of the wilderness but a need to escape from "the spectacle of her eaten father and from
her mother's bright-eyed lies, from all the maniacal respectability with
which the landladies strait-jacketed the life of the town" (227). And here,
again, Stafford provides a twist upon the formula. The tension between society and nature is traditionally in balance: Natty Bumppo respects the civilization that he leaves, and Huck's Aunt Polly and Aunt Sally provide a loving alternative to the Widow Douglas and her sister Miss Watson. In this
balance the traditional Western is a variation upon the epic in which a
hero's actions define the values of a nation. The hero discards his past and
creates himself new as Leatherstocking, the Virginian, or Shane, but far
from seeking anonymity, his quest becomes legendary through his personal exploits. Thus the wandering hero and waiting community are complementary; as the hero's exploits define his existence, repetition of them
provides a community's history. In Stafford's West, language is diseased

and storytelling is a process of contamination. Thus characters seek not simply to discard their past so they can create themselves anew but to cut themselves off completely to save that which they have created: "At the Caribou, there was no one she knew in any other context. Her fellow waitresses were local mountain girls, so chastely green that they were not really sure what a college was and certainly did not care. . . . At Christmas she exchanged cards with them but they did not exist for her, or she for them, before the first of June or after Labor Day. And the dudes whose bathtubs she scoured and whose dietary idiosyncrasies she catered to came from a milieu so rich and foreign and Eastern that she could not even imagine it and therefore did not envy it" (228).

Nature is again a commercial enterprise in "The Mountain Day," whose eighteen-year-old Judy Grayson has advantages that Kitty Winstanley could not even imagine. "Our life was sumptuous and orderly, and we lived it, in the winter, in New York and, in the summer, in the mountains of Colorado" (232), Judy's says, her voice as soft as Kitty's is hard.

"When I woke up that morning, in the fallow light before the sunrise, and remembered that the night before I had got engaged to Rod Stephansson, I could feel my blue eyes growing bluer" (231), Judy Grayson begins, recalling the "storybook summertime romance, woven in the mountain sun and mountain moonlight" (234) that led to her engagement. The next day she announces her engagement to her family, goes on a picnic with Rod, and learns that her grandmother's Irish maids had drowned. The drowning provides the climax of the story, the description of the bodies a shocking contrast to the romantic holiday Judy had been describing: "Mary and Eileen could not have been in the water for more than a few hours, but in that time the hellbenders and the ravenous turtles had eaten their lovely faces and their work-swollen hands; no one, certainly no kinsman, must see them" (247). Momentary silence intensifies the shock of the description. When Judy's grandmother does speak, she momentarily drops her social manner: "By this time of day, I have had enough of the wonders of Colorado," then, "as if she were alone, as if she were speaking to herself or to God, she murmured, 'I won't come here again with innocents'" (248).

She is speaking, however, to another innocent, for Judy is embarking upon a life she understands as little as the Irish servant girls understood the dangers of the lake. The real danger in the story concerns the romantic part of the popular mind in which Judy is caught. The vehicle for it is language. With cliché passing for cleverness, language in "The Mountain Day" is ominous in its numbing superficiality. "The mountain sun had turned him amber and had lightened his leonine hair," Judy says of Rod; "he was tall and lithe and sculptured and violet-eyed, and the bones of his intelligent face were molded perfectly" (231). Love is like being "inoculated by some powerful, sybaritic drug: the aspen leaves were more brilliant than they had ever been before, the upland snow was purer, the pinewoods were more redolent, and the gentle winds in them were more mellifluous; the berries I ate for breakfast came from the bushes of Eden" (235). As Judy speaks, so do those around her. Her mother tells her to "have a skylark" (242), her sister, Camilla, calls Rod "a pet" (242), and her grandmother tells her that "Rod was an Adonis and . . . that she saw no point in marrying if one couldn't marry a handsome man" (239).

The smoothness of the Graysons' manner is as effective in safeguarding against intimacy as the clichés that the landladies in Adams mouth; unlike the landladies, however, the Graysons are also complacent and condescending. Brief excursions beyond their class suggest that the Graysons are comfortable only with themselves and are cruelly critical of outsiders. Following an annual lunch at a nearby field laboratory, Judy and her sister sweepingly dismiss all the young men at the Science Lodge as "stunningly dull" and "nonentities" (233), descriptions more aptly applied to their mother in her comical attempts to discuss flower arrangements with the systematic botanists and the ecologists and to her daughters in their own questions of the young scientists, "Do you know So-and-So at Dartmouth?" (233). Their single contact with westerners is shocking in its ugliness. When the young couples entered the dance hall in nearby Puma, a customer glared at them, spat as they walked by, and "with feral hatred said, 'Goddam yearling dudes!'" The shock lies not in an anonymous and perhaps drunk customer's attitude, however, but in the hostility and hatred Judy expresses when she describes the place as "a squalid, dusty honky-tonk, . . . patronized by subhuman ne'er-do-wells and old wattled trollops" (236).

Despite—or perhaps because of—the practiced skill of their manner, disruptions suggest the pain, frustration, and anger running beneath the story's surface. When Judy's mother tells her daughters to enjoy this time of their life, "the note of disappointment of maturity" in her voice forebodes for their future (241); after Judy tells her father of a friend's plans to study law after college, he reveals his shame "that his life was not consecrated; he had no fixed orbit" (232). A political argument during dinner unleashes anger that unsettles them all: "Daddy protested so violently that you would have thought he might at any moment go and get a gun and shoot to kill. Everyone . . . was frightened by his fuming, stuttering rage" (236).

As for Rod Stephansson—Stafford presents just enough of him to suggest that he is ominously well prepared to marry the daughter of a very wealthy man. His manners are dangerously close to slickness and his ease is suspiciously similar to a lack of purpose. Upon meeting Judy, he ignores her while charming her mother, who invites him to dinner on Sunday; then, hidden from the rest of the party, he takes a blue bandanna handkerchief from his pocket, wipes Judy's boot, and says to her "in a secret voice . . . 'You'll be there Sunday, won't you?'" (234). Complicating the questions surrounding Rod's character, Judy's sister expresses "pity for the girl who married him," saying, "if he's really going to be a doctor, the girl that marries him is in for trouble. What a practice he's going to have among women!" (231). As if confirming doubts, there is the approval of Judy's father, who says that Rod "plays at everything so well and handsomely," as an afterthought adding, "*besides* having medicine and virtue" (235). Most disturbing, however, is that beyond such hints Rod remains drawn in the broadest cliché of social chatter, for as Judy realizes, she was so intent upon his image of her that she was scarcely aware of *him*.

The popularized, indiscriminate language of love merges all too easily with the western setting. To Judy, the West is merely a backdrop for her "storybook summertime romance woven in the mountain sun and mountain moonlight" (234). "Rod had never been West before, and because I had been coming here in the summer ever since my infancy, I was his cicerone, and took him to beaver dams and hidden waterfalls and natural castles of red rock, and to isolated, unmarked tombstones where God knew what murdered prospectors or starved babies were buried" (235). When, emerging from a brief afternoon rain, they "found a vivid rainbow arched over the eastern sky," the habit of cleverness prohibits silence: "This is too much . . . a cheap Chamber of Commerce trick," Camilla's fiancé, Fritzie, says, seconded by Camilla's agreement, "This is the most embarrassing, show-off place in the world. It's like advertisements for summer resorts. Strictly corn" (242–43).

Banality is dangerous, and to present that danger, Stafford created a mountain lake as the unifying symbol of the story. "It was a wonderful lake—limpid, blue, shaped like a heart," Judy says; "Daddy stocked it each year, and the rainbow trout that came from it were so beautiful they looked like idealized paintings of trout. . . . But there were some horrid inhabitants of that lovely water, too—huge turtles and hellbenders, about which [her younger brother] sometimes had screaming nightmares" (237). With this lake Stafford created a symbol for the romantic appearance and cruel reality of the West, for the mannered grace of her characters' lives beneath which runs danger, and for her story, whose language is as limpid as the water but, like the lake, contains horrors that are the stuff of nightmares. It is on this lake that Rod wants to canoe late one night, and on the lake that Judy is overtaken with uncontrollable laughter, as disruptive in its own way as her father's rage was earlier that evening. Rod joins her laughter, and their "gagging, pealing" cries echo (238), recalling the screaming of her brother's nightmares and anticipating the drowning of her grandmother's maids. Back on the shore, while she is lying spent "as if . . . in my casket," Rod asks her to marry him (238).

The image of the maids retrieved from the lake, their "lovely faces and their work-swollen hands" eaten, reflects the danger that lies beneath the surface throughout the story and undercuts with terrible irony the story's conclusion. Handed her first real drink, Judy reflects upon her security in the love of her family and for Rod: "just then standing firmly on my own," not caring how she looked, caring only about Rod's happiness, she thinks, "Love, real love, is just that; it is wanting the beloved to be happy. The simplicity of the equation surprised me, but only for a moment and then it was incorporated into me as naturally as if it had been there all along" (249). In this, the most conventional of definitions of love (on the level of "Love means never having to say you're sorry"), lies the danger that a girl will lose herself in a man, defining herself by him before she has a "personal history," without a "genesis" that is "individual" ("The Liberation" 319). As she revealed at the outset, Judy has inherited her father's "unease", and her preoccupation with what Rod is thinking of her is an intensely focused version of her father's "pressing need for high opinion" (232). In the end she is in a trap disguised as love. Devoting herself to the man she will marry, without a "vocation," and in a "fixed orbit" of her own (232), she will become as faceless as the Irish maids who drowned in the lake.

"The Mountain Day" is about violence and the literary West, seen not in stories of murdered prospectors and starved babies but in the psychic consequences to a girl of a tradition that would relegate identity only to men. The way she describes herself, "like a leaf turning constantly to the sun for its sustenance, so my whole existence had leaned toward Rod's recognition and approval of me, as if without them I would fade and wither" (231), is so deceptively normal that her most perceptive critics dismiss her romantic raptures as "childish hyperbole . . . not to be taken seriously" (Ryan 117) and as "transports" allowed by "the 'storybook' quality of Judy's view of events" (Walsh, *Jean Stafford* 43). As the lake's loveliness masks its danger, the story's familiarity masks its violence. Indeed, it is the familiarity that *is* dangerous. Attitudes so pervasive that we are blind to them are present in their most virulent form in literature of the American West, where they are defining characteristics and where the very existence of women depends upon men, where, when they do appear, women "must complement, not equal" men (235), and where women appear as faceless literary types.

Shortly before she died, Stafford wrote of the diffuse and uncritical quality of American thought seen in the hero of the prototypical Western ("daring, dashing, tall in the saddle and easy on the eye") that resulted in an inability to discriminate among the stories the nation celebrated ("Who was Famous and Why" 196). "Custer, Wild Bill, Billy the Kid, the James brothers and Teddy Roosevelt were confused" when Stafford was growing up, as she expects they were by children before her; she writes that "it is still hard to differentiate between the heroes and the villains who have been immortalized by Hollywood" (196). The confusion is dangerous, Stafford argues, for it means that we ignore the "assiduous slaughter of the Indians and the buffalo" and "the concupiscent mountebanks, the sleazy and murderous scum that accompanied the God-fearing pioneers"; and it means that we ignore too the violence about us today (196). "Who Was Famous and Why" works as a gloss on "The Mountain Day," in which Judy Grayson is caught in the romantic part of the popular mind—her own, but also a product of her family and her class and her nation. It works too as an explanation of Stafford's fundamental indictment of the Western prototype, which lies at the genesis of that romantic part of the popular mind.

In "The Mountain Day" Stafford writes of the danger of popularizing nature; in "The Darkening Moon," she writes of a girl's exclusion from it. It is the story of a double eclipse, that of the moon and that of her character. Stafford opens by contradicting the territorial imperative of the West that would define the lighted kitchen as female space and the unknown of open country and darkness as male space:

There was not a star in the sky, scarcely a sound in the air except for the soft gabbling of the creek. The little girl, when she had shut the kitchen door behind her and so shut in the yellow light, stood for a moment in the yard, taking her breath in sharply as though to suck in the mysterious element that had abruptly transformed day into dark. She was alone beneath the black firmament and between the blacker mountains that loomed up to the right and to the left of her like the blurred figures of fantastic beasts. . . .

Ella was glad that tonight she was going to take a ride on Squaw, who, impatiently stamping one foot, gave voice to a muted whinny as if to show that she, too, was ready for adventure.(251)

Action is simple. Ella rides to the Temples' lonely farmhouse, where she baby-sits. While she is there, the moon goes into an eclipse, and not understanding, she becomes frightened. Following the reemergence of the moon and the return of the Temples, Ella rides home. The events of one night encapsulate the real subject of the story, changes that are inexorably shaping Ella's life. Following her father's recent death that "had made her brother the head of the house" (252) Ella feels emotions as conflicting as the tunes that play simultaneously from the town's two jukeboxes. Speaking as child, sister, companion, daughter, grandmother, Ella in the opening scene reveals her confusion over shifting relationships.

Ella sets out as her father's child: "So long as she was outdoors, she was not afraid at night. Her father had taught her that, long ago, . . . when he had taken her and Fred fishing one night when the grayling were spawning. They had left her alone at the riverbank for half an hour while they went upstream through brush that would have cut her bare legs. Before they left, her father had said, 'There ain't nothing to harm you, sister. The animals is all there is and they won't be looking you up'" (254). Within the Temples' house, however, she is terrified, imagining bobcats closing in and owls warning "Look out!"; and tonight she slows her horse the last mile, wanting "to postpone as long as possible the moment when she would go into the house" (253–54).

Enclosures symbolize the gendered powerlessness of females. Ella leaves her mother inside the house, afraid that the game warden will discover the elk her son has brought inside. At the Temples' farmhouse, where by baby-sitting she will practice the life expected of a woman, Ella sits frozen with fear, "staring at the wall opposite her where hung an oil painting of Mr. Temple's prize bull, Beau Mischief" (254). There she hears a grieving cow in the yard, mourning her calf that Mr. Temple had killed that day, and she is called outside when her mare, Squaw, who she placed inside the pasture, is kicked by Mr. Temple's horse.

Tension builds as Ella moves back and forth between house and nature. From inside, the forms of nature no longer seem true, and she sits in the pink chair as if in a trap. Called outside by the cries of her mare, she comes under the spell of the shrinking moon of the eclipse; back inside, as if the eclipse is reaching into the house, the lamps begin to run out of fuel, yet Ella loathes to leave the house. The Coleman lamps no longer seemed garish to her but instead "cast a warm, saffron glow over the curly cowhide rugs and the serapes on the davenports. For the first time, she reflected that it was an elegant room" (259). But embracing domesticity means estrangement from nature, it would seem. The shadows shooting up in the room remind her of the cattails in the river where she had gone with her father to catch the grayling. Rather than recalling safety, however, it is fear and revulsion she experiences, remembering that her father had made her "pick up the fat slithering blobs in her bare hands" and that he had smeared her wrist with fish blood when he touched her. Crying, "she could not drive away the horror of the reptilian odor, nor could she summon her father's good-natured face" (261).

When the Temples come home, the human constellation has shifted as surely as that in the heavens, and Ella is now aligned with Mrs. Temple. The woman recognizes the girl's fear and reveals that she, too, was once like Ella: "I'm just thinking the way I used to be. Until I was fifteen, wasn't a living thing could give me a turn. And then, later on . . ." (262). Riding Squaw home past Steamboat, Ella sits in the saddle with her eyes closed, trusting the mare to keep to the road, and "a world slipped past her blinded eyes as she traversed a road she would not recognize again, beneath the full, unfaithful moon" (262).

As adolescents become adults, the net of gender conventions tightens about them. Stafford explores the serious and tragic dimensions of that entrapment in "In the Zoo" (1953) and "The Liberation" (1953). "In the Zoo" tells of two middle-aged sisters remembering their childhood in Adams. After their parents died, the girls, eight and ten, were sent from Massachusetts to Adams to live with a landlady, Mrs. Placer. There the girls grew up hearing the "even, martyred voices" of Mrs. Placer, "chairwoman of the victims," and those of her lodgers, "fixed like leeches to their solitary subject and their solitary creed—that life was essentially a matter of being done in, let down, and swindled" (286). Their memory centers on Mrs. Placer's effect on the girls' one friend, Mr. Murphy, "a gentle alcoholic ne'er-do-well" (288), whose small menagerie was the closest thing the girls had to love in a family. Mr. Murphy gave the girls a puppy that they lovingly named Laddie, but Mrs. Placer took it, renamed it Caesar, and it transformed into an animal as mean as she was. Violence takes the form of a chain reaction. When Mr. Murphy and the girls go to "have it out" with Mrs. Placer over the harm done to the dog, Caesar kills the capuchin riding on Mr. Murphy's shoulder; in retaliation the grieving Mr. Murphy poisons the dog. In despair the sisters consider their options: "Flight was the only thing we could think of, but where could we go? We stared west at the mountains and quailed at the look of the stern white glacier; we wildly scanned the prairies for escape. 'If only we were something besides kids! Besides girls!' mourned Daisy. I could not speak at all; I huddled in a niche of the rocks and cried" (299).

Years later the middle-aged sisters ask themselves why they stayed: once they began to work "it would have been no trick at all to vanish one Saturday afternoon with our week's pay, without so much as going home to say goodbye. But it had been infinitely harder than that, for Gran, as we now see, held us trapped by our sense of guilt. We were vitiated, and we had no choice but to wait, flaccidly, for her to die." (301). Yet their belief that they escaped with Gran's death is an illusion, for even in describing that escape the sisters echo Mrs. Placer's phrases ("I had to laugh") and repeat her suspicion. "In the Zoo" offers Stafford's version of violence as a process of corruption triggered by the deprivation of poverty, the impersonality of society, and the helplessness of children. Tuberculars are sent to the West as to a sanitarium, and children are sent there as to an orphanage. Beneath the myth of western adventure and individualism lies the pain of displacement: the unnamed sister who narrates the story recalls being sent to the West by a "man, whose name and face I have forgotten and whose parting speeches to us I have not forgiven" and who "tried to dry our tears with talk of Indians and of buffaloes" (285).

The idea of orphaned childhood appears also in "A Summer Day" (1948), the single story about a boy in the section. The story opens with the conventional western scene of arriving in the West on a train, orphaned, to begin a new life. Jim Littlefield, eight years old and sent alone from Missouri to Oklahoma after his grandmother died, is an unwilling participant in the western script, however: "I don't want to be no orphan," Jim had cried to the preacher, Mr. Wilkins. "Landagoshen, Jim boy, didn't I say you were going to be Uncle Sam's boy?" Mr. Wilkins had replied (346).

Oklahoma is a landscape of devastation, and when Jim arrives there, he has seemingly dropped into hell. He is picked up by a man and woman in a tall, black touring car that says on the door, "Department of the Interior/Indian Service" (349); from the depot, Jim could see the town:

> A wide street went straight through the level middle of it, and it had the same kind of stores and houses and lampposts that any other town had. The trees looked like leftovers, and the peaked brown dogs slinked behind the trash cans in an ornery way. . . . Jim could tell that the men sitting on the curb were Indians, for they had long pigtails and closed-up faces. They sat in a crouch, with their big heads hanging forward and their flat-fingered hands motionless between their knees. . . . The wooden cupola on the red brick courthouse was painted yellow-green and in the yard men lay with their hats over their eyes or sat limply on the iron benches under the runty trees, whose leaves were gray with dust or lice. A few children with ice-cream cones skulked in the doorways, like abused cats. Everyone looked ailing.
>
> The man from the school gestured with the hand that wore the heavy turquoise, and he said, "Son, this is your ancestors' town. This here is the capital of the Cherokee nation." (350–51)

It is little solace to tell a child that "Uncle Sam takes care of us all just as well as he can, so we should be polite to him and not let him see that we are homesick" (353). When they arrive at a group of buildings, Jim sees "a slide and some swings and a teeter-totter, but they looked as deserted as bones, and over the whole place there hung a tight feeling, as if a twister were coming" (353). The story unfolds with the inexorable logic of a landscape of devastation laying waste. Jim learns that "the water is poisonous" (357) and that there is an epidemic at the school; he meets a Navajo boy sitting alone in the shade of a tree, who is being punished for stealing the gun of the boys' counselor and who is passing time by plotting revenge "when I get a six-gun of my own" (359). Imagining that he, too, is planning to escape, Jim falls asleep.

In its isolation, discontinuity, lack of tradition, impersonality, disease, and violence the reservation represents Stafford's West more generally. Like Jim Littlefield, the sisters in "In the Zoo" were sent as orphans to Adams. Only decision, not action, distinguishes the boy from the girls. As Walsh has noted, Jim's decision to escape, "although he does not carry it out . . . separates him from the orphaned girls in Stafford's fiction, who generally accept their fates and do not expect to escape—and usually are unable even to fantasize about such a possibility" (*Jean Stafford* 14). Even so, the landscape in "A Summer Day" is the most barren and the horror the starkest of her section in *Collected Stories,* "Cowboys and Indians, and Magic Mountains." Characters do not act, they survive; at best they react.

Escape is the theme of "The Liberation," the story of the spinster Polly Bay, nearly thirty and living with her aunt and uncle in the Bays' ancestral house in Adams. Her announcement that she is going move to Boston, where she will marry and remain, brings forth all her relatives' familial and regional chauvinism; "too busy honoring their family to love it, too busy defending the West even to look at it. For all their pride in their surroundings, they had never contemplated them at all but had sat with the shades drawn, huddled under the steel engravings" (319). Again, it is speaking out that is liberating. "Don't," Polly says when her aunt Jane asks Uncle Francis to tell Polly about the wreck in the Royal Gorge, by that single word assuming the authority to speak and "without preamble" saying, "I am going to be married ten days from today to a teacher at Harvard and I am going to Boston to live" (312).

The effect that speaking those words has upon Polly is the liberation of the story. When in vain she "called on Robert Fair to materialize in this room," Polly proceeded independently to explain her decision and, upon hearing the chauvinism of her relatives' responses, to feel emotions she had previously denied to herself: "She had not hated the West till now, she had not hated her relatives till now; indeed, till now she had had no experience of hate at all. Surprising as the emotion was—for it came swiftly and authoritatively—it nevertheless cleared her mind and, outraged, she got up . . . to deliver her valediction. 'I don't want Robert to come here because I don't want to live here any longer. I want to live my own life. . . . It's true— I hate, I despise, I abominate the West!'" (316–17).

Alone behind the locked door of her bedroom, Polly realizes that "now that she had finally taken her stand, she was invulnerable" (318). Her words had been the genesis of her personal history. Even when Polly's plans for marriage are cut short when she learns that Robert Fair has died, she says, "I'm going straight to Boston." Once on the train, she thinks how lonely she had been: "And then, not fully knowing what she meant by it but believing in it faithfully, she said half aloud, 'I am not lonely now'" (322). For in taking her stand, she had found herself.

Finally, in "The Philosophy Lesson" Stafford takes female negation inward to tell of another kind of entrapment and escape. Cora Savage, posing nude as model for an art class, "turned herself to stone" (362), or pure object. While posing she sees snow outside: "for the time being, the snow was a private experience; perhaps everything at this moment proceeded from her own mind, even this grubby room with its forest of apparatus and its smell of banana oil, even all these people." Cora "concluded that she would be at peace forever if she could believe that she existed only for herself and possibly for a superior intelligence and that no one existed for her save when he was tangibly present" (365). Hearing of the suicide of a college student, members of the class speculate about him. Cora imagines him and in doing so imagines the darkness of suicide. A woman's helplessness is thus turned to violence against herself; self-destruction becomes liberation for powerlessness. The pain of posing became, for the first time, anger at the pose "in which she held a pole upright like a soldier with a spear." But more than annihilation of herself, philosophy of Bishop Berkeley annihilated the world. "When the snow came, the studio was dematerialized" (363).

Appearing in 1968, "The Philosophy Lesson" was Stafford's last western story published during her lifetime. Only "Woden's Day" was written later, extracted from her unfinished novel, *The Parliament of Women,* and published after her death. Thus with a girl's annihilation of herself and the world, the stories remain as Stafford's exploration of growing up female, gifted, and western, and as such are a complement to *The Mountain Lion,* the novel in which Stafford rewrote the Western.

7 | Stafford Rewrites the Western

Like it or not, reading the West means acknowledging the formula Western. It is indisputably the cultural form with which the region is most identified and arguably the one that bears its most elevated claims. Robert Warshow, for example, looks to the Western for its "serious orientation to the problem of violence which can be found almost nowhere else in our culture" (151), John G. Cawelti reads it as a product of an "epic moment" in our history (*Adventure* 193), and Tompkins turns to it in "an attempt to understand why men act the way they do and to come to terms with it emotionally" (18).

But what is the formula about which such claims are made? After agreeing that its setting is a geographical region transformed into an imaginative landscape, critics give it their personal spins. Cawelti argues that its basic situation develops from binaries—society against wilderness, civilization against violence, and savages against townspeople; through its formulaic action of chase and pursuit, the hero mediates between those forces. For Warshow the point of the Western is "a certain image of man, a style, which expresses itself most clearly in violence"—that of the lonely hero defending the purity of his honor (153). And Leslie Fiedler, drawing upon Freud's theories in *Civilization and its Discontents,* reads the hero's destruction of the savage (native or outlaw) as a modern society's repression of spontaneous sexuality.

What of women and the Western? As characters, we're told, women are scarce, appearing (when they do) as children (Warshow), symbols of civilization (Cawelti), or superegos that disrupt the relationship between hero and savage (Fiedler). As readers, they're sorely underrepresented among the critics, for with the welcome exception of Tompkins, this is territory claimed by men. Indeed, that is Tompkins's point in *West of Everything*. Conceding the Western as written by Owen Wister, Zane Grey, and Louis L'Amour, Tompkins offers a woman's reading of a male formula. Her reading is provocative in its gendered point of view as much as in its substance; any number of critics could have written that "the Western is secular, materialist, and antifeminist; it focuses on conflict in the public space, is obsessed by death, and worships the phallus" (28), but hearing Jane's rather than John's voice gives these words new meaning.

If gender makes a difference in reading the West, it makes an even greater difference in writing it. In *The Mountain Lion* Jean Stafford uses her pen as a divining rod to reveal sources of the psychosexual violence so thinly veiled in western literature. She uses familiar ingredients of the Western, but lays them bare: the cattle ranch is a breeding business, at the heart of male bonding is sexual anxiety, and the hunt takes the form of undisguised aggression against women. Exposed, too, is the experience of women, given voice in the character of a girl who, finding herself in a world structured by the Western formula, is inevitably the victim of its action. *The Mountain Lion* extends as well as exposes the literary West, for it is also Stafford's *Künstlerroman*. It is the novel where she treats directly the theme running as an undercurrent through her oeuvre—the girl destined to be a writer born into a literary tradition that, as Tompkins has argued about the Western, sprang from hostility toward precisely that destiny. As such it is one of the most radical explorations in American literature of gender, creativity, and the significance of the West and is a paradigm for feminist criticism of the field.

Double protagonists, brother and sister Ralph and Molly Fawcett, make dramatic gender divisions of the Western, which rigidly separates male and female cultures.[1] The movement west defines coming of age by this gender separation: growing up, Ralph and Molly do basically the same things in a presexual (and prewestern) state of innocence. In their relationship of friendship and exchange each complements and completes the other. Though in different classrooms both suffer from frequent nosebleeds that nearly always come at the same time; in conversation they speak as if from a common life. Molly repeats Ralph's jokes and tells his dreams, "pretending that they were her own" (6), and Ralph tells her story of eating nitrate fertilizer as if it had happened to him (81). Yet even in childhood there is an awareness that beneath it all, gender makes a primary and fundamental difference. "There was only one thing about Molly he did not like, Ralph decided, and that was the way she copied him. It was natural for her to want to be a boy (who *wouldn't*) but he knew for a fact that she couldn't be" (29–30). As a boy, Ralph recognizes that gender signifies privilege (he long believed that the words in the song "America" were "For spacious guys" [32]). To grow up male is to grow up celebrated by the national anthem. To grow up male is also to go west.

Two trips west structure the novel, dividing it almost exactly in half. The first part tells of Ralph and Molly's loss of childhood innocence when confronted with the mystery of death. Ralph is ten and Molly is eight when their grandpa Kenyon dies while visiting them; as a result of his death, they meet their uncle Claude, and they spend the summer at Claude's Colorado ranch. In the second part, set four years later, both children are initiated into another mystery—sex. So that she can take her older daughters around the world, their mother sends Ralph and Molly to their uncle's ranch for a year. There Ralph joins Claude in a hunt for a female mountain lion while Molly devotes herself to becoming a writer. The action reaches its violent conclusion when, unknown to one another, hunter and hunted meet. Firing simultaneously at the lion, Claude kills the cat and Ralph kills Molly.

As Stafford exposes the sexism inherent in the action of the formula Western, she plumbs implications of its symbolism. "The symbolic landscape of the western formula is a field of action that centers upon the point of encounter between civilization and wilderness, East and West, settled society and lawless openness," writes Cawelti (*Adventure* 193), a tradition Stafford incorporates in *The Mountain Lion*. Cooper's nature versus civilization and Wister's East versus West are echoed in Stafford's contrasting settings. Her story opens in California—a manufactured landscape detached from place; it moves to a cattle ranch in Colorado, the West of literary legend; and it anticipates a future in Connecticut, an East emptied of meaning—civilized or otherwise. For Stafford the point of encounter is between formula and fantasy, literary convention and cultural desire, and the symbolism of her settings is self-reflectively critical of the very formulas that they evoke.

California is located on the other side of the West. It is inhabited by sojourners on their way to someplace else, who comprise a temporary but colorful pastiche: an orange grove sometimes inhabited by bright birds resting on their flight from the South Seas to Japan, a neat dairy run by a fat German, a yard peopled by a postmistress with cartoonlike animal characters. California doesn't qualify as a place, their grandpa Kenyon explains to Ralph and Molly; then, as if defining "place" for them, he tells them a story of divining water on his ranch in the Panhandle. There wasn't a drop of water on his 45,000 acres when he bought it, but he chose a spot where he meant to build his house and took a holly wand, "holding a fork of it in either hand. By and by, the rod bent down: where she showed him, there was a deep clear spring that had never yet gone dry" (8).

The landscape that Ralph and Molly claim for their own is not California but the West, which they identify with a dry creek bed where they play, "a deep, dry arroyo called 'the Wash'" (6). Near their home yet out of time and place, the Wash offers magical possibilities: "On the floor of the Wash, Ralph and Molly could find bright-colored stones, pink and green and yellow and blue. After a heavy rain, there was sometimes fool's gold in the puddles. Strange harsh shallow-rooted flowers grew all over the steep slopes and clumps of mallow that yielded bitter milk. . . . All mystery and evil came from the Wash." (7) The Wash, as their grandpa Kenyon recognized, made a person "think of a place that is a place" (7): that is, it made him think of his ranch. Once their grandpa Kenyon christened the Wash with his story of divining, it became occasion for Molly and Ralph's yearnings. "Golly *Moses,* I'd like to go out West" (8), Ralph would sigh as they passed it, for the Wash reminded them of the West, which was clearly the promised land.

From the Wash sprang stories as rich and endless as the spring their grandfather had divined—family stories of how their father rescued a woman from a flood that swept through the Wash, and stories of their own imagining in which "those smooth colored stones they gathered were really stolen jewels and the thief was a coal-black Skalawag who slept in the daytime in Mr. Vogelman's cornbin but kept watch at night" (7). And why was he so watchful? The Skalawag "feared someone might come with a divining rod and once water was found, all his gems would be washed away" (8).

The parable of the Skalawag introduces the symbolism that informs *The Mountain Lion,* in which the West is a source for storytelling. The West, like the Wash, was occupied by a thief who claimed its storytelling for himself and who feared that someone with inspiration, by divining what lay at its heart, would write truthfully, for truthful writing would disprove his rhetoric as surely as water would wash away the Skalawag's gems.[2] Informed by the parable, *The Mountain Lion* announces that the desire behind its narrative is to divine its own source.

When Ralph and Molly go to Colorado, they enter a West codified by the formula Western, readily recognizable by familiar ingredients. The setting is a cattle ranch (the Bar K) with a spacious, rambling house facing a stream (the Caribou), pastures opening onto foothills leading to the summer range, and beyond them, mountains—remote yet confining—that "wore peril conspicuously on their horny faces" (95). Characters, cowboys we have met in film and fiction, are as familiar as the setting: "The men were skillful, good-humored, living with the present time and on a large scale. When they got drunk on a Saturday night, they did so with abandon, behaving exactly as drunk people in the movies did. Their lawlessness seemed natural. It seemed altogether reasonable that they hunted at all times except during the open season when, as Uncle Claude said, "there was too much danger of getting shot at by them dudes from Denver" (97).

Like its setting and characters, the action of *The Mountain Lion* is codified by the formula. Cooper announced the theme of initiation into heroic identity structured by a hunt, in which, as Cawelti observes in *Adventure, Mystery, and Romance,* a man "kills. . . , receives the name of hunter and warrior, he shows his capacity for adult leadership, he demonstrates his ability to abide by the wilderness code of honor, and he rejects the worldly [woman's] advances in favor of the violent masculine life of the wilderness" (203). These elements remain the important themes of the formula Western, and these are the elements Stafford draws upon. Once at the ranch, ten-year-old Ralph begins the lessons necessary for acceptance in the company of men: he learns how to ride, shoot, butcher, and drink.

Cliché today, the formula Western has been made seductively familiar by its repetition in myriad forms—advertising's Marlboro Man, Hollywood's Clint Eastwood, the political world's Ronald Reagan and George Bush—that merge to create an unmistakably American product. By so self-consciously drawing upon the formula, Stafford instills self-consciousness about the formula itself. Few would object to Cawelti's argument that formulas become "collective cultural products because they successfully articulate a pattern of fantasy that is at least acceptable to if not preferred by . . . cultural groups" (*Adventure* 34). The interesting question concerns asking not *what* that pattern is—but what lies at its source. It is a question that calls for a psychology of the formula and is one to which Stafford responded.

Whereas the Western works by disguising fantasies of sex and violence into a formulaic chase or hunt, *The Mountain Lion* works by removing the disguise to reveal the desire behind the fantasy. Ralph's mentor in the masculine code is Uncle Claude, whose appearance identifies him with the animals he tends: the man's "shoulders were massive, bullish, and his arms hung forward from them in an animal heaviness, terminating in the biggest hands the boy had ever seen . . . scarcely like hands at all but slabs of meat with the rind still on" (59). Contrasting mentors offered to Molly similarly symbolize the desire behind the formula: the housekeeper Mrs. Brotherman, sad and mild-mannered, about whom clings the odor of apples as if in temptation to join a female culture of passive kindness; and Magdalene, the black cook who, speaking of sex and violence, offers not kindness but wisdom. Molly imagines Magdalene to be the wife of the Skalawag, and she imagines herself to be Magdalene's child.

So far as the plot is concerned, there too Stafford removes the disguise behind the familiar initiation story to reveal its source in sexuality. Whereas Ralph and Molly remain good friends in Covina, they become estranged at the ranch their first summer there when Ralph becomes conscious of sexuality that previously he had only sensed in awful comments made by neighbor children and in his uncle's solitary nighttime trips to a particular street in town. In the last days of their first summer at the ranch Ralph witnesses birth: "Uncle Claude took him one day to a deep wet-weather branch where a cow was calving and at the moment he saw the horrible little hoof appear, he felt a painful exultation. . . . He was not in the least embarrassed, only filled with wonder at the bewildered wet calf that was finally born and immediately stood up although it was so small and weak it swayed piteously under its mother's big rosy tongue" (117–18). The experience creates a yearning in Ralph for the language to articulate what he has witnessed: "he tried to remember what Maisol and Maisaka had said that day in the watermelon patch" (118), and he tries to tell Molly about the calving, but words evade retrieval and Molly refuses to hear. Fearful and defensive, Molly "stuck her fingers in her ears and screamed at him, 'You're a dirty liar!' and her nose began to bleed" (118).

When he returns to the West at fourteen, Ralph becomes conscious of his personal sexuality in the biological changes that are inexorably transforming him into a man. Approaching his uncle's ranch, the train on which Ralph is riding passes through fourteen tunnels marking the four-teen years moving him toward manhood. As he passes through each, Ralph's sexual thoughts intensify, culminating in the last, longest tunnel that "he saw . . . as an apotheosis of his own black, sinful mind" (158) that had coveted the half cousin he would see at the ranch and the woman with children in the train with him. Feeling himself on the precipice of a Fall and seeking Redemption (Stafford writes with a fine comic sympathy here), Ralph thinks of his sister beside him, imagining that she might save him and saying "in the lowest voice, 'Molly, tell me all the dirty words you know'" (158).

In describing Ralph's awareness of sexuality as an apotheosis—an el-evation to divine form or a deification—Stafford describes desire seeking form, awareness longing articulation. Here as elsewhere, beneath Ralph's initiation into a manhood that would eschew talk runs the subtext of Ralph's desire to talk, at times a compulsion that leads him to ask inane questions and at other times an invitation to which others respond. Ralph's request for "dirty words" from Molly signals the breech between them made by gender and age, for his younger sister has as yet fiercely re-fused to admit sexuality. Back at the ranch, Molly wraps herself in incom-municability until, in furious retreat, Uncle Claude calls Ralph to a win-dow from which they mutely gaze upon a bull "bellowing with pain and fury" from a hairball in his jaw and, awaiting the vet, pastured near the house (167).

Male bonding—"companionship . . . so complete that it almost fright-ened Ralph"—occurs in "this brief time of their brutal preoccupation" with the bull, who "seemed to stare directly into their eyes with hatred as if they were responsible for their torment" (168). The experience is for Ralph an epiphany—a sudden, clarifying insight into the masculinity that under-lies the code of the West:

> it was as though he had set forth on an adventure whose terms were so inexora-ble that he could not possibly change his mind and go back, as if they were in the middle of a boat in the middle of a landless sea. He looked at the heavy, small-chinned face [of his uncle] in which, as the dark clear eyes studied the sick bull, there was a certain ponderous stupidity, a sort of virile opacity, an undeviating dedication to the sickness and health and the breeding of animals. The bull, by acquiring this infirmity, had temporarily become a nothing since he could not perform his function as a sire. It was almost as if he had made a fool of himself,

for surely the smile that came and went in Uncle Claude's face was a mocking one. While this discovery appalled him, he was determined never to be degraded in the man's eyes as the bull had degraded himself, as Molly had done, simply by being the kind of person she was, bookish and unhealthy. Even so, he was mixed in his feeling about Uncle Claude and his resolution was the result not of a re-freshed admiration but of the desire to go unnoticed by having no shortcom-ings. Because his own masculinity was, in its articulation, so ugly, and he could therefore take no pleasure in himself, neither could he respect it in anyone else. (168)

Again, Stafford relentlessly probes the fantasy at the heart of the Western, revealing its source in the anxiety over articulation of masculinity. Be-neath male bravado is fear of becoming "a nothing" if "he could not per-form his function as a sire." Fear of impotence is made comically clear by wordplay. The name of the bull is Advance Anxiety; and elsewhere, for ex-ample, upon seeing Winifred and her beau, Ralph was afraid he "was going to become too limp to stand up straight" (171).

Negation is the result of such fear. Aware of his uncle Claude's gaze, Ralph refrains from comforting Molly and from lying among flowers lest his manliness be questioned. Obeying his uncle's suggestion that he leave his glasses off, Ralph at first suffers headaches so severe he vomits but then gradually (as Stafford writes with great irony, for eventually Ralph will shoot his sister, mistaking her for a lion) "was able to see almost as well as he had done with his glasses" (117). Most painfully, Ralph must renounce language as a part of a female culture held suspect by a man's man. In Cal-ifornia men use language to dominate, whether under the guise of Ralph's grandfather Bonney's self-satisfied insistence that others defer to his use of "conversation as an art" (21) or of the Reverend Follansbe's speeches that, because he "was a rhetorician and cared little for give and take," were delivered "as if he were in the pulpit" (122). The masculine use of language is similarly repressive at his uncle's western ranch, where among the hands "the talk was endless but it seemed to be made up almost altogether of non sequiturs. The men did not interrupt one another, but they did not listen" (86).[3]

Hunting is the one subject western men talk of freely. Forbidden the lan-guage of love, the men displace the golden girl-woman of cultural myth into the hunt to be pursued as a yellow mountain lion. Mountain lion and woman become indistinguishable in Claude's account of the prey he is tracking: "He thought about her so much that he had given her a name," Claude tells Ralph; "he called her Goldilocks because, running the way she had in the sunlight, she had been as blonde as a movie star" (170). By deciding to let Ralph hunt her too, Claude formalizes their bond; by resolving "that it would be *he,* not the man, who got the lion" (170), Ralph defines the bond as competitive. The hunt as displaced sexuality, driven by fear of its articulation, emerges in the violence of its language as well as in the violence of its action. They name their prey "Goldilocks" because she reminds them of a movie star; they determine to "have her," swear "blast the yellow bitch," identify the housekeeper's daughter with a cat, and with double entendres tell stories of hunting beavers: "I wouldn't think you'd have to go to the mountains to hunt that kind of game. What's the matter with the little lady settin' here? Settin' right here with all us big grown men?" (198).

Given such a code, it is inevitable, perhaps, that Molly is sacrificed, for as Blanche Gelfant has written in "Reconsideration: *The Mountain Lion,*" the male initiation story demands the exclusion of the female. It is, after all, a female mountain lion that the men hunt, its femaleness intensified by Ralph's fantasy of finding her with her cubs in their den and killing them all; and he does come to resent Molly's intrusion into the "pure masculinity" of his friendship with their uncle. However, such an explanation acknowledges only half of Stafford's story, that concerning male initiation. By creating a double, female protagonist, Stafford has presented a second story of initiation—Molly's.

On one level, Molly tells the female version of the male initiation story of the hunt. Like Ralph, Molly is coming of age sexually, and her dawning awareness is as complex as is his, both enticing and foreboding. Beneath Molly's social awkwardness is her secret femininity revealed in her fantasy of herself as beautiful. In a "bag which she kept locked and hidden away on the topmost shelf of her closet," Molly assembles products designed to transport and transfigure her: bath salts that smelled so sweet "she could imagine that she was in a garden" (173–74), soap "in the form of a yellow rose, Armand's talcum power, a bottle of Hind's Honey and Almond, a jar of Daggett and Ramsdell vanishing cream, a bottle of Glostora shampoo, a jar of Dr. Scholl's foot balm, a jar of freckle remover" (174). Were these salts, soaps, powders, and creams to work as their advertising promises, they would transform Molly into a golden girl. The fundamental lesson of growing up female is that to be beautiful is to be desired, and to be desired is to be pursued. And here, chillingly, Molly's fantasy joins with that of the male hunt, but as hunted rather than hunter. When she finally sees the mountain lion and identifies with it, wishing to be golden, small, and beautiful like it,[4] Molly articulates her role in the masculine myth; when she dies because she is mistaken for the lion, she fulfills that role.

Whereas Molly fantasizes of becoming beautiful, in her reality she is becoming a writer. Ralph's initiation into manhood proceeds inevitably from a gendered culture, but Molly's initiation into writing proceeds inevitably from her character. The central fact about Molly (and about *The Mountain Lion*) is that she is truly defined not by her appearance but by her sensitivity to language.[5] Though she might "plan to be a salesman for the *Book of Knowledge,* a grocer, a government walnut inspector, a trolley conductor in Tia Juana; of course, her real vocation was writing and these were to be only sidelines" (187). By giving to Molly the vocation of writing, Stafford announced a second initiation story for which she appropriates the symbolic forms of the literary West. Claiming the metaphor of the hunt in a talk she gave the year that *The Mountain Lion* appeared, Stafford described the vocation of the writer as a "hunt for the proper words" ("Psychological Novel" 225–26). She could have been describing Molly's story.

The competing claims on the metaphor of the hunt appear in the narrative's structure, for Molly's initiation into the life of a writer runs counterpoint to Ralph's initiation into manhood. While Ralph learns to ride, Molly stays "at home to . . . write" (104–05); rather than learning to shoot, she writes of Ralph's doing so (116–17); and when Ralph is out on the range, Molly remains at the ranch composing an article for *Good Housekeeping,* called "My Summer at the Bar K" (104–05). As Ralph's initiation is told by his developing skill with a gun, Molly's is told through her developing skill with words. For Molly as for Ralph, independence signals success—but for Molly, independence is measured by use of language. When young, she and Ralph shared the humor of verbal puns, echoing each other or together repeating a joke, speaking "as a dialogue" (5). Yet, as in childhood awareness of gender separated Ralph from Molly, so in childhood Molly's sensitivity to language separates her from him. Molly's poem "Gravel" illustrates the difference:

> Gravel, gravel on the ground
> Lying there so safe and sound,
> Why is it you look so dead?
> Is it because you have no head? (31)

"It doesn't make any sense," Ralph replies, for gravel hasn't a head. "That's what I said. 'Is it because you have no *head*?'" (31), Molly replies—her words a repetition of the poem as well as an indictment of Ralph for not understanding. The poem becomes a touchstone; repeated by both Molly and Ralph, Ralph never understands it.

At the ranch the breach between them widens, for as Molly enters a writer's realm of words, Ralph remains imprisoned within the literal: "He liked her when they were alone, but she embarrassed him in public because she said such peculiar things. For instance, she said to Mrs. Brotherman this afternoon, 'Do you have any opinion on the false Armistice?' and when Mrs. Brotherman said no, she really had not, Molly had said, 'Oh, of course you don't live in California so you wouldn't have seen the Los Angeles *Gazette*.' What she was talking about was the old newspaper they had with the one word PEACE printed in letters four inches high on the front page, but how was Mrs. Brotherman to know?" (94). The blindness continues as Molly, long conscious of being awkward and skinny, plays upon that idea with a pun on "string bean":

> "Do you like it here?" said Ralph.
>
> "I don't know. I'll tell you later. I don't like the food, I must say. String beans are the bane of my existence."
>
> "I liked the buckskin."
>
> Molly frowned and said nothing for a moment and then she said, "You know, I don't think I'll learn to ride horseback tomorrow. I think I'll wait for a few days as I have an idea for a short story about an amateur kidnapper." (94)

Like Ralph's hunt for the mountain lion, Molly's hunt for words has stages of preparation and tests of worthiness. As if performing an exercise for her imagination, Molly keeps a diary in which she records everything Ralph says and does but inflates her entries with so much creativity and rhetoric that the pack rat he shoots becomes "three Rocky Mountain laughing hyenas" (117). As if in testimony to her patience in her "hunt for the proper words themselves," she writes a long, humorous ballad called "The Fierce Mexican," then tears it up with loathing when "the imperfection of the rhyme of 'Mexican' and 'Mohican' stuck to her mind like paste" (207); and as if carrying out an exercise in narrative logic, she begins a detective novel that is fantastic in its intricate plot. Measured by Stafford's criterion of a writer finding the language adequate to convey exactly what she has seen and what she has deduced from it, Molly's progress is steady. Gradually, puns give way to wit, and rhetoric to the clarity of truth-telling.

Gradually, too, Molly's training moves from the ranch to the mountains, for as with the western hero generally, nature will be the setting for her apotheosis. By moving Molly into nature Stafford again appropriates the western tradition. Like countless western figures before her, Molly enters the wilderness in search of solitude, but the solitude she seeks is for writing and the materials she carries in her knapsack are pen and paper rather than gun and trap. Molly selects as her lookout Garland Peak because "from the summit she commanded a view of the entire valley, of the range as far as the eye could see" (205), thus echoing another heroic tradition. But where the mountain man would use the vista as a lookout for enemies, Molly perfects the observation she will need to write; and where the mountain man feels at home in the forest by taking part in the eternal action of the hunt,[6] Molly does so by finding "an ideal glade for her study" (206). A western equivalent of the room of her own that Virginia Woolf said the woman writer needed, the glade that Molly claims "was very small and surrounded so densely by trees and chokecherry that they were almost like walls, and right in the middle as if planned for her, was a big flat rock" (206).

Molly's version of training herself in the ways of the wild is to observe closely and to record precisely. Gradually, rhetoric drops away and her observations become clear—as when Stafford describes Molly's view from Garland Peak with such precise prose that the effect is of "getting" the experience as surely as any hunter "gets" his quarry: "On a clear day it was possible to see the men on the ricks on the pastures, pitching down feed to the herd which appeared to be hundreds of small red blocks on the glaring snow, as small as her ladybugs. The Caribou was frozen solid and all the trees on either side of it were bare" (208).

As power is at issue in the formulaic Western, power is at stake for Molly. Armed with an arsenal of words, she engages in confrontations familiar to the western hero: she is "fearless and level-headed" in facing down Uncle Claude; she maintains "a vigilant silence" in defending herself against the tyranny of a group (165); and when her mother says she wants to talk with her, Molly replies, "Go ahead. Shoot" (138). Her scenes are structured by verbal battles that provide her occasions to defend truth with a right use of language against its mistreatments by the ignorant, dishonest, and uxorious. When a horse thief comes to the ranch, for example, it is Molly who defeats him in a verbal shoot-out: the stranger is stopped short in the middle of one of his stories when, her voice coming out of the darkness, Molly says, "'I doubt that.' . . . Her voice was firm and clear and its effect upon the stranger was so prompt that sweat came out on his forehead, glittering in the firelight, and his hand trembled" (194).

The overwhelming effect is that Molly establishes words as powerful in ways that others perceive as dangerous. Molly's mother "at times was really afraid" of Molly "and the things she said!" (123). And once Molly is in possession of the words Ralph spoke to her while on the train passing through the tunnel, she terrorizes him by inserting the word "tunnel" into conversations, and he feels panic lest "She has *told!*" (172). Ralph fears their mother's return and their move to Connecticut, where he would be separated from Uncle Claude and where, "always at hand, would be Molly who could ruin him, blow up his world if she chose" (196). He knew she would do nothing against him as long as they were at their uncle's ranch, "but in that bare wasteland where they were to live under the shadow of the trinity of fat men, he must guard himself against her weapon" (196). In ceasing to echo Ralph's thoughts and language as when they were younger, Molly appropriates the stance of the western hero in the story that is unfolding. She is the outsider who is straight-talking, farsighted, and fearless.

The two initiation stories come together in three successive versions of the hunt, each set on Garland Peak, whose name announces its symbolic significance. To reach the peak, the formula promises, is to receive the garland. Garland for what, however, is the question evoked by competing claims upon its symbolism: there the mountain lion lives; there Claude follows her on his hunt; there Ralph follows Claude in his initiation into masculinity; and there Molly goes to finds the solitude to write.

The first hunt is told from Molly's point of view. Uncle Claude and Ralph accompany Molly to Garland Peak, where the mountain lion first reveals herself to them. Molly's response is a moment of artistic possession. With clarity of sight, sensitivity to the moment, and precision of language Molly captures the mountain lion so that she flashes into life on the page, from Stafford through Molly to her reader: "She was honey-colored all over save for her face which was darker, a sort of yellow-brown. They had a perfect view of her, for the mesa there was bare of anything and the sun illuminated her so clearly that it was as if they saw her close up. She allowed them to look at her for only a few seconds and then she bounded across the place where the columbines grew in summer and disappeared among the trees" (211). Molly feels the freedom of forgetting herself: "her wastless grace and her speed did not make Molly think immediately of her fear but of her power" (211), Stafford writes, the antecedent of "her" tellingly ambiguous. The lion and Molly are momentarily one, for in seeing perfectly and translating the moment into language, Molly experiences an artist's "wastless grace" and "power."

The writer must be "patient in waiting for . . . observations to mature," Stafford counseled in an essay on the novel, so that they will "lose their confused immediacy" ("Psychological Novel" 226). On this first hunt Molly is still young, and her artistic impulse toward truth ends in confusion. Immediately following her "perfect view" of the lion, Molly becomes aware of her uncle's anger and her brother's secret smile, and the cat "grew to huge proportions in her reflection. She imagined its claws, its teeth, the way it would hiss" (211). Betraying her own observation in adopting the jargon of pulp fiction, Molly imagines a creature that would corroborate the male script, then casts herself in the formulaic role of a helpless female fearful of entering the wilderness until the men have made it safe by killing the ferocious animals lurking there. She then betrays herself further in thinking, "if only she had yellow hair . . . she would be an entirely different kind of person" (214). But the confusion promises to be temporary, for the first version of the hunt ends with Molly writing with a typewriter. As Ralph and Claude arm themselves with a gun, Molly arms herself with her own weapon.

For her second version of the hunt, Stafford shifts to Ralph's point of view to describe an impulse of love that is displaced into violence. Remembering the household cat he had loved as a child, Ralph dreams of the mountain lion by seeing himself "taking perfect aim, shooting her through her proud head with its wary eyes, and then running across the mesa to stroke her soft saffron flanks and paws" (218). Love and violence interweave, one obscenely justifying the other. Ralph resolves that "if he got her" he would not skin her but "would have her stuffed and keep her in his room all his life" (218). Ralph's image of the animal skinned, stuffed, and caged within his room is grotesquely at odds with Molly's image of her that flashes with the movement and color of life created by words on a page. Ralph's justification of his possessive desire to "have her" is also grotesquely at odds with the exchange of Molly's encounter. Ralph feels that "somehow. . . he had more right to Goldilocks" than his uncle "because he loved her, but Uncle Claude wanted her only because she was something rare" (218); in Molly's scene, love occurred as reciprocity by which the cat "allowed them to look at her."

As Molly's version of the hunt had ended in her confrontation with gender expectations, so Ralph's version of the hunt ends with a similar confrontation. Ralph and his uncle Claude come upon the mountain lion feeding, and she leaps away before they can raise their rifles. Left with the remnant of the hunt, Ralph finds interlocked antlered stag skulls; taking them to Molly and mutely giving them to her, he avoids language when "they exchanged, at last, after these months, a look of understanding and Molly said, 'Thanks, Ralph. I'll shoot them with my Brownie'" (220). It is a painfully brief moment of exchange, however, and a temporary respite from the relentlessly formulaic hunt in which they are both caught.

In the third hunt characters are separated by the distraction of sex and the encumbrance of violence. Because Uncle Claude is taking a mare to stud, he leaves before the others, and because Ralph is carrying a gun, he can't climb up the face of the mountain but must separate from Winifred and Molly. Most important, however, is that because each of them holds memories that distort their experience, they quarrel and separate. Seeking to escape his own confusion and Molly's anger, Ralph goes alone to "a little glade he knew of with a flat rock in the center of it like a table," where he hears a sound, sees "Goldilocks feeding upon a jackrabbit," hears another sound, then shoots (227). Contrary emotions and reactions rush together as Uncle Claude emerges—the men's exultation over shooting the lion, Ralph's tenderness upon turning her over ("She's so little. . . . Why, she isn't any bigger than a dog. She isn't as *big*" [228]), the automatic transformation of his unseemly pity into manly anger that it was his uncle's bullet that killed the lion, not his, and finally Uncle Claude's proposal that they call themselves "a corporation" (229), partners in getting the mountain lion.

Immediately after their formalized bonding, they hear another sound, one "that could come only from a human throat." The sound is Molly's truth-telling articulated as "a bubbling of blood." They "stood up and looked at one another in an agony of terror . . . Somebody . . ."; and then they find Molly: "her glasses lay in fragments on her cheeks and the frame, torn from one ear, stuck up at a raffish angle. The elastic had come out of one leg of her gym bloomers and it hung down to her shin." The sexual violence of the hunt reaches its apotheosis in an image of rape, then extends beyond violence to the female body to Molly's head, where there is "a wound like a burst fruit in her forehead" (229).

Stafford ends *The Mountain Lion* by returning to the parable with which she began. Magdalene, the black cook whom Molly had imagined as "the wife of the Skalawag at the Wash" (98), says upon seeing Molly, "Lord Jesus. The pore little old piece of white trash" (231). Her words, dramatically and radically at variance with the Western formula driving the action, signal the collapse of Ralph and the introduction of the question most commonly asked by critics: Why did Molly have to die?

Critical consensus is that Molly is sacrificed to reestablish the status quo. Walsh writes that Molly "must die" because she "does not cope and is unable to accept the limited life open to her as a female. Consequently . . . she is accidentally shot to death by Ralph, who thus frees himself so that he can reach his full masculine possibilities" ("Young Girl" 241). William T. Pilkington writes that "she and the mountain lion must both die because both are misfits who somehow threaten to disrupt the delicately balanced social arrangements that encircle them" (186). And Gelfant writes that "Her death is demanded by the great masculine myth of the West," for as a female, Molly's "constant presence reminds him [Ralph] of a part of himself he can no longer endure as he grows up, and indeed must kill: the feminine side of his nature" ("Reconsideration" 20). Each assumes that with Molly's death the formula may resume, Walsh of masculine possibilities, Pilkington of social arrangements, and Gelfant of a timeless male initiation into adulthood. Yet the status quo means a return to the formula, and Stafford has irreparably broken with that formula: she has appropriated the hunt for her writer, and in the process she has redefined the territory of its action as language and recast the terms of its struggle into who has possession of storytelling.

The Mountain Lion depicts the West as a reversion to primitive modes of communication. There, the formula promises, people may relate directly to an elemental reality without the intervention of language. At their uncle's ranch, Molly and Ralph can "*look directly* at the ledge from which a packhorse had slipped and fallen to her dreadful, screaming death," and "They *knew the place* where a bold dude had frozen in midsummer" (96; emphases mine). The descriptions recall the method of the formulaic Western, in which a ledge automatically signals danger and a dude signals helplessness. They illustrate also the principle of communication most closely identified with the West, the substitution of thing for word. Uncomfortable discussing sex with her daughter, Mrs. Fawcett decides the breeding ranch would be "good" for Molly "at her age" (136); frustrated over a conversation turned hostile, Claude mutely takes Ralph to see a bull in pain; unable to talk about growing up male, Ralph silently gives to Molly the skulls of stags with their antlers interlocked.

It is a method akin to pantomime, and it is the method fundamental to the hunt, the ritual most celebrated by the Western, wherein men go together into the woods and point to objects in order to express their emotions, indicate their desires, and attempt to control one another.[7] Because the hunt depends upon the object itself for communication, the trophy is its natural extension. A head of a bighorn mounted on Uncle Claude's wall and Ralph's dream of skinning the mountain lion, stuffing it, and keeping it always in his room are similar: both privilege the object itself and, by doing so, both render words superfluous. The physical object is the most real and reliable form of communication; in lieu of such objects, words serve merely as their substitute to signify the object.

But primitive modes of communication satisfy only the most primitive of desires. Whereas pointing to an object and gesturing in pantomime may communicate natural wants and project fantasy, these acts are woefully inadequate to satisfy the human desire to transform experience into concepts—that is, to formulate and express ideas. And this is the desire that runs as a subtext through *The Mountain Lion*. To understand sex, Molly desperately needs not the example of a breeding ranch but the complex association of sense and feeling that language might offer; to assuage his loneliness, Claude desperately needs to articulate the threatening masculinity that he and Ralph share; and the interlocked skulls of stags are a poor substitute for Ralph and Molly's desire to conceive and communicate their experience of growing up.

Into a West that was profoundly hostile to language, Stafford sent Molly, whose primary reality is verbal rather than physical. By creating Molly as a girl whose true vocation was writing, Stafford cast her development in terms of language. Within a year after completing *The Mountain Lion* and speaking as if she were describing Molly, Stafford explained what it means to be a writer:

> probably the reason writing is the most backbreaking of all professions is that it is so very difficult to tell the truth. Even though we may know certainly that our perceptions are accurate and that only one set of conclusions can be drawn from

them, we are still faced with how to communicate the findings perceptively and conclusively. The language seems at times inadequate to convey exactly what we have seen and what we have deduced from it and much too often writers shirk their responsibility and take refuge in rhetoric—as the preaching novelists do—or in snobbish, esoteric reference, as Henry Miller and his followers do, in samples of language other than their own and in jargon, and in elaborate approximations that almost but do not quite say what they mean. But the language is quite able to take care of any of our needs if we are only affectionate and respectful toward it and, above all, patient with ourselves: patient, not only in our hunt for the proper words themselves, but patient in waiting for our observations to mature in us, to lose their confused immediacy so that their timelessness will emerge and their meaning will become available to our reader and applicable to him as well as to ourselves. ("Psychological Novel" 225–26)

Almost thirty years later, Stafford remained firm in her allegiance to language. As she declared in "Miss McKeehan's Pocketbook" (and as Molly might have said), "language is and has always been my principal interest, my principal concern, and my principal delight. I'd rather read a dictionary than go to the moon" (410). For Molly as for her creator, the dictionary offers possibility and power that far exceed that of science. It offers the potential to not only express but to create reality.

A western writer who prefers a dictionary to going to the moon is hardly a western writer of the usual mold. Understanding *The Mountain Lion* means leaving the traditional literary West and turning to philosophy, for Stafford has more in common with philosopher Ernst Cassirer and with Susanne K. Langer than she does with her literary forefathers of the Western. Langer's study of the genesis of cultural myth in language reads as if a gloss upon Stafford's novel generally, and upon Molly Fawcett particularly: "our primary world of reality *is* a verbal one"; language is "the most momentous and at the same time the most mysterious product of the human mind" (*Philosophy* 126, 103). For Langer as for Stafford, to use language symbolically is the most satisfying and the most powerful human experience. By naming we conceive reality, and by using metaphor to make relationships we generate new meaning.

Childhood play in *The Mountain Lion* is play with the possibilities of words—puns that display language's capacity to move from the literal to the figurative, symbolic, and metaphoric. Molly and Ralph enjoy their greatest joy and communion through their shared delight in words. Together they recite a joke that turns upon the word "hide," one moment meaning a thing (the skin of a cow) and the next an act (that of conceal-ing from sight); and they are delighted with one another when they con-nect "Dump" as a man's name with "dump" as a verb, then translate the word by rhyme into "lump." What distinguishes Molly from Ralph—and indeed, from the western literary tradition that he represents—is that she understands that language is through and through symbolic, and only sometimes signific. In her poem "Gravel," Molly plays with the idea of symbolic language; with his objection that "gravel doesn't have any head," Ralph reveals his limitation to signific language—words that stand for a thing and that have practical value.

Conception, generation, and creativity are, according to Langer and Stafford, made possible through language, for "the notion of giving some-thing a *name* is the vastest generative idea that ever was conceived; its in-fluence might well transform the entire mode of living and feeling, in the whole species, within a few generations" (Langer, *Philosophy* 142). The re-sult of approaching creativity through language is identifying power with language. As Langer wrote in an essay on Cassirer, "merely *knowing* a word gives a person the power of using it; thus it is invisibly 'had,' carried about by its possessors" ("On Cassirer's Theory" 390). As if engaging in verbal voodoo, Stafford's Molly uses words like power as Langer discusses it. She places the names of hated persons inside her diary as a means of willing harm to them, she uses the word "'bourgeois' . . . as if it were the most ven-omous in the language" (148), and in using the word "fat" against Ralph she invokes upon him the curse of his ancestry. By naming, "A word fixes something in experience, and makes it the nucleus of memory, an avail-able conception" (*Philosophy* 135)—again, Langer provides insight into Molly's development as she moves past the joy of naming in itself to the re-alization that by recalling the name of an object or person, a whole occa-sion may be retained. Molly knows that to say the words "tunnel" and "dirty" is to recall not only the tunnel through which they were passing when Ralph asked her to tell him dirty words but also the broader expe-riences of going west and of growing up together.

In structuring Molly's story as an appropriation of metaphor, Stafford invests Molly with power of which her young writer is not yet aware. Lan-guage is most vital in metaphor, "the power whereby language, even with a small vocabulary, manages to embrace a multimillion things" (Langer, *Philosophy* 141). Metaphor is to language what myth is to culture—the point at which words take on the power of revolution. Metaphor is "the force that makes [language] essentially *relational,* intellectual, forever showing up new, abstractable *forms* in reality, forever laying down a deposit of old, abstracted concepts in an increasing treasure of general words" (Langer, *Philosophy* 141). Metaphor in *The Mountain Lion* works precisely that way. Stafford begins with the metaphor of the hunt as it has appeared in the formulaic Western, then gives it new life by making Molly both hunted and hunter.

Stafford gave to Molly the writer's task of hunting for the words that would tell the truth. Had she lived (a question far more interesting, I believe, than why she died), what is the truth she would have told? It is that the western myth is not only profoundly hostile to women, but that it is hostile to language, and that the result is a violence of silencing. This is the challenge Stafford faced as Molly's creator: how could she tell the story of growing up in the West as a girl destined to write, when the truth was that such a girl would be silenced? Stafford responded by infusing her character with her own life, thus extending her story beyond the confines of the novel. "Gradually I became Molly," Stafford recalled of writing her story; "I was so much Molly that finally I had to write her book" (qtd. in Goodman, *Jean Stafford* 175). Indeed, Stafford was so much Molly that to read *The Mountain Lion* means reading not only the words on the page—but also the life that lies behind it.

It is a fusion of fiction with fact, creator with created, that Stafford invited the reader to recognize when she infused her story with autobiography. She gave to Molly both her childhood home in Covina complete with the dried-up creek called the Wash and the cat named Budge and her brother Dick, who though renamed Ralph is recognizable in innumerable details. Further, Stafford's gift to Molly of her own precocity with language included "Gravel," the poem Jean composed when she was a child. By embedding into *The Mountain Lion* a code of personal puns, Stafford extended Molly's story into her own adult life. Jean's nickname, "Eanbeaner," which biographer David Roberts says "she proudly wore in its many variations, including Ean, Bean, and Beaner," appears in Molly's pun upon herself as "string bean"; and the fictional reference to Goldilocks echoes the real-life code of "bears" that she and Lowell chose as their literary persona when, young and newly married, they were learning their craft (Roberts 193–94).

To read Stafford's life is to read of continuing silencing, for the critics have remained as watchful over their West as Molly's and Ralph's Scalawags over the Wash. Despite the fact that Stafford is a Pulitzer Prize–winning writer who came from and wrote of the West, she is ignored in major anthologies and bibliographies of western writing: there is no mention of her by Taylor (himself from Stafford's Colorado) in *The Literature of the American West* (1971), no mention by John R. Milton in *The Novel of the American West* (1980), no mention by Fred Erisman and Richard W. Etulain in *Fifty Western Writers: A Bio-Bibliographical Sourcebook* (1982), and no mention by James C. Work in *Prose and Poetry of the American West* (1990).

What happens when Stafford is included? She invites her reader to reread western literature using *The Mountain Lion* as a divining rod to reveal the desire beneath the fantasy as it is revealed in language. The most popular modern Westerns, Owen Wister's *The Virginian* (1902), Zane Grey's *Riders of the Purple Sage* (1912), and Jack Schaefer's *Shane* (1954), provide a sample for such rereadings. The plot of each is typical of the Western: an outsider enters a community, defends the townspeople/settlers/farmers against the Indians/wilderness/ranchers and, after restoring order, departs. Although he departs, he changes the mode of communication from language to pantomime, for the Western celebrates a reversion to the primitive, savage, and elemental.

"Historically, the western represents a moment when the forces of civilization and wilderness are in balance," Cawelti writes, "the epic moment at which the old life and the new confront each other, and individual actions may tip the balance one way or another, thus shaping the future history of the whole settlement" (*Adventure* 193). Jean Stafford rewrites the Western so that it represents a moment when the forces of truth versus falsehood, art versus formula, are in balance, and the future being shaped concerns the settlement that occurs with language. For it is by our language that we claim a country, settle it by certain principles, and make it habitable for ourselves and others; and as I argue in chapter 9, it is by language, too, that we commit, then justify, the cruelest violence.

8

The

Western Hero

as Logos

> Re-vision—the act of looking back, of seeing with fresh eyes, of
> entering an old text from a new critical direction—is for women
> more than a chapter in cultural history: it is an act of survival.
>
> ADRIENNE RICH, "When We Dead Awaken: Writing as Re-Vision"

In the manner of Adrienne Rich, Jean Stafford's *The Mountain Lion* calls for us to look back, to see with fresh eyes, and to enter the popular Western with Molly Fawcett as our companion. Doing so is confirmation that, with its gestalt-like capacity to take on the symbolic shape of our desire and anxieties, the Western has proved itself a ready forum for cultural constructions of identity. During the cold war, critics Warshow and Cawelti looked to the Western for its depiction of violence; when political winds shifted to issues of gender identity, critic Tompkins read the Western for what it told her about "the power that men in our society wield" (*West of Everything* 18), and Lee Clark Mitchell read it for what it reveals of "making the man." Seeking to understand what something means, we look to the Western, where meaning is made.

In this chapter I propose to change the focus from *what* something means to *how* meaning is made in the Western, or (more accurately) how it is *unmade*. I take as my starting point the apparent paradox of a literary genre identified by its hero's reluctance to use language (Cawelti) and hostility toward it (Tompkins). In doing so, I acknowledge that its close identification with a laconic style makes the Western superbly adaptable to the visual medium of film, thus giving rise to the interdisciplinary criticism so characteristic of the field (e.g., Warshow, Cawelti, Tompkins, and L. Mitchell). Returning to the formula's wellspring in literary texts, however, allows a close exploration of the nature and implications of its story of language.

Bestseller lists provide a sample of the literary Western. These are, after all, the books that by their long-standing popularity are the classics of the genre and, therefore, basic to any understanding of it: *The Virginian,* the novel that announced the Western; *Riders of the Purple Sage,* the most popular novel by Zane Grey, who "all but single-handedly confirmed the shape of [the] powerful new narrative form"; and *Shane,* which, through its nostalgic perspective, "offers a distillation of the Western itself" (L. Mitchell, *Westerns* 95, 123, 193).[1]

Each novel, like other conventional Westerns, focuses on regeneration and redemption, which are, as Cawelti has pointed out, the reward "for those protagonists who can respond to [the West's] challenge by recovering basic human and American values" (*Adventure* 233). The regeneration is embodied in the promise of a future, for in "the end, hero and heroine are clearly on their way to marriage, a family, and a settled life thereafter" (235). Beneath this action, what is at issue is language. The three novels are variations upon a single plot, shaped by gender, in which a man enters a situation unsatisfactorily structured by words and displaces language by establishing himself as the Word—the Virginian, Lassiter, Shane. In each variation, the plot concerns silencing and focuses our attention on the "thing" itself, on physical ways of knowing. Knowledge or understanding is revealed not by language but by gesture: by looking, by pointing, by naming in the simplest terms. In this manner, metaphoric generativity is displaced and disproved, and meaning reverts to stasis.

The opening scene of *The Virginian* sets the stage for linguistic regression; in it Wister establishes that entering the West means confronting the inadequacies of language. Alighting from the train, the Tenderfoot overhears a conversation that "resembled none that I had heard in my life so far" (2–3); then while attempting to describe the place in which he finds himself, he realizes that the word "town" hardly applies to places like Medicine Bow, "stark, dotted over a planet of treeless dust, like soiled packs of cards" (8). As eastern language doesn't cover a western reality, so also western words cannot be confined by an eastern lexicon. The Virginian,

Trampas, Shorty, and Steve are all referred to by the word "rustler," for example, a word that those in the East realize

> was not in any dictionary, and current translations of it were inconsistent. A man at Hoosic Falls said that he had passed through Cheyenne, and heard the term applied in a complimentary way to people who were alive and pushing. Another man had always supposed it meant some kind of horse. But the most alarming version of all was that a rustler was a cattle thief.
>
> Now the truth is that all these meanings were right. The word ran a sort of progress in the cattle country, gathering many meanings as it went. (163–64)

The language of the West is as wild and lawless as the country. Words, like individuals, have the potential to be anything at all. When, instead of directly naming Trampas his enemy, the Virginian merely says, "What do yu' make of the proposition yondeh?" as he "point[s] to the cause of this question," his motion causes the narrator to reflect that "[p]roposition in the West does, in fact, mean whatever you at the moment please,—an offer to sell you a mine, a cloudburst, a glass of whiskey, a steamboat. This time it meant a stranger clad in black" (133–34).

When whatever one points to takes the place of words, the important question is who does the pointing—or, in western parlance, who has the say. In both of *The Virginian's* plots—the Virginian's conflict with Trampas and his courtship of Molly—the Virginian does.[2] Only nominally a cattle rustler, Trampas is actually "a talking enemy" (292), and as Lee Clark Mitchell has pointed out, the Virginian's conflicts with him all concern words far more than cattle (*Westerns* 100–01). When Trampas calls the Virginian a son-of-a-———, the Virginian forces him to back down; when Trampas "spoke disrespectfully" of Molly (68), the Virginian demands that he say he lied; when Trampas tries to talk the cowboys into mutiny, the Virginian bests him by telling a tall tale; and when Trampas talks against his good name, the Virginian silences him in a shoot-out.

The courtship of Molly is a variation upon the same theme of language use. "You call yourself a man, I suppose," Molly says during their first conversation, announcing a romantic plot that consists of lessons establishing that he has "a right to say" (82).[3] In their first extended conversation, for example, the Virginian demonstrates his facility with social discourse and then asserts his right to define the words "duty" and "stranger." Having rescued Molly from a stage mired in a river, he disputes her use of "stranger" (though she doesn't know his name) and asserts that her duty is to him: "Don't you think pretendin' yu' don't know a man, his name's nothin', but *him,*—a man whom you were glad enough to let assist yu' when somebody was needed—don't you think that's mighty close to hide-and-seek them children plays?" (82). Reinforcing his lessons, the Tenderfoot reflects that the Virginian's "is the only kind of equality which I recognize" (126); Mrs. Taylor lectures the schoolmarm on "kind" as "a word you shouldn't use, my dear," for Molly has not recognized kindness in the Virginian (203); and the judge instructs Molly in the use of "principle" by arguing that the Virginian's hanging of a man demonstrated the principle of self-governing men (272–74).

Like "duty" and "stranger," "kindness" and "principle" are embodied not in words but in Wister's hero, all reflections upon language that reinforce the single lesson Molly learns—to distrust words and to place her allegiance in the Virginian. It is a ritualized, formal transfer of authority for which Wister isolates both Molly and the Virginian from society, thereby protecting them from gender roles. Having been injured in an Indian attack, the Virginian's weakened condition provides an occasion for his masculine reserve to melt as he is nursed by Molly. His tongue released by unconsciousness and his meaning translated by Mrs. Taylor, the Virginian at last has the "say" with Molly; his muttered words are "fragments of revelation" that disprove her right to language and establish his own. Hearing him utter the name "Trampas," Molly believes he has got her name wrong until Mrs. Taylor tells her that the Virginian had protected the honor of her name by forcing Trampas to retract his words against her. Whereas she previously had defined her "duty" as to her students and had called him a "stranger," she now realizes that the Virginian exemplified duty in defending her and that she is the stranger in the West (211).

As the Virginian slips more deeply into delirium, his revelations become more personal. The Virginian's cry of the name "Steve" reveals a "deep inward tide of feeling" in him, and though he sometimes "broke out in the language of the round-up," never "did the delirium run into . . . intimate, coarse matters. . . . The cow-puncher had lived like his kind, but his natural daily thoughts were clean, and came from the untamed but unstained mind of a man" (210–12). As if looking into the spring from which water flows, Wister describes seeing into the Virginian's character as into language's source. Revelations continue as the Virginian recovers and talks of the books Molly reads to him. Then "the slow cow-puncher unfolded his notions of masculine courage and modesty (though he did not deal in such high-sounding names), and Molly forgot everything to listen to him, as he forgot himself and his inveterate shyness and grew talkative to her" (219). This "luxury of discussion" (218) is notably one-sided, for the Virginian speaks and Molly listens.

The Virginian's talk does more than transfer Molly's allegiance to him, for his authority dispossesses Molly of language. Emptying her mind of everything and opening herself to his, Molly ceases to exist in her own right (if she ever did) and serves merely as a vehicle for the Virginian to express himself. The climax of the scene occurs when he says his thoughts about love, putting "it clear" how it is with him. By doing so, the Virginian claims his right to "love," the word basic to the action of the romantic plot. Hearing him speak about love, she responds in broken phrases—"But . . . But I—you ought—please try to keep me happy," then sinks by his chair, wordlessly hiding her face on his knees. As Molly is dispossessed of spoken words, so she is dispossessed of written ones. When they each write to Bennington to tell Molly's family of their engagement, the Virginian completes his letter naturally and easily, but Molly is unable to begin, for "her mind was among a litter of broken sentences" (229).

The novel's two plots come together when the characters go to town, where the Virginian will kill Trampas and marry Molly. Meeting the Virginian and Molly entering town, Scipio warns his friend of Trampas by saying simply, "Don't change your clothes." Misunderstanding, Molly replies that he's dusty and countrified, "But the Virginian had taken Scipio's meaning. *'Don't change your clothes.'* Innocent Molly appreciated these words no more than the average reader who reads a masterpiece, complacently unaware that its style differs from that of the morning paper" (288–89).

But—and here is the apparent paradox—the Virginian has excelled in rhetoric only to disprove words as inadequate and to displace language by embodying meaning in himself and his actions. Secondary characters establish a principle of meaning by silently pointing to objects in order to communicate; that is, they increasingly defer to the Virginian until it is the fact of himself—undiluted by words—that emerges. Growth of the Tenderfoot is measured by his increasing respect for silence, from his loquacious entry into the West to his maturity, when, following the hanging of Steve, he is among the men bonded in silence. The judge talks to Molly about hanging, though "as all men know, he also knew that many things should be done in this world in silence, and that talking about them is a mistake" (271). The Virginian embodies what "all men know," for "it was his code never to speak ill of any man to any woman. Men's quarrels were not for women's ears. In his scheme, good women were to know only a fragment of men's lives" (284).

The climax to which *The Virginian* builds consists of three showdowns in which the Virginian silences speech and displaces language.[4] The Virginian's first showdown occurs with the bishop and is cast in terms of religion as the bishop speaks God's Word by quoting from the Bible, "Thou shalt not kill" and "vengeance is mine." Contradicting such maxims, however, is the fact of the Virginian, who is described as a good while Trampas is an evil. In light of such a fact, the biblical text is at best irrelevant and possibly corrupting. When the Virginian ends the discussion by declaring, "There's no good in words. Good-by," it is left to the bishop only to give his benediction, "God bless him!" (298).

The Virginian's second showdown occurs with Molly and is cast in terms of the language of love. Again, the Virginian faces down a misuse of words. When Molly objects, "It's murder!" he tells her sternly, "don't call it that name," and when she threatens him with breaking off their engagement, he breaks off their conversation by saying "Good-by," and "at that word she was at his feet, clutching him. 'For my sake,' she begged him. 'For my sake'" (298). As the vanquished bishop sanctions the Virginian by the words "God bless him," so the vanquished Molly sanctions the Virginian after he has shot Trampas, "Oh, thank God!" (303).

The most radical displacement occurs when, in the third showdown, the Virginian confronts Trampas. Framed by short statements of spoken dialogue, the action in this spare account occurs in silence and is described in only three sentences, creating the effect of pure experience unmediated by language:

> "It is quite awhile after sunset," he heard himself say.
> A wind seemed to blow his sleeve off his arm, and he replied to it, and saw Trampas pitch forward. He saw Trampas raise his arm from the ground and fall again, and lie there this time, still. A little smoke was rising from the pistol on the ground, and he looked at his own, and saw the smoke flowing upward out of it.
> "I expect that's all," he said aloud. (302)

The Tenderfoot is absent and the narrator is silent, so that what remains is the fact of the Virginian, neither an object of another's description nor the subject of his own. By framing the action, the brief spoken sentences intensify the quiet surrounding the action. When the Virginian *hears himself say* that sunset is past, his detachment from his own words suggests that he has withdrawn from language. What follows resembles a pantomime in which the gaze displaces both verbal and physical pointing: the verb "replied" refers not to spoken words but to the action of sighting and shooting a gun, and the repetition of verbs "saw" and "looked" describes a gaze so powerful that it causes a physical effect. The Virginian saw Trampas and looked at his pistol, and as if in response, Trampas pitches forward and smoke flows from the gun.[5] His comment, "I expect that's all," conveys the double meaning of "all": the action is final, and its meaning is inclusive.[6]

The shoot-out establishes the authority of the Virginian not only to arbitrate meaning but also to create it. This lesson is reinforced on the honeymoon, a romanticized version of the use of silencing to establish ascendancy over language. Molly's initiation into marriage is also an initiation into silence that begins when the Virginian tells her "nothing" about where they are going for their honeymoon, that is put into effect when he replies with silence to questions to which "she knew that he had thoughts and intentions which she must wait to learn" (305), and that is achieved when "full solitude was around them, so that their words grew scarce" (306) and "she was not thinking." Through this principle of silencing, Molly comes to serve as self-consciousness in the Virginian, and the rest of the scene dramatizes the Virginian's new consciousness of himself. Whereas he had gone alone to the island, "so little was it his way to scan himself, his mind, or his feelings (unless some action called for it) that he first learned his love of the place through his love of her" (305).

As in the shoot-out with Trampas, the principle of meaning is pantomime, now modified so that it is Molly who serves as the projection of the Virginian's will. He points and she sees; the two actions are one: "he drew rein and pointed" and "she looked, and saw the island"; "he pointed upward" and she saw the high mountains they had approached. As she is the projection of his will, the landscape is an emanation of it, the island and the mountains appearing as if in response to his thought. "This is how I have dreamed it would happen," he says (306).

The honeymoon passage is infused with biblical allusions, culminating in echoes of Genesis through which Wister makes explicit the novel's concern with creativity and origins. Leaving Medicine Bow, the Tenderfoot enters "a land without end, on a space across which Noah and Adam might come straight from Genesis" (8); and for their honeymoon biblical cadences reinforce the idea of being at the origin of things, with a New World emanating from the Virginian as the Logos. "All had been as he had seen it in his thoughts beforehand" (308) in this Divine Creator, for whom to think a thing is to will it into being. The universe is created as the Virginian imagined it: the light of day is followed by the darkness of night, and on the first morning "so did it all happen" that they saw their first sunrise (308).

While it is interesting that Wister alludes to Genesis, what is significant is that he turns the allusion back upon itself, to tell an inverse version of creation. Rather than a principle of generativity by which multiple forms unfold, Wister establishes one of degenerativity by which the many are returned to the one. Molly has ceased to exist in herself, so that by the honeymoon scenes she serves solely as a reason for the Virginian to talk "as he had never talked to any one, not even to himself"; without her, "He never would have guessed so much had been stored away in him, unexpressed till now" (310). Stored away in him is the question "What's the gain in being a man?"; "The trouble is," he says "I am responsible. If that could only be forgot forever by you and me. . . . Often when I have camped here, it has made me want to become the ground, become the water, become the trees, mix with the whole thing. Not know myself from it. Never unmix again" (310). There is, as Forrest G. Robinson has argued, an implicit death wish in this culmination of the romantic action that involves a cowboy resisting marriage as an expression of tension between "the natural and the civilized" in American culture (36), but it concerns more than that. The Virginian has become the Logos of the text: meaning has been concentrated in him to the extent that he acts not only as an authority for language (it is he who establishes the right use of words) but as a source for creation (all was as he had seen it in his thoughts). In his wish to return to earth and to "never unmix again" he extends that pattern of reversal, for he would return creation to its original state. Woman has been reabsorbed into man, and now man would return to earth.

The pattern of withdrawal continues in the novel's concluding scenes. Following his wish to return to earth, we seldom see Wister's hero directly. Instead, the narrator generalizes about the Virginian's trip to Bennington, then in a coda refers to him as "an important man, with a strong grip on many enterprises" (316). He is able to give "his wife" (she no longer has a name of her own) whatever she desires, but he no longer rides with her. Indeed, he no longer rides at all, it would seem, now that "the eldest boy rides the horse Monte." But to safeguard against any notion of succession, the narrator adds that "strictly between ourselves, I think his father is going to live a long while" (317). The effect is of stasis: meaning has been withdrawn from language, and the text has become void and without form. Nothing much can happen after the Virginian withdraws, nor (as Grey and Schaefer demonstrate) after the western heroes who follow him withdraw.

Grey's *Riders of the Purple Sage* is a textbook example of hostility to symbolic language in formulaic Westerns. In the tradition of Wister—indeed, Etulain writes that Grey "imitated the formula of *The Virginian*" (36)— Grey's plot concerns a hero's struggle against the use of words to distort and corrupt, this time by "creed bound . . . creed mad" Mormons. Its romantic interest is Jane Withersteen, who has a good heart but who, having been born Mormon then having inherited great wealth, has served as a blind tool for false creeds. Her blindness is illustrated by her indiscriminate use of the word "love" when she describes her feelings for the evil Mormon bishop, Elder Tull, as well as for her gentile hired hand, Venters. Jane both misuses words and is their victim. Attempting to seduce her with a Mormon doctrine of salvation, Tull tries to make Jane one of his wives; arguing a Mormon doctrine of mercy and forgiveness to Venters, Jane induces him to give up his name, horses, cattle—and his guns, until in desperation he cries out to her, "Talk to me no more of mercy or religion. . . . Give me my guns" (17). In short, things are a mess. Desperate, Jane looks to the distant sage-covered slopes and prays, "Whence cometh my help!" In response, a rider appears and approaches them:

> "*Lassiter!*"
> It was Venters's wondering, thrilling cry that bridged the fateful connection between the rider's singular position and the dreaded name. (12)

Unlike in *The Virginian*, action abounds in *Riders*, where shootings, stampedes, and avalanches blur together in frenzied movement. Like the earlier novel, however, the real problem concerns questions of power and gender in the use of language. Like the Virginian, Lassiter becomes the authority on language use. He tells Jane that Mormons "give names to things—bishops, elders, ministers, Mormonism, duty, faith, glory. . . . I'm a man, an' I know. I name fanatics, followers, blind women, oppressors, thieves, ranches, rustlers, riders" (272). The plot centers on Lassiter opening Jane's eyes to the blindness apparent in her question "who is Lassiter?

He's only a name to me—a terrible name" (20). Jane's conversion consists of seeing the power of that terrible name and then transferring her allegiance to it.

Whereas the primary plot of Jane Withersteen and Lassiter concerns corruption of (and through) language, a second plot suggests the power of naming. After Venters shoots the infamous masked rider who rides with outlaw Oldring's gang, he opens his victim's blouse to examine the wound and realizes that he has shot a woman. Not only silent but unconscious, she is a classic version of the Western's ideal woman, beneath whose independent exterior lies a submissive and passive nature. With echoes of Genesis, Venters watches over Bess as Adam over Eve until on the third day he knows she will live. On the sixth day he realizes that he is everything to her, and he claims her as his "possession." By breathtakingly fantastic plot manipulation, Grey moves the young lovers to a hidden valley where, in the Western's equivalent of pastoral retreat, they commune with nature. Like all the settings of *Riders,* the valley is pure wish fulfillment: there Venters has the power of a man-god. He gives the place the name Surprise Valley; in response, it fulfills its name by surprising him with its secrets. It produces long-abandoned homes of Cliff Dwellers that contain the pots and crocks he and Bess need to set up housekeeping, provides abundant game for their food and entertainment, and offers gold to make them rich.

Both plots hinge upon names. Lassiter seeks the name of the man who abducted his sister, Bess seeks to overcome the shame of being nameless, and Jane must learn that names can be false. Plots resolve when characters finally get the names right. Speaking the confessional words "my father," Jane Withersteen reveals who was responsible for the abduction of Lassiter's sister and humbles herself sufficiently to be worthy of Lassiter (239). Whereas the nameless Bess had been an outcast, learning that her name is Elizabeth Erne means that she is redeemed by family, class, and marriage. Hearing that her name is "Erne," Lassiter claims her as his niece. Accepting her given name of Elizabeth, she reveals the fine blood running in her veins; "by this time to-morrow—you will be Elizabeth Venters," (268) Venters says, signaling that he will complete her redemption by giving her his name in marriage.

Women are named; only men have the right to name, a right that has its own hierarchy. By bestowing names, Venters creates relationships: Surprise Valley as his paradise, Balancing Rock as his destiny, and Elizabeth

Venters as his wife. The more powerful naming is restricted to Lassiter, for it is he who arbitrates the names of love, truth, and justice and, by doing so, arbitrates the values that justify action. His showdown with Jane comes when he assumes authority over language. He demands that she "speak names" of the men who have stolen a little girl, and when she replies "Bishop Tull," he demands that if she wants "to talk to me about him—leave off the Bishop. I don't understand that name, or its use." When Jane reminds him that he had foregone vengeance, he renames the action by re-plying, "Jane, now it's justice" (237).

In a verbal landscape consisting largely of nouns, a single verb is instru-mental—"love." "I love her!" Venters says of Bess to the valley, and then, "I love her! . . . I understand now" (159–60). In the romantic formula "love" is all powerful: to conceive the word is to possess; to say it to another is to transform. Venters initially speaks it only to the valley, for to utter the word to Bess would mean he must marry her, and isolated as they are, no minister is available. In a more complicated version of the same principle, Jane Withersteen's conversion from the false worship of Mormonism to the true worship of Lassiter hinges upon her learning the right use of the word "love." Jane initially believes that "In the whirling gulf of her thought there was yet one shining light to guide her, to sustain her in her hope, and it was that, despite her errors and her frailties and her blindness, she had one absolute and unfaltering hold on ultimate and supreme justice. That was love. 'Love your enemies as yourself!' was a divine word, entirely free from any church or creed" (176). But "love" is a divine word only in tribute to Lassiter—that is the lesson Jane must learn. The melodramatic plot builds to its melodramatic crisis when Jane is on her knees before Lassiter begging him in the name of love not to kill Bishop Dyer, and Lassiter replies, "Woman—don't trifle at words! I love you! An' I'll soon prove it!" (238). As in Wister's novel, so here the hero asserts his right to arbitrate the meaning of "love":

> "I'm changing. . . . My master, be merciful—spare him!"
>
> His answer was a ruthless smile.
>
> She clung the closer to him, and leaned her panting breast on him, and lifted her face to his. "Lassiter, *I do love you!* It's leaped out of my agony. It comes sud-denly with a terrible blow of truth. You are a man! I never knew it till now. Some wonderful change came to me when you buckled on those guns and showed that gray, awful face." (238)

It is not his guns (phallic though they may be) but Lassiter (the man and the name are one) to which Jane must give herself. When Jane and Lassiter might save themselves by sealing themselves in the hidden valley, Lassiter will do so only when Jane calls out, "*Roll the stone! . . . Lassiter, I love you!*" (280). As the Virginian had assumed the power of the Logos, so Lassiter does here. To speak his terrible name is to reveal the power of Logos as "the Word [that] has within itself the power of fulfillment" (Bouyer 466), not only announcing *but producing events.* Thus Jane's utterance "I love you, Lassiter," is the dramatic disclosure of the name as divine, a secular, ro- manticized version of "the revelation of the divine Name . . . that Moses received in the burning bush on Mount Horeb (Ex. 3)" (Bouyer 466).

As Jane's relationship with Lassiter and Bess's with Venters involve a pu- rifying of the word "love," so Venters's relationship with Bess involves a clarifying of a word. Hearing Bess say that she is "Oldring's girl," Venters thinks her the outlaw's mistress, whereas Bess meant she was his daughter. Language is suspect because a single word can mean so many different things; like the Mormons, words are "full of tricks" (111). "Girl" can mean innocent daughter or sullied mistress, "elder" can mean older person or church official, and "father" can mean loving parent or defiler of women. Amid a language that is unstable and potentially chaotic, only the name Lassiter is fixed and reliable.

Even though language is unstable, as in *The Virginian,* metaphorical meanings are not expanded. In *Riders* meaning contracts from the chaos of the beginning scenes, wherein Jane thinks that she "loves" her bishop and her hired hand, that "justice" resides in the Mormon creed, and that "mercy" is served when she talks a man out of his guns, to the end, wherein the meaning of love, justice, and mercy resides solely in the West- ern's hero.

Riders accomplishes this transfer of authority with an appeal to the emotions and suspicion of reason. Characters revel in "undefined" emo- tions, stir to "unintelligible" feelings, and quake before "nameless" fears; they suffer as they love "without understanding why" (218). Indeed, it is *not* understanding that qualifies experience as desirable—that is, pure.[7] As always in the formula Western, gender plays its part, for the "purity" of seeing directly, without the interference of thought, is the overriding mea- sure of a woman's worth. Venters comes to value Bess when he can almost believe that she, like Molly in *The Virginian,* "had no thought at all" (113), and he comes to love her when, her "watching, seeing gaze" resting upon him, he realizes that "she saw as the primitive woman without thought" (116). Similarly, Jane Withersteen proves her worthiness by relinquishing thought. Realizing the truth of her feeling for Lassiter, she can still play and dream, "but when I attempt serious thought I'm dazed. I don't think" (225). As does the ideal woman, so does the ideal life reside in primitive experience undiluted by thought. Reflecting upon the appeal of Surprise Valley, Venters muses, "—how glorious it would be to live here always and never think again" (160), a fantasy that Jane and Lassiter fulfill when they seal themselves inside it.

The bewildering effect of chance events and the blurring effect of the setting's generalities reinforce the lesson that thinking is a waste of time. Venters, trying to understand why he is lost amid endless sage and wilderness canyons, realizes that "he did not care," upon which, "tired out by stress of thought, he fell asleep" (40). Later, when he has time to think about his "inexplicable feeling of change," he concludes that he "could not catch the illusive thing that has sadly perplexed as well as elevated his spirit" (91). Venters could be speaking for the frustrated reader seeking any semblance of reason in the plot or any reality in the setting.

As visual markers, names characterize the visual nature of the Western, where experience is overwhelmingly filtered through sight.[8] In considering the fact that he had once loved Jane and now loved Bess, Venters reflects that "His affection for Jane Withersteen had not changed in the least; nevertheless, he seemed *to view* it from another angle and *see* it as another thing—what, he could not exactly define" (111; emphases mine). Lassiter learns Jane's secret by *seeing* it, not by hearing it from her; and the "strange, unintelligible curiosity" Venters experiences before killing Bess's father is "to *see* Oldring alive" (216; emphasis mine).

In *Riders* the most reliable way of orienting oneself is not by reasoning but by seeing things, naming them, and remembering how they look. Although naming is a linguistic act, it focuses attention on the physical object and does not meditate on its meaning. By its simplicity, naming becomes an extension of seeing and pointing, as Venters's approach to Surprise Valley illustrates. Finding himself in a valley about which extends innumerable canyon mouths, Venters recognizes that "There was no reason for a choice of which one to enter" (42), so he arbitrarily rides into one. There "chance . . . directed him to a probable hiding-place" (84), a canyon guarded at its outlet by a huge boulder. Fixing the canyon and boulder in his memory (as well as in the text), he names the canyon Surprise Valley and the boulder

Balancing Rock. Fixing them in the action, Venters marks the rim wall with two stones and "a keen-sighted, remembering gaze" (87), then ties his scarf upon a branch at its base. Like the stones and scarf, names are markers by which one might locate a thing and return to it.

To see is to remove the masks and disguises that *Riders* contains in comic plenitude. Venters takes off Bess's mask to find a woman; Lassiter strips away Jane's authority to reveal her helplessness; Jane sees beneath the names of "Bishop" and "father" to recognize evil desires. Indeed, in *Riders* the Mormons comprise a community of "masked feeling—strange secretiveness—expressionless expression of mystery and hidden power" (211). "[S]eeing truly" is to remove the mask of language to reveal the pure emotion behind it, conveyed by the novel's endless description and exposition. Rather than metaphor, with its expansive connotations, simile works here to reduce emotions to objects and displace urges and impulses onto landscape and horses. The absurdity of the equivalencies stills any critical involvement. Bess "was like Surprise Valley—wild and beautiful" (147); defiance against Mormonism stiffens "like a steel bar" in Jane Withersteen (7); after Venters shoots Oldring, his "being" raged "like a fiery steed with ice-shod feet . . . rioting through his blood" (218), and so on, with mind-numbing profusion.

Settings similarly still thought and appeal to emotion. Surprise Valley is a male fantasy of female space: a canyon entered by its mouth, a secret recess to which Venters alone has access and where he enjoys a drifting existence apart from experience. As Tompkins has written, the novel's landscape is "engorged" with sexual energy (*West of Everything* 169). All that sexual energy makes the severe restrictions upon creativity in *Riders* significant. Grey's novel limits the authority and power of naming to the two male characters, and it excludes generativity/procreativity altogether.

With only slight variations, this pattern of linguistic regression reappears in *Shane*. Though arguably more sophisticated than *Riders, Shane* is similarly suspicious of and hostile to language. Whereas Grey presents words as full of tricks, Schaefer presents them as frivolous, but like his predecessors Schaefer treats language as inadequate and suspicious. Shane talks about women's fashions but not about the important things, as Bob Starrett (the narrator who is nostalgically recalling his childhood encounter with Shane) recognizes: "He was a man like father in whom a boy could believe in the simple knowing that what was beyond comprehension was still clean and solid and right" (91).

As in *The Virginian* and *Riders,* in *Shane* the purest experience is unsullied by language. For the Western's obligatory bonding scene, Starrett and Shane work together to remove the stump on the Starrett place. With their ax blows "talking" to the stump (101), the sound of direct action replaces words. When characters do resort to language, they use it sparingly and to point to an object. Peering under the stump they had been chopping hour after hour, Starrett utters the single words of the scene, "Must be a tap-root" (103); telling Bob how to shoot a gun, Shane says, "Just point it, low and quick and easy, like pointing a finger" (139); and to teach him values, Shane tells Bob to look at the valley: "Hold it in your mind like this. It's a lovely land, Bob. A good place to be a boy and grow straight inside as a man should. . . . My gaze followed his, and I saw our valley as though for the first time and the emotion in me was more than I could stand." (250).

Unlike other characters' use of language—muted and spare as it is—to point to objects outside themselves, Shane uses it to point to himself, so that the words take on his own physical reality. When asked if he knows about violence, Shane replies simply, "I do," as if wedding himself to the idea; then "Shane let the words lie there, plain and short and ugly" (218). Similarly, when Shane tells Marian to "Tell him no man need be ashamed of being beat by Shane," Bob reflects that "the name sounded queer like that, the man speaking of himself," not a boast because "He was stating a fact, simple and elemental as the power that dwelled in him" (245).

As in other Westerns, silencing in *Shane* occurs physically, when the hero kills the outlaw, and also metaphorically, when others relinquish language in tribute to him. The action builds to Shane's confrontation with Stark Wilson, a confrontation framed by reflections upon Shane displacing and disproving language. As Shane rides to town, Bob reflects that he "was the symbol of all the dim, formless imaginings of danger and terror in the untested realm of human potentialities beyond my understanding" (249). As Shane rides away, Bob realizes "that no word or thought could hold him" (263). Shane has appropriated the experience of the novel: he/it (the man and the name are one) are in the places and people he leaves behind:

> I guess that is all there is to tell. The folks in town and the kids at school liked to talk about Shane, to spin tales and speculate about him. I never did. . . .
>
> For mother was right. He was there. He was there in our place and in us. . . .
>
> And when I would hear the men in town talking among themselves and trying

to pin him down to a definite past, I would smile quietly to myself. . . . But when they talked like that, I simply smiled because I knew he could have been none of these.

He was the man who rode into our little valley out of the heart of the great glowing West and when his work was done rode back whence he had come and he was Shane. (273–74)

The effect is yet another form of the linguistic regression seen in *The Virginian* and *Riders*. Meaning has been concentrated in a single figure, and that figure concentrated in a name. SHANE. With deific power and as the sole authority for and source of meaning, the character has become the Word; when he disappears, he takes that authority and possibility of meaning with him. What remains after Shane has left? Characters find themselves inside a fence secured by the post Shane set; when they try to move it, they cannot, and they understand that "we have roots here now that we can never tear loose."

The fence is an image of confinement and stasis reinforced by the larger setting of the valley, and of the text itself. "I guess that is all there is to tell," Bob concludes, then explains that he never talked about Shane, for he could have been none of the stories about him. "He was there in our place and in us. . . . he was Shane." Thus the book ends with "Shane" as the name in which meaning has been concentrated.

The pattern seems clear.[9] I am suggesting that in these novels meaning works by a process of degeneration: the use of language reverts to ever simpler principles until it resides solely in the hero as Logos, the Word. The hero assumes this authority of meaning in an absolute and static way. In this respect, the formula Western represents American literature's most radically regressive response to the charge to create a national epic or (in the metaphorical terms so expressive of issues of creativity) to give birth to a nation. This pattern is especially dramatic when seen in contrast with two related conceptions of language: the Greek/Jewish/Christian Logos and the Native American oral tradition.

The Western sprang from a Eurocentric tradition in which Logos and the Word are aligned with creativity and generation.[10] From the Greek Stoics to Christian doctrines, the Logos is associated with creativity and generativity and with an unfolding of an idea in manifold form as a world and meaning without end. It is the capacity for generations of a plant to produce unique blossoms and of a human family to create individuals; it is also the capacity of language to create the infinite variety of meaning in metaphor. Logos comes from the root of the Greek verb *lego,* meaning "to say," a root that suggests the active, generative, and ever-changing forms emanating from it. In Greek and Christian doctrines the Logos is a "conception of a germinative principle . . . which manifests itself in the universe" (*Encyclopaedia* 135). In Jewish-Alexandrian theology, a deity lies at this source of the generative power of the thought expressed as word. "God spoke the word, and the worlds were made; then at once His spirit, or breath, gives life to what the Word creates." (*Encyclopaedia* 135). The Old Testament account of Genesis is of setting in motion procreativity when God said, "let the earth bring forth living creatures according to their kinds" and then said to man and woman, "be fruitful and multiply." In the New Testament the principle of generativity is personalized when the Gospel of John describes the Logos as God, the creative Word, who took on flesh in the man Jesus Christ: "In the beginning was the Word, and the Word was with God, and the Word was God" (*New Oxford,* John 1.1); and the *Word* (Logos) of God is more than speech; it is God in action, creating (Gen. 1.3; Ps. 33.6), revealing (Amos 3.7–8), redeeming (Ps. 107–20).

Whereas the Logos of Greek philosophy and the Bible gives rise to generativity and creativity, the Western's Logos restricts meaning, denies generativity, and excludes procreativity.[11] Superficially the Western's hostility toward change is demonstrated in the hero's single status and laconic manner, characteristics long acknowledged by critics,[12] but this hostility is also demonstrated in the text's hostility to metaphor. Through a pattern of silencings, the text disproves the varied possibilities of symbolic and metaphoric language and returns meaning to a single concentrated authority—the Virginian, Lassiter, Shane—a static name/word/hero that displaces alternatives and defies change.

The novels' conclusions illustrate the implications of this regressive principle. *The Virginian*'s last major scene ends with the Virginian's wish to return to earth, never to unmix again, and though the novel's coda makes him the exception among Western heroes in establishing that he has had the first of "many children," these progeny exist as the merest aside to a description of an all-powerful figure who is occupying himself elsewhere. Grey and Schaefer are more blatant in their depiction of stasis: *Riders* concludes with Lassiter sealed in Deception Pass, its outlet "closed forever"

(280); and *Shane*, with the hero riding into the country until "he was gone," after which the narrator reflects that "that is all there is to tell" (264, 273).

When we look past the Western's written antecedents to the native oral traditions that it ignores and, in doing so, would erase, the Western's hostility to creativity is even more dramatic. The orality central to the Native American tradition is "the other side of the miracle of language," (81) N. Scott Momaday writes in *Man Made of Words*, in that it treats the intrinsically efficacious role of language with profound awe and its tentativeness with profound respect. "Nothing exists beyond the influence of words"; by language, we imagine ourselves into being, for "Words are the names of Creation. To give one's word is to give oneself, wholly—to place a name, than which nothing is more sacred, in the balance. One stands for his word; his word stand for him" (104). Because "words and the things that are made of words are tentative, extreme care is granted to language in an oral tradition. A song, or a prayer, or a story, is always but one generation removed from extinction. The risk of loss is constant, therefore, and language is never to be taken for granted" (28).

The dichotomy informing the history of Indian-white relations is realized by this difference in language (52). The written tradition gives an illusion of permanence and, by doing so, encourages indifference to language and blindness to the sacred aspect of words that would erase the oral tradition from mainstream culture. However, the oral tradition inheres within itself the knowledge that "a song, or a prayer, or a story, is always but one remove from extinction," and because the risk of loss is constant, "language is never to be taken for granted" (28). In an oral tradition, the formulation of meaning is given ritualistic sanction in storytelling: when the storyteller has created himself and us, his listeners, in the creative act of story, he resurrects in his words meanings that are vital and complex and that are as tentative as breath itself.

Man Made of Words exists as a series of moments—prayers chanted, stories told, and experiences remembered, all as nearly as possible told, albeit in a written text. In this manner the text embodies itself, approximating an oral tradition in which words are powerful, beautiful, and magical and—by the complexity of language—achieve their great vitality and inexhaustible power. "Where language touches the earth, there is the holy, there is the sacred. In our deepest intelligence we know this: that names and being are indivisible. That which has no name cannot truly be said to exist, to be" (124). Describing his existence as "a man made of words," Momaday retraces the act of language by which we imagine ourselves into being and by which to speak truly is to speak of the deepest, oldest racial memories. In re-creating the vision of that memory, the speaker re-creates himself as "a spiritual sense so ancient as to be primordial, so pervasive as to be definitive—not an idea, but a perception on the far side of ideas, an act of understanding as original and originative as the Word" (52). Significantly, Momaday re-creates himself as one whose identity fluidly emerges from a long-standing and ever-shifting web of communal stories; unlike the Western hero, he discovers meaning within language.

The Western shares with its antecedents in written and oral traditions Genesis as a site of origins for the Word, but there the similarity stops.[13] Whereas the biblical Genesis sets in motion a principle of procreativity by calling forth living creatures from the earth, creating woman from man, calling upon them to "be fruitful and multiply," and granting to them access to knowledge, the Western genesis reabsorbs woman into man, withdraws knowledge, and returns man to matter. And where the Native American genesis has its profound, mysterious origin in the creative act of language, the Western flattens language and removes the mystery. In the end, meaning has been restricted to the Word (the Virginian, Lassiter, Shane), and that Word has been returned to the earth, with the Virginian involved in his enterprises, Lassiter sealed in a secret canyon, and Shane absorbed in a valley. What remains is the silence and stasis of a world from which creativity has withdrawn.

To end with biblical allusions and native spirituality is to misrepresent, for despite the frequency of such allusions, these Westerns are, as Tompkins has argued, profoundly secular. They (and the Western more generally) are concerned with power rather than spirituality, and rather than serving a god in action, their heroes usurp the power of creativity. It is, therefore, with political terms that I wish to end my discussion of them. The tension in their treatment of language contrasts fear of instability with faith in a single authority and resolves these by concentrating meaning in the Word, a concentration accomplished by appealing to emotion and holding reason in suspicion. Power that resides absolutely within a single authority is despotism; an appeal to emotion and prejudice plus hostility to reason is demagoguery.

The Western is about language far more than it is about land, and its claims concern the right to make a myth far more than they do to settle a frontier. It is a claim to author/ity in the most basic sense—that is, to author an identity for a nation. It is a claim that warrants our engagement with how meaning is made and unmade. Recalling Molly Fawcett from the dead, and rereading *The Virginian, Riders,* and *Shane* with her as my companion, I grieve for her anew, for she didn't have a chance. Of course, that is the point. She is Jean Stafford's favorite child, and as such, she is the one that Stafford entrusted with her understanding that revision, in the words of Adrienne Rich, "is for women more than a chapter in cultural history: it is an act of survival" (35).

Robinson's Politics of Meditation

"We have busied ourselves so long exploding assumptions that it is by now an interesting experiment to try reassembling them again in plausible forms." MARILYNNE ROBINSON, "Fiction in Review"

With her phenomenally successful 1980 novel *Housekeeping,* Marilynne Robinson announced her engagement with epistemological and political questions of the literary West. In her matter *Housekeeping* recalls the staples of the literary West—lighting out for the territory, leaving civilization behind, and embracing a life of wandering. The difference—called radical by some—is that Robinson's wanderers are women. Yet it is in her manner that Robinson is most radical, for she has imported to the literary West a meditative tradition that disproves any notion of that West as a site of new beginnings. She does so by reencoding the birth metaphor into her western narrative, then extending its implications backward until it becomes a myth of origin to which we have access through metaphor. Unlike the formula Western with its hostility to language, *Housekeeping* privileges language as a way of knowing, and in her subsequent writing Robinson articulates the role of language in political issues of epic proportions. Whereas Jean Stafford wrote about the literary Western as an act of survival for women, Marilynne Robinson appropriates the patterns of the Western as an act of survival for the world.

"My name is Ruth." The opening sentence of *Housekeeping* announces the allusive depth to Robinson's surface plot. Her narrator's name echoes the Old Testament and the cadence of her sentence mirrors Melville's opening for *Moby-Dick*. With the pull of allusion functioning as an undertow, recent historical episodes are present only as faint traces and fleeting memories: moving west, building a sod house, and laying a railroad are recalled as incidents that, once acknowledged, vanish in the narrative as completely as the train carrying Ruth's grandfather vanished in Fingerbone Lake. Men, who figure so largely in history, similarly vanish. Though Ruth sometimes attaches a vestigial "Mrs." to her grandmother's name, it is with no apparent connection to a husband; and though Ruth possesses two snapshots of her "putative father," they are of a man about whom she has "no memory at all" (14). "I didn't intend to leave men out originally," Robinson reflected, "but at a certain point I realized there were not going to be male characters, and I thought that's fine" ("Life of Perished Things" 176).

What there was going to be was a family of women. Drawn ever more strongly toward Genesis by the cadences as well as the content of her reflection, Ruth recounts that "I grew up with my younger sister, Lucille, under the care of my grandmother, Mrs. Sylvia Foster, and when she died, of her sisters-in-law, Misses Lily and Nona Foster, and when they fled, of her daughter, Mrs. Sylvia Fisher" (3). Having traced her lineage through women, Ruth's theology follows suit. In the early years of their childhoods, Ruth and Lucille live with their grandmother, a magisterial figure who is omnipresence rather than person and who tends her orchard and presides over the children with silent watchfulness. Released from the linearity of narrative, Ruth begins her inward drama of memory.

That inward drama begins when the biblical story of the Fall reappears as Ruth's story of her grandmother's death. As in Genesis, separation yields knowledge, which is to say the conflict of the mind that results from awareness of loss. Arriving to care for the orphaned girls, Ruth's two great-aunts appear as female versions of Beckett's Gogo and Didi in that they serve as a narrative bridge by creating an awareness of need—an existential gap, one might say. They flee in relief upon the arrival of Sylvie, Ruth's aunt and her grandmother's third daughter. "With Sylvie, I simply got the idea," Robinson has said. "I don't know how it happened. I suddenly *knew* certain things about her. . . . she was an atmosphere before she was any specific character" (qtd. in Pinsker 126). In *Housekeeping*, Sylvie functions as the private inner self, the alternative to the conforming public self represented by Lucille—not so much a character as a form of self-address by which the dramatic action of Ruth's memory unfolds.

Reflections upon Sylvie set Ruth's meditation on its radical course. As a catalyst there are the ordinary activities of housekeeping made extraordinary by reversal, for Sylvie's idea of housekeeping is to let nature in rather than to keep it at bay: "She preferred it sunk in the very element it was meant to exclude. We had crickets in the pantry, squirrels in the eaves, sparrows in the attic" (99). Given such a premise, the surface plot moves inexorably toward dispossession. Lucille, fixing her sights on respectability and increasingly embarrassed at her sister's and aunt's eccentricities, eventually leaves them to live in town with the high-school home economics teacher. Ruth, ever more alone with Sylvie, gradually assumes habits of vagrancy, and the townspeople, concerned over Ruth's welfare, begin custody proceedings. To remain together Ruth and Sylvie light fire to their house one night and set off across the railroad bridge to take up a life of wandering.

Such a synopsis of *Housekeeping* is akin to summarizing *Moby-Dick* as a man's hunt for a whale, however, for it is not events but rather reflections structured as extended metaphors that make up both novels. Whereas Melville extended and pushed forward the metaphor of a hunt, Robinson extends and pushes backward the metaphor of birth until it delivers itself into a new articulation.[1]

How might one reenact one's birth? Imagine oneself at conception? Conceive of one's self before creation? These are the questions to which Robinson responds in *Housekeeping*. Whereas the biblical Genesis establishes a forward movement of creation *ex nihilo* driven by acts that divide and separate (God makes heaven and earth out of nothing, then separates darkness from light, matter from air, woman from man), *Housekeeping* reverses the movement. It returns light to darkness, form to void, and the many to the one when Ruth pursues the memory of a lake and its associations with birth until she reaches the void and discovers the loneliness from which arises the need of analogue. *Housekeeping* is, I am suggesting, a record of a mind finding what will suffice. Robinson draws upon spiritual exercises basic to three centuries of meditative poetry to address the central problem of our time—the survival of a living planet.

The meditative poem is, Louis Martz writes, "a work that creates an interior drama of the mind; this dramatic action is usually . . . created by some form of self-address, in which the mind grasps firmly a problem or situation deliberately evoked by the memory, brings it forward toward the full light of consciousness, and concludes with a moment of illumination, where the speaker's self has, for a time, found an answer to its conflicts" (*Poetry of Meditation* 330). The poem of meditation was given form in the spiritual exercises of St. Ignatius; adopted by seventeenth-century British poets—Southwell, Donne, Crashaw, and Herbert; transplanted to America by Puritans such as Edward Taylor; and continued in Emerson, Emily Dickinson, and Wallace Stevens, who in "Of Modern Poetry" provided the "perfect definition" as

> The poem of the mind in the act of finding
> What will suffice (174–75)

What these poets have in common is their deliberate evocation of a threefold meditative structure consisting of memory, analysis, and understanding. A prelude to meditation characteristically consists of a composition of place, in which the author calls upon the reader to imagine "a concrete, dramatic setting with which the meditative action may develop" (Martz, *Poem of the Mind* 36). The meditative exercise itself consists of three "operations of the mind." First, in Robinson's words, "memory makes the essential choices; it is the inventory of meaning" in recalling the imaginary composition (qtd. in Pinsker 120). Second, the reason engages in the analytical acts of understanding; and third, the will draws forth emotions and acts conforming to that which the understanding has meditated. A conclusion characteristically consists of a colloquy in which the three faculties, now integrated by the meditative exercise, make up a self engaged in conversation. In the seventeenth century that conversation was with God, but in modern times it usually takes the more secular form of the inner self addressing the whole self or the reader.[2] For Robinson, it takes the form of the self in conversation with the landscape.

Adaptations and inventions upon the meditative threefold structure are as varied as its individual practitioners. The meditative exercise allows for fluidity of form; the vehicle may be a sermon, an essay, a sonnet, or (as for *Housekeeping*) a prose-poem presented as a novel. Along with allowing fluidity of form, the meditative exercise ensures enormous flexibility by calling for a language "based on that of common men, *but including whatever in its own experience is unique and individual*" (Martz, *Poetry of Meditation* 323; emphasis mine). From the outset, Robinson was aware of bringing her individual experience to *Housekeeping,* which she conceived as "a novel about the West, in the sense that that's the part of the country where I grew up. . . . my own experience of living in a Western family was matriarchal, and I think this is unusual," and so she thought of creating "a world that had the feeling of . . . femaleness about it to the extent that my experience did" ("An Interview" 233). Robinson, who received a doctoral degree in English literature, also brought a distinctive literary and learned allusiveness to her writing of *Housekeeping*.

When asked about her influences, Robinson refers not to particulars of gender, place, or education but rather to the meditative tradition by which she reflected upon those particulars. Reading Melville, Dickinson, Thoreau, and Stevens was "like finding a genetic strand that opens a whole genealogy" ("An Interview" 239), she said in one interview. Her explanation of this affinity serves well as a definition of the meditative tradition: "Nothing in literature appeals to me more than the rigor with which they fasten on problems of language, of consciousness—bending form to their purposes, ransacking ordinary speech and common experience, rummaging through the exotic and recondite . . . always, to borrow a phrase from Wallace Stevens, in the act of finding what will suffice. . . . I believe they wished to declare the intrinsic dignity of all experience and to declare the senses bathed in revelation—true, serious revelation, the kind that terrifies" ("Writers" 30). When Robinson described *Housekeeping* as "a meditation on that lake and the memories that accompany it," she not only places her prose-poem within that tradition but also invites her readers to find through it the genetic strand that will open a genealogy to discourse today.

"One is always aware of the lake in Fingerbone, or the deeps of the lake, the lightless, airless waters below." Ruth thus begins her composition of place:

> When the ground is plowed in the spring, cut and laid open, what exhales from the furrows but that same, sharp, watery smell. The wind is watery, and all the pumps and creeks and ditches smell of water unalloyed by any other element. At the foundation is the old lake, which is smothered and nameless and altogether black. Then there is Fingerbone, the lake of charts and photographs, which is permeated by sunlight and sustains green life and innumerable fish. . . . And above that, the lake that rises in the spring and turns the grass dark and coarse as reeds. And above that the water suspended in sunlight, sharp as the breath of an animal, which brims inside this circle of mountains. (9)

As the composition of place ensures the specific and dramatic setting from which the meditative action of a poem may develop, so Robinson's meditation upon the lake in Fingerbone sets the problem and establishes the premise for the meditative action in *Housekeeping*. Whereas the biblical Genesis proceeds from a premise of "in the beginning," the nonhieratic central proposition of Robinson's genesis is an ancient lake residing "At the foundation," from which life emerges by transmutation rather than by division and separation. Water moves from liquid to gas and from ground to air as it arises from "the lightless, airless waters below"; it issues forth as the breath of Earth; upon meeting sunlight, it "sustains green life and innumerable fish"; frozen in winter, it flows again in the spring and "turns the grass dark and coarse as reeds." Suspended in sunlight as air, it envelops the planet, ever-present in inhaling and exhaling motions "sharp as the breath of an animal" (9).

Robinson's composition of place also fulfills an epistemological function in that she conceives of the lake as a symbol so powerful that it functions in her narrative as a gravitational field to which the characters, the plot, and language itself are attracted. Fragmented and multiple images collapse into one another as if pulled downward and inward toward their genesis, and genesis itself is returned to its Latin and Greek meanings of generation, origin, and birth.

Sylvie, the dramatic form of Ruth's self-address, sets the extended metaphor in motion when, newly arrived in Fingerbone, "she sat there in a wooden chair in the white kitchen, sustaining all our stares with the placid modesty of a virgin who has conceived, her happiness . . . palpable" (49). Gendered connotations of conception (women conceive a pregnancy; men conceive ideas) converge, and the enlarged, encompassing "conception" lies behind the expanded metaphor of birth. As Sylvie's housekeeping provides the catalyst for the surface plot, so her silence provides the catalyst for the meditation pushing that metaphor. Responding to the inner self involves what Robinson elsewhere calls "hearing silence," by "an intense, continuous, and typically wordless conversation between attentive people and the landscape they inhabit" ("Hearing Silence" 149).

A reprise of the biblical flood provides an exercise in hearing silence. "It's like the end of the world!" Sylvie comments, then falls silent. "Guessing that she must be listening to something, we were silent, too," Ruth reflects, then describes what follows: "The lake still thundered and groaned, the flood waters still brimmed and simmered. When we did not move or speak, there was no proof that we were there at all. The wind and the water brought sounds intact from any imaginable distance. Deprived of all perspective and horizon, I found myself reduced to an intuition, and my sister and my aunt to something less than that. I was afraid to put out my hand, for fear it would touch nothing, or to speak, for fear that no one would answer. We all stood there silently for a long moment" (69–70). To hear silence is to experience the reduction of self to intuition, a return to origins, and an intension of meaning—the passage prepares for the experience of *Housekeeping* more broadly.

Pulled into deep memory, Ruth imagines her birth and conception in the two extended meditations that form the heart of *Housekeeping*. In the first, Ruth remembers walking with Lucille to the lake and on its shore building a driftwood shelter in which they spent the night together. The sisters slept in their womblike space with their chins on their knees until, Ruth remembered, "I woke up in absolute darkness. I could feel the branches at my side and the damp at my back, and Lucille asleep against me, but I could see nothing." Scrambling out, Ruth returns "into darkness no less absolute. There was no moon" (114).

In a meditative exercise, analysis follows memory, and in *Housekeeping* Ruth analyzes the experience that memory provided: "I simply let the darkness in the sky become coextensive with the darkness in my skull and bowels and bones" (116). As in meditation, so in *Housekeeping* analysis yields understanding when Ruth reflects upon what Derrida might call the "erasure of differánce": "it seemed to me that there need not be relic, remnant, margin, residue, memento, bequest, memory, thought, track, or trace, if only the darkness could be perfect and permanent. . . . Everything that falls upon the eye is apparition, a sheet dropped over the world's true workings" (116).

Referring to nineteenth-century American writers Melville, Dickinson, and Poe, Robinson said, "I've always found that to be a very rich period, but it seems to me that it ended before it was completed in a way. I was very interested in taking up what seemed to be philosophical or theosophical or aesthetic issues which they brought up, but too few people carried forward" ("Life of Perished Things" 157). In *Housekeeping* she carries forward these issues in a second extended birth meditation, set in motion when Ruth accompanies Sylvie onto the lake in order to reach an island. Her thoughts forming the drama of the scene as they walk toward the water, Ruth imagines herself Sylvie's shadow, thinking, "we are the same. She could as well be my mother"; "I crouched and slept in her very shape like an unborn child" (145) until, while in the boat crossing the lake, "I crawled under her body and out between her legs" (146).

The backward pull of memory continues when, reaching the island in early morning, Ruth follows Sylvie to a desolate and frozen valley where a stunted orchard and fallen house are remnants of the Edenic life that once filled the place. Quietly, patiently, they withdraw, then when it was surely noon, Ruth follows Sylvie "up into the valley again and found it much changed." Before them lies a scene of creation; the experience is an illumination of life created on this island, on this planet. "It was as if the light had coaxed a flowering from the frost, which before seemed barren and parched as salt. The grass shown with petal colors, and water drops spilled from all the trees as innumerably as petals. . . . Imagine a Carthage sown with salt, and all the sowers gone, and the seeds lain however long in the earth, till there rose finally in vegetable profusion leaves and trees of rine and brine." Ruth's question "What flowering would there be in such a garden?" begins her analysis, which yields the understanding that "Light would force each . . . bright globe of water—peaches and grapes are little more than that, and where the world was salt there would be greater need of slaking. . . . For need can blossom into all the compensations it requires. To crave and to have are as like as a thing and its shadow" (152). Separation yields longing that is knowledge: "So whatever we may lose, very craving gives it back to us again" (153).

In the meditative exercise, understanding produces emotions and acts of will in an extension of the self to other human beings, nature, and the supernatural. Without Lucille (her public self) and without Sylvie (the dramatic form of her self-address), Ruth achieves the heightened receptivity of a solitary self. Sylvie's stories of ghost children return to her, and when Ruth reasons that "there was neither threshold nor sill between me and these cold, solitary children who almost breathed against my cheek and almost touched my hair" (154) illumination and understanding follow: "once alone, it is impossible to believe that one could ever have been otherwise. Loneliness is an absolute discovery" (157). An extension of the self based upon her understanding of loneliness occurs when Ruth thinks that she would have made a snow statue of a woman, had there been snow, to "be more than mother to them, she so calm, so still, and they such wild and orphan things" (153). A silent form of colloquy concludes the meditative exercise when Sylvie appears, puts her hand on Ruth's back, and envelops her in her coat while crooning to her and rocking her with her body.

Having pushed the birth metaphor to its paradox in which the nurturing womb expels its inhabitant into a life of exile, Robinson prepares to push it further to conceive of birth as a way of knowing: "The only true birth would be the final one, which would free us from watery darkness and the thought of watery darkness, but could such a birth be imagined? What is thought, after all, what is dreaming, but swim and flow, and the images they seem to animate?" (162). Behind the imaginings of conception is need, that is, desire for "a law of completion—that everything must finally be made comprehensible. . . . For why do our thoughts turn to some gesture of a hand, the fall of a sleeve, some corner of a room on a particular anonymous afternoon, even when we are asleep, and even when we are so old that our thoughts have abandoned other business, What are all these fragments for, if not to be knit up finally?" (92). Such fragments are "a foreshadowing—the world will be made whole" (152–53).

To write metaphorically, Robinson has said, is to write in the characteristic mode of most classic American writers whose work is "based on the assumption that the only way to understand the world is metaphorical, and all metaphors are inadequate, and . . . you press them far enough and you're delivered into something that requires a new articulation" ("Life of Perished Things" 159).[3] Explaining, Robinson again places herself within the meditative tradition that perceives the world as a metaphor. Melville, Dickinson, and Thoreau used metaphor as "a highly legitimate strategy for real epistemological questions to be dealt with in fiction and poetry"; "Wallace Stevens, it seems to me, was still doing a very similar thing. That was a large part of my interest in writing [*Housekeeping*] . . . the feeling that there was something to the idea of experience as emblematic, not a simple 'Puritan notion,' but that as Thoreau suggests over and over in his book, and as they all do, in some profound sense, reality is of a piece. . . . It seems to me that reality must somehow be describable as linked through analogue—I mean that rather than a structure in the Euclidean sense, it has a signature quality, and that's basically what [Ruth] does and why she does it and what that mind is" ("An Interview" 239).

At first glance Robinson's reflection that "all metaphors are inadequate" resembles the modernist's critical commonplace that exploring metaphorical thinking means revealing "a fundamental imaginative instability" signifying "a failure . . . to create coherent metaphorical structures of any sort" (Guetti 1).[4] Pursued far enough, the metaphor will break

down into instability; and the instability of metaphor signifies the instability of order, as the order of metaphor is a creative act imposed upon
chaos. In reflecting upon Ahab's pursuit of Moby-Dick, Ishmael is stabbed
by "the thought of annihilation" in the whiteness of the whale as "dumb
blankness, full of meaning" (63); in extending the metaphor of a mind
traveling alone on water "like a man lured on by a syllable without any
meaning," Stevens reaches the point that "the metaphor stirred his fear"
when

> The object with which he was compared
> Was beyond his recognizing ("Prologues to What is Possible" 377)

For the modernist, finding what will suffice means looking to a created order—a metaphor or an image, for example, as Frost observed, "a momentary stay against confusion" (17). In extending the metaphor of

> the mind in the act of finding
> What will suffice,

Stevens first compares the mind to an actor and then compares the actor
to

> A metaphysician in the dark, twanging
> An instrument

that allows the "finding of a satisfaction" in the image of

> a woman
> Combing

he creates ("Of Modern Poetry" 174–75).

"The images are the worst of it." Ruth's reflection responds to Stevens,
pressing his metaphor further by imagining what it is to stand outside in
the dark through a window watching (not creating) a woman in a lighted
room studying her own reflection in that window. "It would be terrible . . .
to throw a stone at her, shattering the glass, and then to watch the window
knit itself up again and the bright bits of lip and throat and hair piece
themselves seamlessly again into that unknown, indifferent woman. It
would be terrible to see a shattered mirror heal to show a dreaming woman
tucking up her hair" (162). Thus Stevens's image of a woman combing is
extended by Robinson into a woman who completes her toilet, and Stevens's satisfaction in the created (and therefore dependent) image be-

comes the "terrible" independence involved in conception. Whereas for Stevens pressing the metaphor of creation means reaching the threat of annihilation, for Robinson pressing the metaphor of conception means reaching loneliness, that "absolute discovery" that delivers a new meaning in the compensatory response that "there will be a garden where all of us as one child will sleep in our mother Eve, hooped in her ribs and staved by her spine" (192).

At the conclusion of *Housekeeping* the townspeople threaten to assume custody of Ruth; to remain with Sylvie, Ruth follows her across the bridge above Fingerbone Lake and disappears from the narrative. In a coda Ruth imagines Lucille imagining her, then engages the reader in colloquy: "Of my conception I know only what you know of yours. It occurred in darkness and I was unconsenting. I (and that slenderest word is too gross for the rare thing I was then) walked forever through reachless oblivion, in the mood of one smelling night-blooming flowers, and suddenly—My ravishers left their traces in me, male and female, and over the months I rounded, grew heavy, until the scandal could no longer be concealed and oblivion expelled me" (214-15).

I am amused at speculations that Ruth and Sylvie died in their attempt to cross the bridge above Fingerbone Lake, so that they never reached the other side.[5] The question of their death is quite beside the point in a novel that breaks down divisions of men/women, East/West, culture/nature, and life/death. The pertinent question has to do with language. Do Ruth and Sylvie inhabit our language and thus our consciousness? Is the Ruth of *Housekeeping* free of Robinson, having become part of the stories now growing inside her readers? Do we recognize ourselves in her and become her ghost children, pulled toward a conception of ourselves?

Like Margaret Fuller and Willa Cather, Robinson places female creativity at the center of her myth of origins and makes birth her central metaphor. The difference is that where Fuller and Cather wrote from the outside looking in (Fuller wrote *Summer* before she had given birth and Cather wrote *My Ántonia* without the prospect of doing so), Robinson writes from knowledge gained from the experience itself. Because her stance is so deeply female, critics have embraced her with an outpouring of feminist readings. She has challenged "the oedipal master plot" (Sprengnether) and displaced the Creation story by making woman the creator (Walker). To read her as usurping the myths to which she alludes, however, is to misread by the contentiousness of our time, when, in "our collective eagerness" . . . [we] disparage "without knowledge or information about the thing disparaged" (Robinson, "Puritans" 38). The result is that "Now we assume a posture of judgment and censure toward our fellows, as our best writers never did" (Robinson, "Writers" 34).

"We have busied ourselves so long exploding assumptions that it is by now an interesting experiment to try reassembling them again in plausible forms" (Robinson, "Fiction" 228). The form she adopts, colloquy, signifies the meditative exercise's conclusion in action. In the talks and interviews she has given, as well as in the reviews and essays she has written, Robinson models how texts might be read together to "seem almost collaborative, like an ideal conversation in which one of those present might propose a way of speaking—of how value exists, for example—and another might say, you are right, and yet we can turn the question again and see it differently" ("Fiction" 227). In describing how she came to write *Housekeeping,* for example, Robinson declares her "affinity" with Poe, considers herself "in the company of commentators" on the Old and New Testaments, and speaks of the nineteenth-century transcendentalists as her "aunts and uncles" to whom she "will always answer" ("Life of Perished Things" 158).

The densely allusive manner of *Housekeeping* is a form of colloquy. In describing herself as taking to the woods, Ruth echoes Thoreau; in writing of clouds of glory, she is Wordsworth's child; and in the manner of Dickinson, she hears a fly buzz. The conversation itself, the exchange of colloquy, is what is important, not its resolution in agreement or disproof: the pleasure "is that whatever *it* is, whatever *we* are, whatever is passing between us, there *is* something passing between us, there's some kind of conversation" ("An Interview" 239). Expand the conversation, and the effect is of a diaspora that Robinson sees in Angela Carter's *Wise Children* but that also applies to her own writing: it "is about the boundary-less community of shared culture. It is a meditation on the benign aspects of the fact that our common preconceptions travel ahead of us to colonize and domesticate future experience so that we are never truly disowned or estranged—our twin waits on the shore where we must be shipwrecked" ("Fiction in Review" 234–35).

With collaborative conversation as her ideal, Robinson utterly rejects the divisions maintained by party agendas. Her relationship with Melville is a case in point. *Housekeeping* "was such a sort of joke to myself," Robinson remarks and then explains that "the book I admire most in the world is *Moby-Dick,* after the Bible of course." She had been encouraged to believe that Melville's book was hostile to women and *"told* that I was pointedly excluded as a woman from *Moby-Dick.* . . . but I never felt that this was true, and I thought if I could write a book in which there were no male characters that men could read—comfortably—then I get *Moby-Dick."* Asked whether she felt she'd "gotten *Moby-Dick* now," Robinson responded, "I think I have some claim on *Moby-Dick* at this point because men have been very receptive readers of *Housekeeping"* ("An Interview" 234–35).

In this manner Robinson includes others' voices and acknowledges the values of what they are saying, yet she "turn[s] the question again and sees it differently" (Robinson, "Fiction in Review" 227). Describing Wallace Stevens as one of the poets who most influenced her and describing herself as engaged

> in the act of finding
> What will suffice,

Robinson engages him in conversation about the issues he articulates (the problem of belief, the role of the poet, and the nature of the creative act) in the tradition he represents (including that of meditation). Stevens brings to his part of the dialogue premises reminiscent of the biblical idea of creation *ex nihilo.* "The mind that in heaven created the earth and the mind that on earth created heaven were, as it happened, one," he states (*Opus Posthumous* 176); and as in Genesis, so for Stevens the imagination "Creates a fresh universe out of nothingness by adding itself" ("Prologues to What Is Possible" 378). "The imagination is man's power over nature" (*Opus Posthumous* 179), and metaphor, which Stevens defines as "the creation of resemblance by the imagination" (*Necessary Angel* 72), is the mind's way of momentarily imposing order upon unending chaos.[6]

By grounding creativity in conception rather than creation, Robinson sees the question differently. She couldn't have written *Housekeeping* if she hadn't given birth, Robinson has said, because "I just wouldn't have known all the sorts of strange emotional dynamics of having your identity invested in another person. I wouldn't have known the disparity between how you perceive yourself and how you are perceived by the people that are very dear to you" ("Life of Perished Things"160). It is this emotional dynamic that lies behind Robinson's methodology of metaphor. Approached from within the female experience of conception and birth, creativity is freed from anxiety over possession and control. "Might we not have been kinder and saner if we had said that discontent is our natural condition," Robinson reflects elsewhere, "that we are the Ishmael of species, that, while we belong in the world, we have no place in the world" ("Puritans and Prigs" 48).

By putting connection rather than isolation and kinship rather than autonomy at the center of her story, Robinson challenges notions of the United States as unique in its destiny, questions its claim to happiness as a worthy ideal, and reclaims the metaphor of birth from its fragmented and divisive appropriation as "the birth of a nation" by American jingoists. Loneliness, that "absolute discovery" yielded by the meditative exercises of *Housekeeping,* undergirds Robinson's subsequent writing, which is—not surprisingly—intensely political in the sense not of particular party interests but of polity, or how a people interact in a community to collaborate and solve problems. "[T]he genius of democracy was always respect for people in general," she says; "If you read Lincoln, it's fascinating how he dealt with that war, how he never ever said anything injurious about southerners. His respect for them was absolute so far as he would express it, beginning to end. And this respect was, I think, to a large extent a result of the fact that the culture supported a very humane imagination of the content of other people's souls" ("An Interview" 238).

In an essay she titles "Puritans and Prigs," Robinson aligns herself with the seventeenth-century Puritans in commenting upon the prigs of today. Priggishness stems from "overvaluing oneself or one's ideas, habits, notions, . . . and by small disparagement of others," and Americans are so helpless against it "because we cherish a myth of conversion in which we throw off the character our society gives us and put on a new one in all ways vastly superior." Salvation ("this great change" of conversion), she continues, is normally "achieved by education, enhanced by travel, refined by reading certain publications, manifested in the approved array of scruples"; conversion is then proved by disparagement and disavowal of others, and also in claims to economic and social distinctions, and—especially and most dangerously—moral superiority. The result is that "Americans never think of themselves as sharing fully in the human condition, and therefore beset as all humankind is beset" (39). The pervasive cultural arrogance described by Robinson is rooted to a great degree in the popular Western formula. The Virginian, Lassiter, and Shane present virtuousness as difference and display heroism by (in Robinson's words) "contempt for the art of suasion": "They do not really want to enlist or persuade—they want to maintain difference. . . . Certainly they are not open to other points of view" (50).

In place of priggishness Robinson offers "the true, abiding myth of the West [which] is that there is an intense, continuous, and typically wordless conversation between attentive people and the landscape they inhabit, and that this can be the major business of a very rich life" ("Hearing Silence" 149). It is the meditative tradition reinvented by the circumstances of Robinson's place and time. Whereas Francois de Sales counseled meditation as an exercise "to arouse the will to holy and wholesome affections and resolutions" and Stevens practiced meditation "with the aim of developing an affectionate understanding of how good it is to be alive" (Martz, *Poem of the Mind* 218), Robinson uses the meditative exercise to return the United States to the global community and to develop a polity of responsibility to the planet. "When I think about the degradation of the world and the loss of the world," she says, "I think specifically in terms of the loss of the conversation that's going on between humankind and the world since Genesis. To me everything that's beautiful about humankind is derived absolutely out of its response to the atmosphere of questioning difficulty that's generated out of the world. I think that a true understanding of what a human being *is* is based on an understanding of this rapt conversation in which people are *all* engrossed, and that re-establishing a sense of the sacredness of what is occurring here is probably the *only* antidote, because without that there is no final urgency about the rescue of either one" ("An Interview" 251).

Robinson aligns herself with the Puritans, drawing Calvin into the conversation by quoting his answer to the question "Who is our neighbor?": "It is the common habit of mankind that the more closely men are bound together by the ties of kinship, of acquaintanceship, or of neighborhood, the more responsibilities for one another they share. This does not offend God; for his providence, as it were, leads us to it. But I say: we ought to embrace the whole human race without exception in a single feeling of love; here there is no distinction between barbarian and Greek, worthy and unworthy, friend and enemy, since all should be contemplated in God, not in themselves" ("Puritans and Prigs" 53).

The meditative exercise is part of a disciplined and rigorous training in social responsibility based upon spiritual revelation: the first two steps of that exercise (memory and analysis) are followed by the will's extension of the self in emotions and acts. Seen thus, Robinson's second book, the non-fiction study *Mother Country*, is a logical sequel to *Housekeeping*. In *Housekeeping* a meditation upon a lake serves as a basis for extending the metaphors of birth and conception until they require a new articulation as a myth of origins. Released from its debased nationalistic connotations, "birth" returns to its genesis in conception; and released from its fragmented connotation of women's domestic sphere, "house" returns to its primary meaning as a habitation for something living—the planet that is our home.

"The world's interests have not been properly respected," Robinson writes in her introduction to *Mother Country*, and "I am angry to the depths of my soul that the earth has been so injured" (9). Her subject is the "apocalyptic tale" (153) of the British-run industry Sellafield, the world's largest source of radioactive contamination and the greatest commercial producer of plutonium in the world. The action involved is audaciously simple: Sellafield accepts wastes generated in other countries, "extracting as much usable plutonium and uranium as they find practical [i.e., profitable] and flushing the rest into the sea or venting it through smokestacks into the air" (5). Robinson's response is similarly straightforward: she interprets this action as a narrative, which is to say as initiating a sequence of events. Doing so means responding with moral and ethical outrage: "I am forced to confront the epic scale of my narrative," for "there is, so far as we can know, only one living planet. And even if there were another, nothing in our present state of consciousness would save it from the abuse that threatens to kill this one" (30).

To make her case, Robinson turns to the texts that compose national discourse: legal and public proceedings as reported in newspapers, magazines, and books. In these texts she traces policies by which Great Britain defined values in opposition to the conditions of life of poor people, from the poor laws of the fourteenth century to its present welfare state. Against this backdrop she tells the narrative of Windscale/Sellafield (its name was changed when a core fire and "accidents" made the original a public relations problem). For her standard of judgment, she appeals to common sense. One doesn't have to be a physicist to know better than to pour plutonium into the environment nor does one have to be an epidemiologist to respond to elevated incidents of disease and death associated with Sellafield (one child in sixty dies of leukemia in one village, for example).

The complicating factor in this narrative is, according to Robinson, the mystery of how Sellafield "has remained unknown to us for so many years" (7). "Moral aphasia" might be a useful concept here (193), she suggests, as if only the loss of an ability to articulate ideas or comprehend language could account for our complicity. Robinson's denouement concerns language. "One of the disillusionments suffered by a wanderer from fiction into the world of Great Ideas is the discovery that the conceptual vocabulary is a slovenly grafting of incompatible parts" (228). Beyond the metaphoric incompatibility of casting Great Britain as a Mother Country, there is the disjunction of casting the world's survival in terms of a political confrontation between the Soviet Union and the United States and then of proposing solutions in terms of democratic processes. "The problem," she writes, "has been and is now outside democratic political control, first of all because books about nuclear issues do not tell the public the problem exists" (229).

As for the United States, Robinson continues, "The world's most favored public, our own, is educated thoroughly and badly, starved of information, and flattered as to its own importance, while it is made incompetent in the use of the power it has" (230). "If Russia ceased to appear to us as a threat," Robinson wrote presciently in 1989, "we would probably simply forget it, as we do most of the world most of the time. The tendency of this country to be engrossed in itself makes it ill suited to sustaining large-scale, long-term interest of any kind in the outside world" (231).

Preacher, orator, conscience, Robinson reinvents the meditative tradition to evoke wonder at the miracle of the living planet and to issue action in its defense. "I think one of the reasons the world is so badly defended is that there's been a fantastic erosion of loyalty to it," she observed in an interview; "heaping contempt on whatever's presently existing . . . [is] a ridiculous way to proceed, but it's had an enormous impact on the imagination. And I think it's produced a resignation almost to the point of connivance to the process of actually acting these things out, actually debasing the world" ("An Interview" 248–51). To save the world—and this is what she is about—Robinson reenlists the imagination in a noble—some would say sacred—politics of meditation and a language of social conscience.

Afterword

I began this book when preparing a presidential address for the Western Literature Association meant asking why I felt I belonged in a prototypically male field. Writing this afterword means asking what I've learned in the past decade.

Despite all our talk of change, some things remain the same. Frederick Jackson Turner's "theories are still with us," as Barbara Howard Meldrum has observed (2), his thesis given new life most recently in *The Legacy of Conquest,* Patricia Nelson Limerick's exposé of the dark underside of the Turner myth that has inspired its own progeny of conferences, exhibitions, and publications. The stakes are indisputably high, for they concern identity: who we are, where we came from, and what we value as a nation—indeed, whether there is a "we" at all in this nation's identity. That is the question with which Limerick concludes her argument. The Turnerian frontier myth embraced by white Americans as a creation myth has an "undeniable charm of simplicity," she writes, then continues that "Simplicitly, alas, is the one quality that cannot be found in the story of the American West" (322-23). As Limerick acknowledges, however, discrediting Turner is one thing and finding an alternative is quite another: "The cast of characters who inherit the West's complex past is as diverse as ever," she writes: "Indians, Hispanics, Asians, blacks, Anglos, businesspeople, workers, politicians, bureaucrats, natives, and newcomers, we share the same region and its history, but we wait to be introduced" (349).

Propelled by principles of diversity, the cast of characters will continue to expand (What about farmers and factory workers? Gays and lesbians? Children? Women?), yet we will remain waiting to be introduced so long as we proceed by variations upon the conflict of a single plot. Here I refer to the frontier thesis not for the story that it tells but rather for the manner of its telling: a dialectic by which thesis, antithesis, and synthesis occur most famously as a conflict between civilization and wilderness from which emerges a new American. It is not simply that by dating the closing of the frontier in the 1890s Turner's thesis closed the frontier to others (i.e., women and minorities) but rather that by adopting the form of dialectic he closed the telling of history to others. "Let us dream as our fathers dreamt, and let us make our dreams come true," Turner challenged his reader, articulating a closed system by which authority passes from father to son, dreamer to doer ("The West and American Ideals" 301). Turner reinforced that closed system by positioning himself within it as both writer and reader; that is, he based his writing of history upon his reading of the country that he imagined spread before him "like a huge page in the history of society" ("The Significance of the Frontier" 11).

In recent decades we've grown increasingly skeptical about the notion of a synthesis and correspondingly hesitant to assume the pronoun "we," but the dialectic's opposition has remained with us. Women versus men, white versus color, victor versus victim, rural versus urban, and the country versus the academy are some of the variations of that plot that are given narrative form as the gender wars, the canon wars, and the culture wars. We've now embarked upon "the science wars," a popular magazine informs us (Begley). The possibilities are endless.

The MLA-sponsored volume *Redrawing the Boundaries: The Transformation of English and American Literary Studies* illustrates my point. The volume consists of essays responding to the premise that we're "in a period of rapid and sometimes disorienting change" (1). Editors Stephen Greenblatt and Giles Gunn challenge academics in various areas of literary studies to reconsider "their constitutive interpretive paradigms" (1). They then argue for redrawing boundaries by describing two contrasting definitions of frontier: a frontier representing a notion of limit (such as those that devolve from "impassable rivers or mountains") versus a frontier conceived "as the zone between antagonists," negotiated by appropriation, confrontation, and ambition (6). Proposing their own idea for literary studies, they specify that "what is meant here by *frontier* is not a fixed line but the furthest point to which you can push your forces, extend your influence" (6). Consider civilization and wilderness antagonists in this context and this frontier sounds unnervingly familiar. As Tompkins said, while reflecting upon other reenactments of the Western's violence in academic discourse, "There has to be some better way" (*West of Everything* 233).

A decade ago I hoped to find a better way as I set out in search of women who responded in terms of the West to the call to give birth to a nation. Instead of finding a challenge to the masterplot, however, I found a challenge to the very premise of a plot. Margaret Fuller, Willa Cather, Jean Stafford, and Marilynne Robinson suggest that what matters is not *which* story we tell but rather *the manner of our telling*. Each in her own way probes the frontier plot of opposition and, exposing the violence at its heart, discards the plot. Having cleared the stage, each offers a principle of relationship embodied in the conversation as it is articulated in the West, where communities are formed rather than inherited and where the importance of the land mandates that community be understood by ecological principles.

Conversation as a national epic? I find the idea intriguing as it emerges from these four disparate writers, who demonstrate the potential range, flexibility, and rigor of the conversation. Fuller designed her Conversations as a forum to prepare women to take up action, and then she extends the manner of those Conversations into *Summer on the Lakes*. Cather posits the genesis of *My Ántonia* as a conversation between herself and a childhood friend, extends the manner of conversation into reading by receiving the manuscript he brings to her, and structures the narrative to climax in the kinship aesthetics of a family in conversation. Stafford structures *The Mountain Lion* as a conversation between a brother and sister that upon adolescence is cleaved by gendered conventions, and Robinson draws upon the meditative tradition in writing *Housekeeping* as the self in conversation with the landscape and then extends the colloquy in *Mother Country*'s call to action.

By their uses of conversation, these writers disprove frontier plots of opposition. Merging the gendered space of private versus public, each wrote from her personal life with a self-consciously public impulse to articulate the identity of a nation; together they offer conversations as a female Bildungsroman that is a voyage out as well as in. Disregarding opposition between high and low art, they use the conversation—that seemingly most casual of genres—as the form for an epic. The ranking of canonical versus noncanonical is rendered similarly ludicrous by the vagaries of literary reputation. Fuller has achieved longevity largely through her reincarnations in the pop culture of literary personalities; Cather has been elevated from marginal to canonical status with the light speed of a single decade; Stafford remains unread within the academy, known (if at all) as Robert Lowell's first wife; and though critics hailed Robinson's first book as an instant classic, they have scarcely acknowledged that she wrote a second. In terms of male versus female and white versus color, perhaps it should not have surprised me—as it initially did—that the women who responded to the challenge to give birth to this nation in terms of the West were white and educated. As such, however, they contribute to diversity in our national discourse. From their cultural role of Other in the westering myth, they probe the sources and effects of cultural alterity; by virtue of their dual status—mainstream and marginalized—they provide an alternative discourse that both provides access and accommodates difference.

What is at issue in such a discourse is language, and each invites the rigorous close reading that trains one's ear to hear the nuances of words as they are culturally, historically, and individually inflected. Observing daily examples of the leveling effects of mass media (what Robinson calls the "moral aphasia" that describes the failure of a populace to engage with issues that threaten its humanity and, indeed, that threaten the survival of life on our planet), I am convinced that such training is critically important. Talking about Stafford's "The Mountain Day" in a recent graduate seminar, for example, I was horrified to realize that my students were reading its clichéd language straight. Like the story's character Judy Grayson, they were unsettled by the mutilated bodies of maids recovered from the lake, but like Judy, they found comfort in the love plot of a western sojourn. That was our first discussion of Stafford; by month's end her stories had awakened these readers to cultural inflections of language and engaged them with issues of power conveyed through those inflections. Such stories are the best antidote to moral aphasia that I know.

The westering quest that Fuller, Cather, Stafford, and Robinson embark upon is a search for the genesis of cultural myth in language. Keeping a journal of her travels, Fuller sets out toward the frontier to "woo the mighty meaning of the scene." Placing herself in the tradition of Virgil bringing the Muse to her neighborhood, Cather recovers fertility myth from classical, Native American, and European permutations and, combining pro/creativity, celebrates an immigrant woman as a New World's Earth Mother. By placing her fictional daughters within cultural myths of the West, Stafford exposes the psychosexual violence at the heart of those myths. After freeing her characters from domestic plots of the gendered West, Robinson explores the birth metaphor, pushing it back before conception and finding in loneliness a new articulation of the epistemology of language's generativity.

By resisting closure, the reciprocity of conversation reinforces language's generativity. "My Friends! May they see and do more," Fuller writes at the end of *Summer on the Lakes* (96); in giving his manuscript to Cather, Jim Burden asks, "Now, what about yours?" (xiii); in taking Molly Fawcett inside the literary West, Stafford challenges us to revisit its language with her as our companion; and in the final pages of Robinson's *Housekeeping,* Ruth tells the reader to imagine Lucille imagining her. In this manner conversation models the give-and-take at the heart of every moral system: social reciprocity means taking turns, listening as well as speaking. Surely it is a better way.

Notes

Preface

1. I am paraphrasing Edward Said's argument that Orientalism is "indebted to various Western techniques of representation that make the Orient visible, clear, 'there' in discourse about it" (22).

Introduction

1. "In what according to critic Stephen A. Whicher is 'probably his strongest essay,' Emerson announced the following year in 'Experience' (1844) that even though these limitations—Illusion, Temperament, Succession, Surface, Surprise, Reality, Subjectiveness—were obstacles, he accepted their 'clangor and jangle.' Perceiving things different now from his perspective in 'Nature' and 'The American Scholar,' he shows that experience belies reconciliation, and that wisdom consists in one's living with what he calls 'the middle region,' 'the temperate zone,' 'the mid-world,' where the limitations upon the human spirit find their analogy in a close frontier. It must be noted that Emerson, not ready to accept a tragic view of life, manifests far less torment in his facing the wall than did Herman Melville. In fact, Emerson calls these limitations 'beautiful,' and then, in what seems more contradiction and paradox, announces in this same essay that indeed 'we have not arrived at a wall.' He will envision the time when he might 'die out of nature,' transcend the not-Me, and 'be born again into this new yet unapproachable American I have found in the West'" (qtd. in Simonson 5).

2. Using Frederick Jackson Turner's theory of the frontier as his starting point, Gay Wilson Allen compares the attitudes of Emerson, Thoreau, and Whitman to the "Frontier": Emerson responded with moral revulsion against the frontier, Thoreau

expressed ambiguity concerning the frontier, and Whitman celebrated it as heroic and epic.

3. This period is not only generally but specifically described as nine months. Using the criterion of when Walden "was first completely open" as announcing spring, Thoreau records seven years of dates marking that event. The median of these dates (23 March to 18 April) is 4 April, or precisely nine months following the onset of his sojourn.

Interestingly, the final date, "in 54, about the 7th of April," "is not on ms. 1094. The date is so late that it must have been one of the last things put into the book, for we know that Thoreau began to receive proofs on March 28. *Journal* for that day, VI, 176" (Stern 422).

4. Here I differ from Max Westbrook, who interprets the mother as "a whore in the sense that she allowed her legal husband to sleep with her without giving him love" (102). What is significant, I suggest, is not so much whether or not a woman is a whore or in what sense she is but the charge that indiscriminately runs through Clark's plot in response to women.

1. Fuller and the West as Muse

1. Miller interprets Fuller's self-culture as an American, domestic version of Continental romanticism (xii–xiii), and Eakin interprets it as "an expression of the New England mind in romantic dress" (*New England Girl* 50). I would add that to understand Fuller's self-culture we must recognize not only Continental and New England influences upon Fuller but also those of the American West.

2. Exceptions are Annette Kolodny's interpretation of Fuller's journey to the West as an attempt to restore the domesticity and stability of her mother's garden (*Land before Her*) and McKinsey's reading of the Niagara Falls passage (and, by extension, of *Summer* more generally) as the "psychological lesson of the sublime . . . [which is] the union of two aspects, of instinct and spirit, or in more modern terms, of unconscious and conscious" (*Niagara Falls* 225).

3. Though they retreat, the transcendentalists continued to link the West imaginatively with a national literature. McKinsey describes this impulse as found in the writing of the *Western Messenger,* a monthly Unitarian journal founded by Ephraim Peabody in 1835 and edited by Clarke, to which Channing and Cranch as well as Fuller contributed: "All 'artists' to some degree—Clarke in his sermons and essays, Channing in his journalism, and Cranch in poetry and later in painting—they sought a personal artistic opportunity in the West, as well as fulfillment of the promise for a national literature" (*Western Experiment* 16).

4. See also MF to Clarke, 19 Apr. 1836, 1:248, and 1 Feb. 1835, 1:219; MF to William H.

Channing, 9 Dec. 1838, 1:353; and MF to Eugene Fuller, 8 June 1839, 2:70, all in *Letters*.

5. Medea's story is, of course, not only of a powerful woman but also of her defiance of a patriarchal order. Fuller here refers to Medea's destroying the usurping King Pelias, upon returning with her husband, Jason, and the Golden Fleece she had helped him to obtain. To demonstrate her power and gain ascendancy, Medea cut up an old ram into pieces and boiled them in a cauldron with magic herbs, and the ram came forth as a new lamb. Pelias's daughters cut apart their father and boiled the pieces, but Medea withheld the magic herbs.

Kolodny offers a psychological interpretation of Fuller's redefinition of the West in female terms as springing from a search for Eden, imagined as the "stable and contented domesticity" she had once known in her mother's garden. Kolodny argues that "what Fuller was able to repossess on the parklike and flowered prairies of the middle west was her unmediated pleasure in 'the dear little garden' remembered from childhood" and that she discovered in frontier cabins she visited no Edenic return at all, but "her own horrific residence at Groton." Thus women's "newfound frontier fantasies might, in fact, turn into domestic captivity—even in Eden" (117, 119, 121, 130).

6. Reading *Summer* as conversation is interesting in terms of Stephen Adams's perceptive argument that the "experimental form" of romantic aesthetics figures in its deliberately loose structure (see esp. 248). Allen's survey of the complex "issue of Fuller the conversationalist versus Fuller the writer" (67) is useful as general background for *Summer,* and Urbanski's argument that Fuller wrote *Woman* in the oral tradition of the sermon provides another interpretation of Fuller's efforts to write in the manner of oral discourse.

7. Urbanski writes, "comparison of the two texts reveals that the first 130 pages of the 179-page text of *Woman* are a close adaptation of the 47 pages of 'Lawsuit,'" then notes that "there are, however, forty-nine pages of new materials. The portion she adds contains the most daring subject matter in the book because much of it is contemporary application of her thesis," including "frank discussions of sex," "the double standard of morality," "property rights for married women: and her ideas that 'ladies' are responsible for rehabilitating prostitutes" (269–70). Chevigny describes Fuller's increased focus upon women's autonomy: while she retained "virtually all" of "The Great Lawsuit" in her revised *Woman,* she added examples of women's heroism, a call for women to act against slavery, and an extended discussion of prostitution ("Growing" 91).

The generally favorable reception that "Lawsuit" received "among the *Dial*'s small coterie of readers" may well have contributed to Fuller's "courage to treat inflammatory subject matter," as Urbanski argues. Yet in *Summer* Fuller reveals that her western trip was far more important than has been recognized. *Summer* is Fuller's account of the politicizing effect of the West, where she tested expectation against experience and from which she returned with a more impassioned, immediate, and (above all) gendered vision of woman's destiny. She returned from the West, in other words, ready to revise "Lawsuit" into *Woman*.

8. Here I interpret self-culture rather than celibacy or virginity as the issue. For an alternate reading, see Blanchard 218–24. See also Chevigny's note that Fuller changed her autobiographical story of herself from one of dependency upon her father to her "dignified sense of self-dependence." Clearly, Fuller had changed since she wrote the 1840 romance. "This heroic assertion of independence, equaled nowhere else in her work" is seen in her "second autobiography, thinly disguised in the description of 'Miranda,'" drafted immediately before her journey to the West and published in *Woman* immediately after returning from it (Chevigny, "Daughters" 363). Fuller's revision further suggests the influence of the West upon her.

9. As if searching for her place in the American myth she was helping to create, Fuller casts herself in a confusing (confused?) variety of roles: Holy Mother, Muse, wife, sister, midwife, nurse, mother. Through her descriptions run lip service to relationship, yet there remains a contrary impulse toward autonomy. For example, Fuller wrote to Caroline Sturgis of longing to inseminate herself and give birth independently, her version of a virgin birth: "I cannot plunge into myself enough. I cannot dedicate myself sufficiently. The life that flows in upon me from so many quarters is too beautiful to be checked. I would not check a single pulsation. It all ought to be;—if caused by any apparition of the Divine in me I could bless myself like the holy Mother. But like her I long to be virgin" (*Letters* 2:167).

10. Tompkins argues that the sentimental novelists were capable of being both subversive and conformist ("Sentimental Designs" 122–46, 218 n.15, 220 n.31).

2. The Long Foreground to Cather's West

1. In seeking historical reality, Elizabeth Hampsten cautions, one must ask what documents are missing. In seeking family history we might best ask what the family kept—what it wished to preserve in the letters it keeps as in the stories it tells.

2. See Hampsten, who writes, "what women—the ordinary women whose casual writings I have been describing—have written least about is the one subject that our schooling in literature has taught us to expect writers to begin with: their place, locale, the landscape of wherever they are" (29).

3. As Susan Parry describes the fluxes of this emigration, "John Smith went to Nebraska in April 1874 to homestead near the George Cathers (Franc's letter of 6/26: 'I suppose you have heard that Jno. took 320 acres a mile south of us'). Smith re-

turned to Frederick County in Aug. or Sept. 1874 upon receiving word of Rettie's im-pending death; he sold his Nebraska claim and never went back. Two other Virginia friends of Geo. Cather (Henry Lockhart and Johnson Wisecarver) settled in Web-ster County in 1874, but most of the Frederick County friends and neighbors settled there in 1875–76" (Letter to author, 27 October 1993).

4. Alverna Clutter filed for divorce in Webster County on grounds of desertion.

5. Carroll Smith-Rosenberg suggests that from the 1760s to the 1870s, letters be-tween women "retained a constancy and predictability" that provided women with continuity in a time of significant social change (60–61).

6. Robert L. Griswold discusses domestic ideology as "less a cult or a rigid orthodoxy and more a flexible vocabulary about gender ideals" that provided women with "a much needed sense of stability, community, and generational continuity in a new region" (28–29).

3. Cather's Western Stories

1. Asking "What is desire?" in the introduction to his book on the subject, Eugene Goodheart acknowledges that the term in our daily use is so clearly "akin to words like 'want' and 'need' that it may seem pedantic to ask for a definition of it. What is striking, however, is the way the word in what I call the discourse of desire resists definition. . . . In its vernacular expressions, we desire particular satisfactions: food, sex, pleasure, happiness. But the word, when used by writers like Bersani and Kris-teva, does not require a predicate. Desire moves, floats, negates, shatters, aspires, it is itself a subject. Its freedom, if that is what we wish to call it, consists in its refusal to be constrained by the satisfactions that would extinguish it" (2–3).

2. In interpreting Jim Burden's experience in *My Ántonia* with Margaret Homans's argument of gender orientation to language (i.e., language based on the male's dif-ference from and loss of the mother), Ann Fisher-Wirth acknowledges that "Ho-mans's theory, like the gender-based psycholinguistic theories from which it de-rives, is highly controversial, but whether or not one accepts it, it is remarkably pertinent to a study of *My Ántonia*" (68 n.2). I agree that we should acknowledge the controversy over essentialism in such theories and acknowledge their useful-ness—albeit limited—in interpreting Cather's novel.

3. I scarcely need to say that Turner's 1893 address, "The Significance of the Frontier in American History," has been the subject of enormous controversy. Nevertheless, the fact that Turner remains a touchstone for dispute testifies to his ongoing in-fluence. Patricia Nelson Limerick, for example, writes against Turner in *The Legacy of Conquest*, which has become a standard for revisionist history. Turner's chal-lenge, which is infuriating to many, lies in his method. As Ben Merchant Vorpahl

writes, "Turner's detractors and supporters alike have only rarely taken into account [that] Turner aimed to convince not by arguing, citing authorities or amassing and analyzing facts, but by the far more ambitious means of establishing and manipulating points of view" (286).

4. In *Revolution in Poetic Language* Kristeva distinguishes between the symbolic and the semiotic. Whereas the symbolic is associated with syntax or grammar and is the element of meaning that signifies, "The semiotic elements within the signifying process are the drives as they discharge within language. This drive discharge is associated with rhythm and tone. The semiotic is this subterranean element of meaning within signification that does not signify" (*The Johns Hopkins Guide* 446).

5. Levy perceptively comments upon the frontier as the site of pervasive American (male) hostility to women's creativity: "Widely diverse commentators in a variety of disciplines have remarked on the cultural prevalence of this free-standing hero who is a law unto himself *and who has created himself*. For example, Erik Erikson sees a historical basis in America's frontier past for this figure, exemplified by the folk hero John Henry in *Childhood and Society*: "But wherever our methods permit us to look deeper, we find at the bottom of it all the conviction, the mortal self-accusation, that it was *the child who abandoned the mother*, because he had been in such a hurry to become independent. . . . John Henry thus is one of the occupational models of the stray men on the expanding frontier who faced new geographical and technological worlds as men and with out a past. The last remaining model seems to be the cowboy. . . . These workmen developed to its very emotional and societal limits the image of the man without roots, the motherless man, the womanless man" (296, 299; emphasis mine).

6. Cather's counterrevolutionary strategy was remarkably consistent, in fact. With *O Pioneers!* she displaced Whitman by writing her own epic song of America, and in *My Ántonia* she displaced Virgil by positioning herself as "the first . . . to bring the Muse into my country," thus transforming his "patria" into her "matria."

7. Bringing the Muse to life—letting her speak for herself—led to Lena Lingard and, as I have argued elsewhere, more dramatically to the writing of "Coming, Aphrodite!" ("Cather's Manifesto for Art"). For another dimension of revisioning the western romance adventure, see Cather's response to H. Rider Haggard's *She* (1886), the adventure "universally read because the world has not yet outgrown the liking for fairy tales" and because of its charms, consisting of "weird suggestions of unknown lands and peoples, of mystery and awful age, of reckless daring and of careless love" (*World and the Parish* 132, 240). "A Tale of the White Pyramid" is Cather's response to *She*, as if anticipating Showalter's observation "The quest for She is . . . both a quest for the Ur-Mother, who holds the secret of life, and the quest to usurp her power" (85).

8. The device of a twinned protagonist is familiar in Cather's work, as Charlotte Goodman was among the first to point out in "The Lost Brother/The Twin."

9. Though she is not writing of Cather specifically, Susan Griffin's "parody of a voice with such presumptions" (xv) in *Woman and Nature: The Roaring Inside Her* describes well Cather's parody with the "strange love letter" in "Eric Hermannson's Soul."

10. With this story, Cather responds to the debate over the dilemma of the woman artist. In *The Daughters of Danaus* (1894) Mona Caird "dramatizes the contradictions of motherhood and art, femininity and artistic creativity," writes Showalter (66). The story is of bright, gifted women "subjected to a domestic routine that takes away their time for concentrated work. . . . The sisters debate Emerson's dictum that 'genius will triumph over circumstances.' . . . But, they point out, Emerson leaves out the question of gender. 'Emerson never was a girl! . . . If he had been a girl, he would have known that circumstances DO count hideously in one's life'" (67).

11. For a complementary view, see Tom Quirk's perceptive argument that in *O Pioneers!* Cather reimagined the conventionally understood east to west movement of American history and in fact reversed it so that the past is in the West and the future in the East (see, e.g., 130).

12. Goodheart could be writing of Cather: "In *Death in Venice, Heart of Darkness, The Metamorphosis, The Immoralist,* the authors Mann, Conrad, Kafka, Gide, though they *write* their deaths in the figures of Aschenbach, Kurtz, Gregor Samsa, and Michel, respectively, survive their surrogate counterparts" (8). Cather, significantly, by taking Godfrey St. Peter into death when he falls unconscious from inhaling gas fumes of his stove and then reviving him, writes beyond the ending in *The Professor's House,* her most concentrated and developed modernist narrative acting out of desire "from the writer's point of view . . . [by] the courting of suffering and death" (8).

4. Pro/Creativity and a Kinship Aesthetic

1. Cather in *Death Comes for the Archbishop* creates another richly symbolic female space in the cave called Stone Lips. Latour descends into it for shelter during a storm, and Cather describes his horror over the experience as so intense that, despite the fact that it saved his life, he resolves to never again venture into such a place. Whereas Thea Kronborg, in *The Song of the Lark,* and Ántonia are nurtured by the cave spaces they inhabit, Cather's male characters characteristically feel revulsion over such direct contact with the earth and the primitive.

2. Gunn's book on Laguna and Acoma history, traditions, and narratives is now

among the holdings of the Willa Cather Pioneer Memorial and Educational Foundation. For discussion of this myth see Weigle 214–18 and Hindehede.

3. Reading *My Ántonia* in terms of Homans's argument that Western metaphysics is founded on the myth that "language and culture depend on the death or absence of the mother and on the quest for substitutes for her," Ann Fisher-Wirth interprets Jim's narrative as "a form of desire, which constantly seeks but can never arrive at that lost body" (41). "In the gendered myth that informs *My Ántonia, Ántonia* represents the body of the world. The narrative of Jim's life describes his fall away from union with worldbody, into the Law of the Father. But his act of narrative itself constitutes a perpetual desirous return toward the lost motherbody from which his life necessarily departed" (67).

4. Wendy Lesser demonstrates that Beauvoir's point is still relevant. Addressing mothers as the initial subject of male artists, Lesser writes, "If to be an artist, a writer, is to fly unburdened with the weight of reality, then to think about one's mother—to attempt to think oneself *into* one's mother—is to be brought with a crash down to Mother Earth" (33).

5. *My Secret Life*'s narrator-hero, Walter, "sums up Victorian attitudes with a series of displacements: he reaches a turning point in his sexual knowledge when he has 'learnt enough . . . to know that among men of his class the term lacemaker, along with actress and seamstress, was virtually synonymous with prostitute'" (qtd. in Michie 67).

6. As Gerda Lerner writes, the Goddess's "frequent association with the moon symbolized her mystical powers over nature and the seasons" (148).

7. In discussing "biblical borrowings" in *My Ántonia,* John J. Murphy perceptively traces Cather's use of Christian iconography to describe Ántonia: "The Christmas story of Matthew and Luke echoes in Widow Steavens's account of the birth of Ántonia's child, and Jim's subsequent farewell scene with Ántonia, . . . recalls Revelation 12:1, traditionally applied to the Virgin Mary" (40); the orchard scene describes a "della robbia image of maternity clothed in light and blossoms [that] recalls Dante's dawn-bright vision of Mary in *Paradise*" (93); and for Jim's return twenty years later, Cather "reworks the icon into a kind of Coronation of the Virgin" (103).

8. Here Cather reverses novelistic tradition of gendered authority. Whereas "The poetry of troubadours, like popular tales, stories of voyages, and other kinds of narratives, often introduces at the end the speaker as a witness to or participant in the narrated 'facts,'" writes Julia Kristeva, "in novelistic conclusions, the author speaks not as a witness to some 'event' (as in folk tales), not to express his 'feelings' or his 'art' (as in troubadour poetry); rather, he speaks in order to assume ownership of

the discourse that he appeared at first to have given to someone else (a character)" (Kristeva, *Desire in Language* 63).

9. The title of book 5, "Cuzak's Boys," unsettles expectations that a patriarchal principle would be replaced by a matriarchal one. Cuzak's boys or Ántonia's? Jim's story or Cather's? Such questions are made irrelevant by a kinship aesthetics of exchange and connectivity.

5. Stafford's Inherited West

1. See *West of Everything*, esp. 7.

2. Among the many explorations of the cultural significance of literary formula, John G. Cawelti and Tompkins are particularly important here. In *Adventure, Mystery, and Romance* Cawelti traces the evolution of the formula Western as a projection of cultural tensions and concerns; in *West of Everything* Tompkins explores what it is as a woman to encounter those tensions and concerns in the Western.

3. The structure of Stafford's novel can be compared to Woolf's idea of life as a "semi-transparent envelope"—not a single reality but a series of sensations and perceptions. See Woolf's "Modern Fiction" 103–10.

4. I note without comment the contrast of Shura Marburg to Freud's description of a mother's love for her son as ideal. "A mother is only brought unlimited satisfaction by her relation to a son; this is altogether the most perfect, the most free from ambivalence of all human relationships" (*Standard Edition* 22:133). This point is discussed by Madelon Sprengnether as "the concept of maternal plenitude which Freud evokes as a defense against his darker vision of seduction and aggression" (80–81).

5. Changes in her name extend the metamorphosis, as Sonia recognizes. Asked by a friend of Miss Pride, "By the way, I don't understand your name, Sonie. Is it short for Euphrosyne?" Sonia reflects. "Through a misreading of the word, she had metathesized the vowels and pronounced it 'Euphrysone.' I explained that Sonie was my own childish corruption of Sonia. 'What a pity,' she said. 'Not that I don't love Sonia for you, but it would have been so delightful if you *had* been named for the goddess of Mirth'" (303).

6. Originally published in 1946, only two years after *The Boston Adventure,* Viola Klein's *The Feminine Character* is particularly useful in illuminating precursors to feminist critiques of Freudianism.

7. As the single critical essay devoted to it acknowledges, *Boston Adventure* is a psychological novel, but it is not enough to point out that its structure follows Eric Neumann's "psycho-mythological patterns" of female transformation. This would

define the highest female potential as becoming "the Mother in her benevolent form," devoted to nurturing the male and forever denied the consciousness of wisdom that results from the masculine process of individuation (Mann 291, 292).

8. My description of psychoanalytical terms paraphrases Sprengnether, 227.

6. Stafford's Western Stories

1. Though Alfred Habegger, in *Gender, Fantasy, and Realism in American Literature,* discusses mid-nineteenth-century women's fiction, his point about realism is relevant here. Habegger supplements René Wellek's description of realism as "the objective representation of contemporary social reality" "with a more explicit recognition of the dialectical nature of realism. . . . [Realism] belonged to the mid-nineteenth-century genre of the novel, but bore in part an adversary or corrective relation to a major type of novel, women's fiction." Objectively presented and detailed verisimilitude was "all part of a strategy of argument, an adversary polemic. These techniques were the only way to tell the truth about, to test, to *get at,* the ideal gender types, daydreams, and lies that were poisoning society and the novel. Realism was an analysis of quiet desperation. Attempting to break out, and to help their readers break out, of a suffocated, half-conscious state, Howells and James had to be circumstantial" (103–06).

2. In "Jean Stafford's Western Childhood: Huck Finn Joins the Camp Fire Girls," Melody Graulich argues similarly that because Stafford has given "much of her own childhood character" to Molly and Emily, each character "helps illuminate her struggles as a woman writer using male conventions and writing within a male tradition" (40).

7. Stafford Rewrites the Western

1. Goodman has written on this point: "Like other male-female double Bildungsroman by women writers, such as George Eliot's *The Mill on the Floss,* Willa Cather's *My Ántonia,* and Joyce Carol Oates's *Them, The Mountain Lion* contrasts the coming of age of a male and a female character in a patriarchal society" (*Jean Stafford* 174; see also "The Lost Brother/The Twin").

2. When reading Stafford's work, a dictionary is often useful as a reminder of nuances of meaning. A divining rod is "a forked branch or stick that allegedly indicates subterranean water or minerals by bending downward when held over a source"; it relates to the verb "divine," which is "to . . . reveal through the art of divination" and "to know by inspiration, intuition, or reflection." Both relate to the adjective "divine": "being or having the nature of a deity . . . sacred; holy; supremely good; magnificent" (*American Heritage Dictionary*). As Margaret Laurence has reminded

us in using divining as the unifying metaphor for *The Diviners,* it also has to do with creative inspiration.

3. In so portraying masculine culture, Stafford exposes a negative quality similar to what Terence Martin has called "the negative character in American fiction." Martin argues that "Americans have long found a series of compelling negatives the surest way of claiming identity," explaining that "to be sure of what they were, Americans . . . acquired a habit of asserting what they were not, both nationally and personally." "[F]ictional characters who enact the negative impulse"—"Natty Bumppo, Huckleberry Finn, Isaac McCaslin, and Randle Patrick McMurphy—exist in novels that virtually recapitulate the experience of America" (230). Flight to a wilderness is antagonism to community, "for the social conception and the negative conception are antithetical in nature. Neither can accommodate the other" (235).

Martin describes American experience as represented by male writers. Once gender is factored in, we see that it is the masculine tradition of the West that is negative, defining itself by negating an "other" and representing the "other" as women. It is not flight from civilization that is essential to the negative character but negation of civilization; it is not freedom from women but negation of women.

4. Stafford felt in her own life that being a woman and being a writer were incompatible. Writing to Lowell after their marriage failed and *The Mountain Lion* had received successful reviews, Stafford dismissed the reviews: "What should it console me to be praised as a good writer? These stripped bones are not enough to feed a starving woman. I know this, Cal, and the knowledge eats me like an inward animal. There is no thing worse for a woman than to be deprived of her womanliness. For me, there is nothing worse than the knowledge that my life holds nothing for me but being a writer." (qtd. in Goodman, *Jean Stafford* 176).

5. Pilkington writes that "The central fact about Molly is her physical ugliness. She has 'thin, freckled arms' and an 'ugly little face framed by black hair with which . . . nothing could be done'" (92). Isolated and lonely because of her appearance, "she finds refuge only in books and in the company of Ralph" (185). Pilkington interprets Molly as becoming "transformed into a young Miss Watson, complete with exacting Victorian morality," then pleads that the reader grant her compassion because she can't be blamed for what she has become because "the scars of ugliness and isolation are irremovable" (185). I suggest, however, that Stafford is challenging the expectation that we might judge character by appearance and exposing the sexism of assuming that the central fact about a girl is her appearance.

In her perceptive argument that Molly Fawcett suggests a "new breed of female" in the feminization of quest romance, Dana A. Heller argues that "Although Stafford puts an abrupt end to the growing pains of Molly Fawcett, . . . the point of the devastation is to transfer growing pains to the reader. For it is we who must now come to terms with our literature's annihilation of the female and the end of her development. It is we who must initiate a movement beyond the limits of social expectations" (55).

6. A. B. Guthrie's "Mountain Medicine" illustrates the everlasting negotiation of hunted/hunter that composes the masculine myth. Guthrie's hero, John Clell, enters the mountain as a hunter-trapper but becomes prey when he is captured by the Blackfeet, who formalize the game of a chase. Symbolism such as a beaver removed from a trap and an eagle gliding overhead as well as the hero's constant negotiation of his role—hunted or hunter—reinforces the action of an eternal hunt in the wilderness.

7. I am paraphrasing Langer's description of animals' communication without speech (*Philosophy* 104).

8. The Western Hero as Logos

1. Lee Clark Mitchell confirms and extends Cawelti's assessment of the influence of these Westerns by looking at their sales figures: *The Virginian* was a bestseller during the year following its publication and has remained so, with total sales by 1976 at 1,736,299; Grey was "Wister's successor as the most popular author of Westerns"; and *Shane* was "the most popular of recent Westerns" (Cawelti, *Six-Gun* 2).

2. In *The Virginian* Wister retained the Western's formulaic chase-and-pursuit pattern even while he prepared for the modern Western by transmuting the theme of nature versus civilization into a conflict between East versus West and by replacing the mountain man hero with a romanticized cowboy (Cawelti, *Six-Gun*, esp. 67). The standard readings of Wister are, with a few exceptions, variations upon the assumption that the Western is grounded in action. The most important challenge to that assumption has been made by Lee Clark Mitchell, who argues that "words shape consequence in this novel as powerfully as action does" (*Westerns* 100). Our conventional focus upon action in *The Virginian*, he states, ignores the fact that its "encounters consist more of wordplay than gunplay" and that "far from depicting a conventional male violence tamed at last by a feminized East, the novel celebrates the Virginian's rhetorical triumph over the school-marm and the silencing of her feminism in favor of a 'logic' of patriarchy" ("When You Call"). While positioning myself in the tradition of Mitchell, I suggest that in *The Virginian* not only do words shape consequences but Wister's hero displaces words by becoming the Word—the Virginian.

3. I am not disagreeing here with critics who point out that the Virginian picks up skills from the schoolmarm. As Donald E. Houghton has written, the Virginian improves his spelling and penmanship under Molly's tutelage. With such skills he fills

in the gaps of his education; but even while doing so, it is he who has authority and in the end it is he who educates Molly about life's important lessons. So Wister would have it.

4. Nesbitt writes that "Wister's most frequently cited contribution to the Western is the showdown, a formal and detached killing through which the hero resolves a culturally defined conflict" (208).

5. Here my interpretation differs from that of Lee Clark Mitchell, who writes, "the accumulated conjunctions and repetitive syntax draw attention to the process of the prose itself, a prose no longer transparent or comfortably outside the experience it purports to describe. In a sense, action here *becomes* language through a transition so radical that the fatal gunshot is identified in conversational terms: 'he replied'" (*Westerns* 102).

6. While I agree with Houghton and others that the character of the Virginian contains "two Virginians, one who succeeds in terms of Western values, the other in terms of Eastern values," I interpret this duality not as a split "into two stories with two heroes" but as inclusiveness (498). What appears as duality is resolved in the Virginian as All. While Cawelti argues that the Virginian is "both an exponent of natural law and of the major ideals of American society," Wister "resolved the old ambiguity between nature and civilization" and presented "the West . . . as an environment in which the American dream could be born again" (*Adventure* 224–25). I go further to argue that the Virginian is revealed as the Logos, the source of all meaning.

This principle of inclusiveness lies behind the diversity of elements, types, and traditions running through *The Virginian*. Nesbitt, for example, argues that Wister synthesizes "the tradition of frontier adventure with a more sophisticated and genteel Anglo-American literary tradition," the novel of manners (202), and concludes that "it is a novel containing a marriage of two literary traditions, with historical romance and social realism at odds with one another for the last word" (208). Forrest G. Robinson argues that the Virginian "waffles" "in a culturally consistent way," "because his dual, incomplete, and finally incompatible allegiances to the natural and the civilized mirror our own" (36).

Rather than evaluate whether or not Wister manages consistency (as do Houghton, Nesbitt, and Robinson), I suggest that Wister was radically and reductively claiming authority for creativity of all things, and all meaning.

7. Forrest G. Robinson reads such passages as examples of bad faith by which characters raise issues that they then ignore, so that "they secretly embrace confusion" (10). He interprets in the Western "contrary impulses to see and not see, to address painful issues and to turn away from them" that are "always delicately, dialectically poised in these texts, and never fully 'managed' or resolved" (114). I agree that ten-

sions and ambiguities are not resolved but argue that the linguistic act of making sense is both disproved and negated.

8. In each case the plot concerns silencing, The stress on the thing itself incorporates landscape but is not limited to it: action, setting, and characterization exemplify a stress on the thing itself. The principle of pointing and pantomime takes various forms: hunting prey, tracking a path, shooting an enemy. Its strong stress on sight results in a genre particularly well suited for adaptation to film.

9. But what about the Western more generally? To test further the new sight offered by Molly Fawcett, we might go to the first Western, where we find Deerslayer, establishing his distrust of language: "'Have the governor's or the king's people given this lake a name?' he suddenly asked, as if struck with a new idea. 'If they've not begun to blaze their trees, and set upon their compasses, and line off their maps, it's likely they've not bethought them to disturb Natur' with a name'" (Cooper, *Deerslayer* 21). "'I'm glad it has no name,' resumed Deerslayer, 'or, at least, no pale-face name, for their christenings always foretell waste and destruction'" (21). For the "high" or literary Western, we might turn to Walter Clark's *The Track of the Cat,* a novel with chilling similarities to *The Mountain Lion.* By its content as well as its chronology, Clark's novel invites further comparison with Stafford's *The Mountain Lion.* The novels offer a male and a female writer's contrasting treatments of a common subject (gender roles displaced into the hunt for a mountain lion), and *The Track of the Cat*'s composition brackets Stafford's *The Mountain Lion* (1947). Interestingly, Clark's short first version in 1935 was without any female characters; its revised form published in 1949 gives them prominence.

As Stafford did, Clark uses the metaphor of hunting a lion to write of male responses to a women's independent sexuality and creativity. Again, it is in its language that its violence against women is most dramatically revealed in the charge that runs through men's responses to women: father, mother, and Curt call Gwen a whore; the father calls the mother a whore; the son (Hal) thinks his mother a whore; the father calls all women whores. The effect is a leveling and a silencing.

The pulp Western presents a principle of silencing in even more obvious form, for a character's use of language serves as a shorthand to his or her worth: a hero expresses himself through action, not words; a quiet woman is good, a talkative man weak, and a talkative woman trouble. Bill Gulick's story "Squaw Fever" illustrates the suspicion of language that runs through pulp westerns. The story of Charley Smith, an illiterate and inarticulate man whose knowledge of the land saves the wagon train from the mess of following a false map and who is saved from being talked into marriage to a white woman by his friend Bear Claw (Indian and, therefore, strongly silent), who acquires for him a squaw who works hard and "no talk at all."

10. See *The Westminster Dictionary of Christian Theology, The New Oxford Annotated Bible,* and *Encyclopaedia of Religion and Ethics.*

11. In American literature, male authors' appropriation of creativity through language takes us back to Cooper, among others. In *The Crater* (1848), Cooper writes of IDEA as that upon which the birth and survival of a New World depended—the New World appears in response to the narrator-writer's idea and disappears when he withdraws.

12. See Cawelti, who includes the Western hero's "oft-noted laconic style" in his interpretation of the hero's role "as middleman between the pacifistic townspeople and the violent savages" (*Six-Gun* 61). And he notes, "Reluctance with words often matches the hero's reluctance toward women" (61).

13. The conventional Western presents a plot of regeneration and redemption even as each denies change and generation. Cawelti writes of the romantic Western tradition of Wister, Grey, and Hart as portraying "the West as a distinctive moral and symbolic landscape with strong implications of regeneration or redemption for those protagonists who can respond to its challenge by recovering basic human and American values" (*Adventure* 233). "In the end," he writes, "hero and heroine are clearly on their way to marriage, a family and a settled life thereafter" (235).

9. Robinson's Politics of Meditation

1. Discussions of birth imagery, which are standard to discussions of *Housekeeping,* demonstrate the range of interpretations that the novel invites. For Martha Ravits *Housekeeping* is a female version of the American theme of wilderness rebirth; for Madelon Sprengnether, who reads psychoanalytically, it is a reformulation of the Fall as mother-daughter separation; for Nancy Walker it contributes to a reworking of the Genesis story in which literal and symbolic birth is part of the larger theme of generation and regeneration, so that "the infinite possibility of rebirth . . . directly counters the finality of the Fall and the expulsion from the Garden, and which thus challenges the authority of the biblical story" (39).

2. Robinson describes a similar form of self-address when she tells of writing *Housekeeping*: "when I was writing I was aware of movements of mind not mine, that I didn't know the solution to. It's sort of like, If you put *this* in relation to *that,* what is implied? And the first thing I would think is, Not much, or nothing, and then—it was strange—it felt almost like a physical kind of problem, in the sense that it was like there *has* to be, there *has* to be, I mean I could *intuit* something I felt was like a movement or a principle of unity, but I didn't know what it was. If I knew what it was, I didn't proceed. The whole interest of the book for me was in trying to be beyond my own grasp or outside my own experience. I tried to set problems for myself

that I truly experienced as real problems, and in a way what I was doing was testing my method, finding what I could make it yield. Of course if I had any commitment beforehand to what it should have yielded, then I would have been ruining my experiment. Which of course is probably quite thoroughly self-deceived. But that was the experience of it. I thought my solutions tended to be recognizably my solutions, there's no doubt about it" ("An Interview" 241-42).

3. Referring to Ishmael's skepticism when he's aloft in the crow's nest, Robinson says, "It seems to me that in a way the masthead chapter is a classic demonstration of the sort of Emersonian method which is based on the assumption of the inadequacy of the method. That's what's so brilliant about it. You can create an absolutely dazzling metaphor that seems to be resolving things and pulling things together and reconciling things and making sense of things, and then you can collapse the metaphor, and what you're left with is an understanding that's larger than you had before, but finally it is a legitimate understanding because you know it's wrong or you know it's imperfectly partial. I mean, what they are all trying to do is use language as a method of comprehension on the largest scale, at the same time using all the resources of language and absolutely insisting that language is not an appropriate tool. . . . It's inadequate. It's also inappropriate because it has its own logic, because it wants to go its own way. There's always the drift toward self-invited order in language that makes resolutions that are too neat or too small or beside the point. This is what happens most of the time with most attempts to deal with anything in language." ("An Interview" 240-241).

4. James Guetti represented this position three decades ago in *The Limits of Metaphor* by defining metaphor as "the fundamental imaginative process of creating, discarding, and re-creating order" and then arguing that verbal difficulties arising from this imaginative process of creating order "appear to be implicit in the very nature of language and become obvious as the imagination is called upon more and more frequently to create, by manipulating the diversities of its perceptions, new and stable order" (2).

5. Asked about disagreement among critics "whether Ruth and Sylvie are still alive at the end of the novel," Robinson responded obliquely (which is to say, very much in the manner of Sylvie): "Critics sometimes do point out things I never noticed before" ("Life of Perished Things" 172).

6. In terms relevant to *Housekeeping*, Jacqueline Vaught Brogan discusses the long theoretical interest in metaphor by its "impulse . . . toward an Adamic naming and/or creating" following "the assumption that metaphor illustrates, or is itself a metaphor for, the original creative act" (6). Her discussion of Wallace Stevens's "Prologues to What Is Possible" is relevant to Robinson: "This poem is particularly interesting because it explores what is often ignored in the discussion of meta-

phor—the frightening potential of the impulse toward unity: annihilation of individuality in the 'one-ness.' The 'metaphor' is frightening because . . . If the impulse toward unity were realized, . . . we would have only 'quiet,' the unspoken where being and essence are joined, that which is 'more than human' and cannot be said 'with human voice.' As a result, such unity or 'one-ness' ironically means utter isolation, traveling 'alone,' voyaging out of and beyond the familiar" (16–17).

Works Cited

Adams, Stephen. "'That Tidiness We Always Look for in Woman': Fuller's *Summer on the Lakes* and Romantic Aesthetics." *Studies in the American Renaissance* (1987): 247–64.

Aldrich, Marcia. "The Poetics of Transience: Marilynne Robinson's *Housekeeping*." *Essays in Literature* 16.1 (1989): 127–40.

Allen, Gay Wilson. "How Emerson, Thoreau, and Whitman Viewed the 'Frontier.'" *Toward a New American Literary History: Essays in Honor of Arlin Turner*. Ed. Louis J. Budd, Edwin H. Cady, and Carl L. Anderson. Durham, N.C.: Duke UP, 1980. 111–29.

Allen, Margaret Vanderhaar. *The Achievement of Margaret Fuller*. University Park: Pennsylvania State UP, 1979.

Allen, Paula Gunn. *Grandmothers of Light: A Medicine Woman's Sourcebook*. Boston: Beacon, 1991.

The American Heritage Dictionary of the English Language. Boston: Houghton, 1976.

Anderson, David D. "A Transcendental View of Niagara," *Niagara Frontier* 8 (1961): 24–27.

Baym, Nina. "Melodramas of Beset Manhood: How Theories of American Fiction Exclude Women Authors." *Feminism and American Literary History: Essays*. New Brunswick, N.J.: Rutgers UP, 1992. 3–18.

Beauvoir, de Simone. *The Second Sex*. Trans. H. M. Parshley. New York: Knopf, 1953.

Beaver, Harold. *Huckleberry Finn*. London: Allen, 1987.

Begley, Sharon. "The Science Wars." *Newsweek* 21 Apr. 1997: 54–57.

Bennett, Mildred R. "What Happened to the Rest of the Charles Cather Family?" *Nebraska History* 54 (1973): 619–24.

———. *The World of Willa Cather*. New ed. with notes and index. Lincoln: U Nebraska P, 1961.

Bersani, Leo. *A Future for Astyanax: Character and Desire in Literature*. Boston: Little, 1976.

Blake, Forrester. Interview. Taylor 38–40.

Blanchard, Paula. *Margaret Fuller: From Transcendentalism to Revolution*. Radcliffe Biography Ser. New York: Delta/Seymour Lawrence-Dell, 1978.

Bohlke, L Brent. *Willa Cather in Person: Interviews, Speeches, and Letters*. Lincoln: U Nebraska P, 1986.

Rev. of *Boston Adventure*, by Jean Stafford. *Catholic World*. Dec. 1944: 283.

Rev. of *Boston Adventure*, by Jean Stafford. *Commonweal*. Dec. 1944: 20.

Brogan, Jacqueline Vaught. *Stevens and Simile: A Theory of Language*. Princeton: Princeton UP, 1986.

Brooks, Peter. *Reading for the Plot: Design and Intention in Narrative*. New York: Knopf, 1984.

Brown, Arthur W. *Margaret Fuller*. New York: Twayne, 1964.

Brown, Charles Brockden. "To the Public." Introductory note to *Edgar Huntly; Or, Memoirs of a Sleepwalker*. 1799. *The Novels and Related Works of Charles Brockden Brown*. Bicentennial ed. Ed. Sydney J. Krause and S. W. Reid. Vol. 4. Kent, Ohio: Kent State UP, 1984. 3.

Bucco, Martin. *Western American Literary Criticism*. Boise, Idaho: Boise State U, 1984.

Carruthers, Mary. "The Re-Vision of the Muse: Adrienne Rich, Audre Lorde, Judy Grahn, Olga Broumas." *Hudson Review* 36 (1983): 293–322.

Cather family letters. Nebraska State Historical Society, Lincoln. Collection no. RG3890.AM.

Cather, Willa. *Collected Short Fiction, 1892-1912*. Ed. Virginia Faulkner. Introd. Mildred R. Bennett. Rev. ed. Lincoln: U Nebraska P, 1970.

———. *Death Comes for the Archbishop*. New York, Knopf, 1927.

———. "Katherine Mansfield." *On Writing: Critical Studies on Writing as an Art*. Fwd. Stephen Tennant. Lincoln: U Nebraska P, 1988.

———. *Kingdom of Art: Willa Cather's First Principles and Critical Statements, 1893-1896*. Ed. Bernice Slote. Lincoln: U Nebraska P, 1967.

———. *Lucy Gayheart*. New York: Knopf, 1935.

———. *My Ántonia*. Ed. Charles Mignon with Kari Ronning. Hist. essay by James Woodress. Lincoln: U Nebraska P, 1994.

———. *O Pioneers!* Ed. Susan J. Rosowski and Charles W. Mignon with Kathleen Danker. Hist. essay by David Stouck. Lincoln: U Nebraska P, 1992.

———. *The Song of the Lark*. Boston: Houghton, 1915.

———. *The World and the Parish: Willa Cather's Articles and Reviews, 1893-1902.* Ed. William M. Curtin. 2 vols. Lincoln: U Nebraska P, 1970.

Cawelti, John G. *Adventure, Mystery, and Romance: Formula Stories as Art and Popular Culture.* Chicago: U Chicago P, 1976.

———. *The Six-Gun Mystique.* Bowling Green, Ohio: Bowling Green UP, 1971.

Channing, Ellery. "The Importance and Means of a National Literature." *Christian Examiner* Jan. 1830: 269-93.

Charnon-Deutsch, Lou. *Narratives of Desire: Nineteenth-Century Spanish Fiction by Women.* University Park: Pennsylvania State UP, 1994.

Chevigny, Bell G. "Daughters Writing: Toward a Theory of Women's Biography." *Between Women: Biographers, Novelists, Critics, Teachers and Artists Write about Their Work on Women.* Ed. Carol Ascher, Louise DeSalvo, and Sara Ruddick. Boston: Beacon, 1984. 357-79.

———. "Growing out of New England: The Emergence of Margaret Fuller's Radicalism." *Women's Studies* 5 (1977): 65-100.

———. *The Woman and the Myth: Margaret Fuller's Life and Writings.* Old Westbury, N.Y.: Feminist, 1976.

Chodorow, Nancy. *Reproduction and Mothering: Psychoanalysis and the Sociology of Gender.* Berkeley: U California P, 1978.

Cixous, Hélène. "Reaching the Point of Wheat, or a Portrait of the Artist as a Maturing Woman." *New Literary History* 19 (1987): 1-21.

Clark, Walter Van Tilburg. "On *The Track of the Cat.*" *Walter Van Tilburg Clark: Critiques.* Ed. Charlton Laird. Reno: U Nevada P, 1983. 181-86.

———. *The Track of the Cat.* Lincoln: U Nebraska P, 1949.

———. "The Watchful Gods." Taylor 183-244.

Clarke, James Freeman. *The Letters of James Freeman Clarke to Margaret Fuller.* Ed. John Wesley Thomas. Hamburg, Ger.: Cram, de Gruyter, 1957.

The Concise Oxford Dictionary of Literary Terms. Comp. Christ Baldick. Oxford, Eng.: Oxford UP, 1990.

Cook-Lynn, Elizabeth. *Why I Can't Read Wallace Stegner and Other Essays: A Tribal Voice.* Madison: U Wisconsin P, 1996.

Cooper, James Fenimore. *The Crater, or Vulcan's Peak.* Ed. Thomas Philbrick. Cambridge: Belknap-Harvard UP, 1962.

———. *The Deerslayer, or The First War-Path. Works of James Fenimore Cooper.* Vol. 1. New York: Greenwood, 1969. 293.

Crowell's Handbook of Classical Mythology. New York: Crowell, 1970.

Dale, E. E. "Turner: The Man and the Teacher." *University of Kansas City Review* 18 (1951): 18-28.

Dall, Caroline Wells Healy. *Margaret and Her Friends; or, Ten Conversations with*

Margaret Fuller upon the Mythology of the Greeks and Its Expression in Art. Boston: Roberts, 1895.

Douglas, Ann. *The Feminization of American Culture*. New York: Knopf, 1977.

Eakin, Paul John. "Margaret Fuller, Hawthorne, James, and Sexual Politics." *South Atlantic Quarterly* 75 (1976): 323–38.

———. *The New England Girl: Cultural Ideals in Hawthorne, Stowe, Howells, and James*. Athens: U Georgia P, 1976.

Emerson, Ralph Waldo. *The Collected Works of Ralph Waldo Emerson*. Notes and hist. introd. by Joseph Slater. Text established by Alfred R. Ferguson and Jean Ferguson Carr. Apparatus and textual introd. by Jean Ferguson Carr. 5 vols. Cambridge: Belknap-Harvard UP, 1971–94.

Encyclopaedia of Religion and Ethics. Ed. James Hastings with J. A. Selbie and L. H. Gray. Vol. 8. New York: Scribner's, 1956–60. 13 vols.

Erikson, Erick. *Childhood and Society*. 2nd ed. New York: Norton, 1963.

Erisman, Fred and Richard W. Etulain, eds. *Fifty Western Writers: A Bio-Bibliographical Sourcebook*. Westport, Conn.: Greenwood, 1992.

Etulain, Richard W. *Owen Wister*. Boise, Idaho: Boise State College, 1973.

Fetterley, Judith. *The Resisting Reader: A Feminist Approach to American Fiction*. Bloomington: Indiana UP, 1978.

Fiedler, Leslie. *Love and Death in the American Novel*. New York: Criterion, 1960.

Fisher, Vardis. Interview. Taylor 34–37.

Fisher-Wirth, Ann. "Out of the Mother: Loss in *My Ántonia*." *Cather Studies 2*. Ed. Susan J. Rosowski. Lincoln: U Nebraska P, 1993. 41–71.

Fowler, Rowena. "Feminist Criticism: The Common Pursuit." *New Literary History* 19 (1987): 51–62.

Freud, Sigmund. *The Standard Edition of the Complete Psychological Works of Sigmund Freud*. Trans. James Strachey in collaboration with Anna Freud and assisted by Alix Strachey and Alan Tyson. 23 vols. London: Hogarth, 1955–64.

Friedman, Susan Stanford. "Creativity and the Childbirth Metaphor: Gender Differences in Literary Discourse." *Feminist Studies* 13 (1987): 49–82.

Frost, Robert. "The Figure a Poem Makes." *Selected Prose of Robert Frost*. Ed. Hyde Cox and Edward Connery Lathem. New York: Holt, 1956. 17–20.

Fuller, Margaret. "American Literature: Its Position in the Present Time, and Prospects for the Future." *Papers on Literature and Art*. Vol. 2. London: Wiley, 1846. 122–43.

———. "The Great Lawsuit: Man versus Men, Woman versus Women." *The Dial* 4 (1843): 1–47.

———. *The Letters of Margaret Fuller*. Ed. Robert N. Hudspeth. 4 vols. Ithaca: Cornell UP, 1983–87.

———. *Memoirs of Margaret Fuller Ossoli*. 2 vols. Boston, 1858.

———. *Summer on the Lakes, in 1843. The Writings of Margaret Fuller*. Selected and ed. Mason Wade. New York: Viking, 1941. 3–104

———. *Woman in the Nineteenth Century, and Kindred Papers*. Introd. Horace Greeley. New York: Source, 1970.

———. "The Wrongs of American Women. The Duty of American Women." Rev. of *The Wrongs of American Women*, by Charles Burdett, and *The Duty of American Women to Their Country*, by Catharine Beecher and/or Harriet Beecher Stowe. *New York Daily Tribune* 30 Sept. 1845. Rpt. in *Woman in the Nineteenth Century, and Kindred Papers Relating to the Sphere, Condition, and Duties of Woman*. Ed. Arthur B. Fuller. Boston: Jewett, 1855. 217–27.

Fussell, Edwin. *Frontier: American Literature and the American West*. Princeton: Princeton UP, 1965.

Gelfant, Blanche H. "Reconsideration: *The Mountain Lion*." *New Republic* 10 May 1975: 22–25.

———. "Revolutionary Turnings: *The Mountain Lion* Reread." *Massachusetts Review* 20 (1979): 117–25.

Goodheart, Eugene. *Desire and Its Discontents*. New York: Columbia UP, 1991.

Goodman, Charlotte Margolis. *Jean Stafford: The Savage Heart*. Austin: U Texas P, 1990.

———. "The Lost Brother/The Twin: Women Novelists and Male-Female Double Bildungsroman." *Novel* 17 (1983): 28–43.

Graulich, Melody. "Jean Stafford's Western Childhood: Huck Finn Joins the Camp Fire Girls." *Denver Quarterly* 18.1 (1983): 39–55.

———. "Violence against Women." *The Women's West*. Ed. Susan Armitage and Elizabeth Jameson. Norman: U Oklahoma P, 1987.

"The Great Nation of Futurity." *United States Magazine and Democratic Review* 6 (1839): 426–30.

Greenblatt, Stephen and Giles Gunn, eds. Introduction. *Redrawing the Boundaries: The Transformation of English and American Literary Studies*. New York: MLA, 1992.

Grey, Zane. *Riders of the Purple Sage: A Novel*. New York: Penguin, 1990.

Griffin, Susan. *Woman and Nature: The Roaring Inside Her*. New York: Harper, 1980.

Griswold, Robert L. "Anglo Women and Domestic Ideology in the American West in the Nineteenth and Early Twentieth Centuries." *Western Women: Their Land, Their Lives*. Ed. Lillian Schlissel, Vicki L. Ruiz, and Janice Monk. Albuquerque: U of New Mexico P, 1988.

Guetti, James. *The Limits of Metaphor: A Study of Melville, Conrad, and Faulkner*. Ithaca: Cornell UP, 1967.

Gulick, Bill. "Squaw Fever." *White Men, Red Men, and Mountain Men*. Ithaca: Cornell UP, 1967.

Gunn, John M. *Schat-Chen: History, Traditions and Narratives of the Queres Indians of Laguna and Acoma*. Albuquerque: Albright, 1917.

Guthrie, A. B. "Mountain Medicine." Taylor 299–307.

Habegger, Alfred. *Gender, Fantasy, and Realism in American Literature*. New York: Columbia UP, 1982.

Haggard, H. Rider. *She: A History of Adventure*. London: Longmans, 1925.

Hampsten, Elizabeth. *Read This Only to Yourself: The Private Writings of Midwestern Women, 1880–1910*. Bloomington: Indiana UP, 1982.

Harrison, Fraser. *The Dark Angel: Aspects of Victorian Sexuality*. New York: Universe, 1978.

Haslam, Gerald W., ed. Introduction. *Many Californias: Literature from the Golden State*. Reno: U Nevada P, 1992. 1–2.

Hawthorne, Nathaniel. *The Scarlet Letter*. Ed. William Charvat et al. Centenary ed. Vol. 1. Columbus: Ohio State UP, 1962.

Heller, Dana A. "Remembering Molly: Jean Stafford's *The Mountain Lion*." *The Feminization of Quest-Romance: Radical Departures*. Austin: U Texas P, 1990. 40–55.

Hindehede, Karen M. "Allusions and Echoes: Multi-Cultural Blending and Feminine Spirituality in *Death Comes for the Archbishop*." *Heritage of the Great Plains* 28.1 (1995): 11–19.

Holman, C. Hugh and William Harman. *A Handbook to Literature*. New York: Macmillan, 1986.

Hooker, Tho[mas]. *A Survey of the Summe of Church-Discipline. Wherein, The Way of the Churches of New-England is warranted out of the Word*. London: Bellamy, 1648.

Houghton, Donald E. "Two Heroes in One: Reflections on the Popularity of *The Virginian*." *Critical Essays on the Western American Novel*. Ed. William T. Pilkington. Boston: Hall, 1980. 118–24.

Humphreys, D[avid]. *A Poem on the Happiness of America Addressed to the Citizens of the United States*. London: Hartford, 1786.

Jeffrey, Julie R. *Frontier Women: The Trans-Mississippi West, 1840–1880*. New York: Hill, 1979.

The Johns Hopkins Guide to Literary Theory and Criticism. Ed. Michael Groden and Martin Kreiswirth. Baltimore: Johns Hopkins UP, 1994.

Jones, Howard M. "The Artistry of Jean Stafford." *Saturday Review* 23 Sept. 1944: 10.

Kenner, Hugh. *The Pound Era*. Berkeley: U California P, 1971.

Kirby, Joan. "Is There Life After Art? The Metaphysics of Marilynne Robinson's *Housekeeping*." *Tulsa Studies in Women's Literature* 5.1 (1986): 91–109.

Klein, Viola. *The Feminine Character: History of an Ideology*. 1946. Urbana: U Illinois P, 1971.

Knapp, John. Untitled essay. Ruland 109–13.

Kolodny, Annette. *The Land before Her: Fantasy and Experience of the American Frontiers, 1630-1860*. Chapel Hill: U North Carolina P, 1984.

———. *The Lay of the Land: Metaphor as Experience and History in American Life and Letters*. Chapel Hill: U North Carolina P, 1975.

Kristeva, Julia. *Desire in Language: A Semiotic Approach to Literature and Art*. Ed. Leon S. Roudiez. Trans. Thomas Gora, Alice Jardine, and Leon S. Roudiez. New York: Columbia UP, 1980.

Krutch, Joseph Wood. *Henry David Thoreau*. New York: Sloane, 1848.

Langer, Susanne K. "On Cassirer's Theory of Language and Myth." *The Philosophy of Ernst Cassirer*. Ed. Paul Arthur Schilpp. New York: Tudor, 1958. 381-400.

———. *Philosophy in a New Key: A Study in the Symbolism of Reason, Rite, and Art*. Cambridge: Harvard UP, 1967.

Laurence, Margaret. *The Diviners*. Toronto: McClelland, 1978.

Leland, Charles. "The Bohemian." Wedeck.

Lerner, Gerda. *The Creation of Patriarchy*. New York: Oxford UP, 1986.

Lesser, Wendy. *His Other Half: Men Looking at Women through Art*. Cambridge: Harvard UP, 1991.

Levy, Helen Fiddlymont. *Fiction of the Home Place: Jewett, Cather, Glasgow, Porter, Welty, and Naylor*. Jackson: UP of Mississippi, 1992.

Lewis, R. W. B. *The American Adam*. Chicago: U Chicago P, 1955.

Limerick, Patricia Nelson. *The Legacy of Conquest: The Unbroken Past of the American West*. New York: Norton, 1987.

London, Jack. *The Call of the Wild*. Norman: U Oklahoma P, 1995.

Manfred, Frederick. Interview. Taylor 24-27.

Mann, Jeanette W. "Toward New Archetypal Forms: *Boston Adventure*." *Studies in the Novel* 8.3 (1976): 291-303.

Marchand, Ernest. "Emerson and the Frontier." *American Literature* 3 (1931): 149-74.

Martin, Terence. "The Negative Character in American Fiction." *Parables of Possibility: The American Need for Beginnings*. New York: Columbia UP, 1995. 83-129.

Martz, Louis L. *The Poem of the Mind*. New York: Oxford UP, 1966.

———. *The Poetry of Meditation: A Study in English Religious Literature of the Seventeenth Century*. 1954. Rev. ed. New Haven: Yale UP, 1962.

McKinsey, Elizabeth R. *Niagara Falls: Icon of the American Sublime*. Cambridge, Eng.: Cambridge UP, 1985.

———. *The Western Experiment: New England Transcendentalists in the Ohio Valley*. Cambridge: Harvard UP, 1973.

Meldrum, Barbara Howard, ed. Introduction. *Old West-New West: Centennial Essays*. Moscow, Idaho: U Idaho P, 1993. 1-11.

Melville, Herman. *Moby-Dick*. Boston: Houghton. 1956.

Michie, Helena R. *The Flesh Made Word: Female Figures and Women's Bodies*. New York: Oxford UP, 1987.

Miller, Perry, ed. *Margaret Fuller: American Romantic*. Garden City, N.Y.: Doubleday, 1963.

Milton, John R. *The Novel of the American West*. Lincoln: U Nebraska P, 1988.

Mitchell, Juliet. *Psychoanalysis and Feminism*. New York: Pantheon, 1974.

Mitchell, Lee Clark. *Westerns: Making the Man in Fiction and Film*. Chicago: U Chicago P, 1996.

———. "'When You Call Me that . . . ' Tall Talk and Male Hegemony in *The Virginian*." *PMLA* 102 (1987): 8. Abstract.

Momaday, N. Scott. *The Man Made of Words*. New York: St. Martin's, 1997.

Morrison, Tony. *Beloved: A Novel*. New York: Knopf, 1987.

Murphy, John J. *My Ántonia: The Road Home*. Boston: Twayne, 1989.

My Secret Life. New York: Grove, 1966.

Nesbitt, John D. "Owen Wister's Achievement in Literary Tradition." *Western American Literature* 18 (1983): 199–208.

The New Oxford Annotated Bible. Ed. H. G. May and Bruce Metzger. New York: Oxford UP, 1973.

Norris, Frank. *McTeague, A Story of San Francisco*. Ed. Donal Pizer. New York: Norton, 1977.

———. *The Octopus: A Story of California*. Ed. Kenneth S. Lynn. Boston: Houghton, 1958.

The Oxford English Dictionary. Ed. James A. H. Murray et al. Oxford, Eng.: Clarendon, 1933.

Parry, Susan. Letter to the author. 27 October 1993.

Pilkington, William T. "On Jean Stafford's *The Mountain Lion*." *Critical Essays on the Western American Novel*. Ed. William T. Pilkington. Boston: Hall, 1980. 182–86.

Pinsker, Sanford. "Conversation with Marilynne Robinson." *Conversations with Contemporary American Writers*. Amsterdam, Neth.: Rodopi, 1985. 119–27.

Poe, Edgar Allan. "The Literati of New York City." *The Complete Works of Edgar Allan Poe*. Ed. J. A. Harrison. Vol. 15. New York: Crowell, 1902. 1–137.

Quirk, Tom. *Bergson and American Culture: The Worlds of Willa Cather and Wallace Stevens*. Chapel Hill: U North Carolina P, 1990.

Ravits, Martha. "Extending the American Range: Marilynne Robinson's *Housekeeping*." *American Literature* 61.4 (1989): 644–66.

Rich, Adrienne. *Of Woman Born*. 1976. New York: Norton, 1997.

Riley, Glenda. *Frontierswomen: The Iowa Experience*. Ames: Iowa State UP, 1981.

Riley, Paul. "Cather Family Letters, 1895." *Nebraska History* 54 (1973): 585–618.

Roberts, David. *Jean Stafford*. Boston: Little, 1988.

Robinson, David M. "Margaret Fuller and the Transcendental Ethos: *Woman in the Nineteenth Century*." *PMLA* 97 (1982): 83–98.

Robinson, Forrest G. "The Virginian and Molly in Paradise: How Sweet Is It?" *Western American Literature* 21 (1986): 27–38. Rpt. in *Having It Both Ways: Self-Subversion in Western Popular Classics*. Albuquerque: U New Mexico P, 1993. 41–54.

Robinson, Marilynne. "Fiction in Review." *Yale Review* 80.1–2 (1992): 227–35.

———. "Hearing Silence: Western Myth Reconsidered (In the Thoreau Tradition)." *The True Subject: Writers on Life and Craft*. Ed. Kurt Brown. St. Paul, Minn.: Greywolf, 1993.

———. *Housekeeping*. Toronto: Bantam, 1982.

———. "An Interview with Marilynne Robinson." By Thomas Schaub. *Contemporary Literature* 35.2 (1994): 231–51.

———. "A Life of Perished Things." Interview in *Face to Face: Interviews with Contemporary Novelists*. Ed. Allan Vordfa. Houston: Rice UP, 1993. 154–83.

———. *Mother Country*. New York: Farrar, 1989.

———. "Puritans and Prigs: An Anatomy of Zealotry." *Salmagundi* 101.2 (1994): 36–54.

———. "*Wise Children* by Angela Carter." *Yale Review* 80 (1992): 237.

———. "Writers and the Nostalgic Fallacy." *New York Times Book Review* 13 Oct. 1985: 1+.

Rosowski, Susan J. "Cather's Manifesto for Art—'Coming, Aphrodite!'" *Willa Cather Pioneer Memorial Newsletter* 38.3 (1994): 51–56.

———. "The Novel of Awakening." *Genre* 12 (1979): 313–32. Rpt. in *The Voyage in: Fictions of Female Development*. Ed. Elizabeth Abel, Marianne Hirsch, and Elizabeth Langland. UP of New England for Dartmouth College, 1983. 49–68.

Ruland, Richard, ed. *The Native Muse: Theories of American Literature*. New York: Dutton, 1972.

Ryan, Maureen. *Innocence and Estrangement in the Fiction of Jean Stafford*. Baton Rouge: Louisiana State UP, 1987.

Said, Edward W. *Orientalism*. New York: Pantheon, 1978.

Schaefer, Jack. *Shane: The Critical Edition*. Ed. James C. Work. Lincoln: U Nebraska P, 1984.

Schlissel, Lillian, Vicki L. Ruiz, and Janice Monk. Introduction. *Western Women: Their Land, Their Lives*. Lillian Schlissel, Vicki L. Ruiz, and Janice Monk. 1–9.

Showalter, Elaine. *Sexual Anarchy: Gender and Culture at the Fin de Siècle*. New York: Viking, 1990.

Simonson, Harold P. *Beyond the Frontier: Writers, Western Regionalism, and a Sense of Place*. Fort Worth: Texas Christian UP, 1989.

Slotkin, Richard. *The Fatal Environment: The Myth of the Frontier in the Age of Indus-*
trialization 1800–1890. New York: Atheneum, 1985.

———. *Regeneration through Violence: The Mythology of the American Frontier,*
1688-1860. Middletown, Conn.: Wesleyan UP, 1973.

Smith, Henry Nash. *The Virgin Land: The American West as Symbol and Myth*. Cambridge: Harvard UP, 1950.

Smith-Rosenberg, Carroll. "Female World of Love and Ritual, Relationships between Women in Nineteenth-Century America." *Signs* 1 (1975): 1–30. Rpt. in
Disorderly Conduct: Visions of Gender in Victorian England. New York: Knopf,
1985. 53–76.

Spacks, Patricia Meyer. *Desire and Truth: Functions of Plot in Eighteenth-Century Eng-*
lish Novels. Chicago: U Chicago P, 1990.

Sprengnether, Madelon. *The Spectral Mother: Freud, Feminism, and Psychoanalysis*.
Ithaca: Cornell UP, 1990.

Stafford, Jean. *Boston Adventure*. New York: Harcourt, 1944.

———. *The Collected Stories of Jean Stafford*. New York: Farrar, 1969.

———. "Heroes and Villains: Who Was Famous and Why." *McCall's* Apr. 1976:
196+.

———. "Miss McKeehan's Pocketbook." *Colorado Quarterly* 24 (1976): 407–11.

———. *The Mountain Lion*. New York: Random, 1947.

———. "The Psychological Novel." *Kenyon Review* 10 (1948): 214–27.

———. Review of *A Lost Lady*. *Book World, Washington Post*, 26 Aug. 1973: 1+

———. "The Scarlet Letter." *Mademoiselle* July 1959: 62+

———. "The Violet Rock." *New Yorker* 26 Apr.1952: 34–42.

Stern, Philip Van Doren, ed. *The Annotated* Walden, *by Henry D. Thoreau*. New York:
Potter, 1970.

Stevens, Wallace. *The Necessary Angel: Essays on Reality and the Imagination*. New
York: Random, 1951.

———. *Opus Posthumous*. New York: Knopf, 1966.

———. "Of Modern Poetry." *The Palm at the End of the Mind: Selected Poems and a*
Play by Wallace Stevens. Ed. Holly Stevens. New York: Knopf, 1971. 174–75.

———. *Parts of a World*. New York: Knopf, 1945.

———. "Prologues to What is Possible." *The Palm at the End of the Mind: Selected Po-*
ems and a Play by Wallace Stevens. Ed. Holly Stevens. New York: Knopf, 1971.
174–75.

Taylor, J. Golden, ed. *The Literature of the American West*. New York: Houghton,
1970.

Thoreau, Henry. *Familiar Letters of Henry David Thoreau*. Ed. F. B. Sanborn. Boston:
Houghton, 1894.

———. "Walking." *The Writings of Henry David Thoreau: Excursions*. Boston: Houghton, 1893.

———. *The Variorum Walden*. Annotated and introd. Walter Harding. New York: Twayne, 1962.

Tompkins, Jane. "Sentimental Power: *Uncle Tom's Cabin* and the Politics of Literary History." *Sensational Designs: The Cultural Work of American Fiction, 1790-1860*. New York: Oxford UP, 1985.

———. *West of Everything: The Inner Life of Westerns*. New York: Oxford UP, 1992.

Turner, Frederick Jackson. "The Significance of the Frontier in American History." Rpt. in *The Frontier in American History*. New York: Holt, 1921. 1–38.

Turner, Frederick Jackson. "The West and American Ideals." *The Frontier in American History*. New York: Holt, 1921. 290–310.

Twain, Mark. *Adventures of Huckleberry Finn*. Ed. Walter Blair and Victor Fischer. Berkeley: U California P, 1985.

Urbanski, Marie Olesen. "The Genesis, Form, Tone, and Rhetorical Devices of *Woman in the Nineteenth Century*." *Critical Essays on Margaret Fuller*. Ed. Joel Myerson. Boston: Hall, 1980. 268–80.

Vorpahl, Ben Merchant. "Roosevelt, Wister, Turner, and Remington." *A Literary History of the American West*. Ed. J. Golden Taylor. Fort Worth: Texas Christian UP, 1987. 276–302.

Wade, Mason. *Margaret Fuller: Whetstone of Genius*. New York: Viking, 1940.

Walker, Nancy A. *The Disobedient Writer: Women and Narrative Tradition*. Austin: U Texas P, 1995.

Walsh, Mary Ellen Williams. *Jean Stafford*. Ed. Warren French. Boston: Twayne, 1985.

———. "The Young Girl in the West: Disenchantment in Jean Stafford's Short Fiction." *Women and Western American Literature*. Ed. Helen Winter Stauffer and Susan J. Rosowski. Troy, N.Y.: Whitston, 1982. 230–43.

Warshow, Robert. "Movie Chronicle: The Westerner." *The Immediate Experience: Movies, Comics, Theatre, and Other Aspects of Popular Culture*. Garden City, N.Y.: Doubleday, 1964. 135–61.

Waters, Frank. Interview. Taylor 27–32.

Wedeck, H. E. with Wade Baskin. *Dictionary of Gypsy Life and Lore*. New York: Philosophical, 1973.

Weigle, Marta. *Creation and Procreation: Feminist Reflections on Mythologies of Cosmogony and Parturition*. Philadelphia: U Pennsylvania P, 1989.

Welter, Barbara. "The Cult of True Womanhood: 1820-1860." *American Quarterly* 18 (1966): 151–74.

Westbrook, Max. *Walter Van Tilburg Clark*. New York: Twayne, 1969.

The Westminster Dictionary of Christian Theology. Ed. Alan Richardson and John S. Bowden. Philadelphia: Westminster, 1983.

Whitman, Walt. *Leaves of Grass*. Ed. James E. Miller, Jr. Boston: Houghton, 1959.

Williams, Gary. "Resurrecting Carthage: *Housekeeping* and Cultural History." *English Language Notes* 29 (1991): 70–78.

Wister, Owen. *The Virginian: A Horseman of the Plains*. New York: New American, 1979.

Woodress, James. *Willa Cather: A Literary Life*. Lincoln: U Nebraska P, 1987.

Woolf, Virginia. "Modern Fiction." *Collected Essays*. Vol. 2. London: Hogarth, 1966. 103–10.

———. "Professions for Women." *Collected Essays*. Vol. 2. 284–89.

Work, James C., ed. *Prose and Poetry of the American West*. Lincoln: U Nebraska P, 1990.

Wunder, John R. "What's Old about the New Western History." *Pacific Northwest Quarterly* 85.2 (1994): 50–58.

Index